D0872241

PROPERTY OUTLAWS

PROPERTY OUTLAWS

How Squatters, Pirates, and Protesters Improve the Law of Ownership

Eduardo Moisés Peñalver
Sonia K. Katyal

Yale University Press
New Haven & London

Copyright © 2010 by Eduardo Moisés Peñalver and Sonia K. Katyal.

All rights reserved.
This book may not be reproduced, in whole or in part, including illustrations, in any form (beyond that copying permitted by Sections 107 and 108 of the U.S. Copyright Law and except by reviewers for the public press), without written permission from the publishers.

Set in Galliard Roman and Copperplate 33 types by The Composing Room of Michigan, Inc. Printed in the United States of America.

Library of Congress Cataloging-in-Publication Data
Peñalver, Eduardo Moisés, 1973–
    Property outlaws : how squatters, pirates, and protesters improve the law of ownership / Eduardo Moisés Peñalver, Sonia K. Katyal.
        p. cm.
    Includes bibliographical references and index.
    ISBN 978-0-300-12295-4 (pbk. : alk. paper)   1. Right of property.   2. Intellectual property.
3. Civil disobedience.   4. Rule of law.   I. Katyal, Sonia K., 1972–   II. Title.
    K721.5.P445 2010
    346.04'8—dc22

                                                                        2009023582

A catalogue record for this book is available from the British Library.

This paper meets the requirements of ANSI/NISO Z39.48-1992 (Permanence of Paper).

10 9 8 7 6 5 4 3

CONTENTS

PREFACE

On November 20, 1969, early in the morning, a group of eighty-nine Native American activists landed on the federally abandoned property of Alcatraz Island in the San Francisco Bay.[1] They claimed the land "by right of discovery" and under the terms of a treaty signed in 1868, the Treaty of Fort Laramie, which gave Native Americans the right to unused federal government property that had previously been theirs.[2] Their occupation became the longest and most visible occupation of any federal facility until the federal government forcibly removed fifteen remaining protesters nineteen months later. Although the occupation did not result in a shift of title, it was, by any account, a watershed moment in American history. Alcatraz was an opening shot in the Red Power movement, which repeatedly employed the tactic of property occupations to draw attention to Native American issues. Between 1969 and the late 1970s, Native American activists carried out over seventy occupations of property, including the Trail of Broken Treaties, which involved the occupation of the Bureau of Indian Affairs (BIA) headquarters.[3]

Although their protests, like other civil rights demonstrations, were occasionally characterized by sporadic violence and controversy, there is no question that the Red Power movement contributed to a fundamental shift in government policy.[4] As the nation took note of what was happening at Alcatraz, President Nixon announced a formal reversal of previous federal policy toward Native Americans, proclaiming that the government would now fully support tribal self-determination and return 48,000 acres of land that had been taken without compensation to the Taos people.[5] That year, Congress passed fifty-two legislative proposals that dramatically increased funding for the BIA, scholarships, water rights, housing, and health care.[6] In one communication, Alcatraz resident Grace Thorpe wrote, "Our seizure of Alcatraz is the awakening of Indian self-determinism and Indian unity. It is the beginning of the Indian's rightful claim, not only to his land, but also his own destiny and power."[7]

The same pattern has been borne out, again and again, by the complex phenomenon of property disobedience. The actual number of property-outlaw movements, both in the United States and abroad, is truly astonishing. Countless movements, well known and obscure, have resorted to unauthorized tactics to achieve their property goals. In many cases, they have been successful, obtaining for their participants the desired access to, possession of, or even title to property. Whether they fail or succeed, however, outlaws reveal an essential ambiguity at property's core. For the people occupying Alcatraz, property was both the object and the subject of their disobedience, the instrumental tool upon which the protest was based as well as the proverbial "brass ring" they hoped to gain in the event that their action succeeded.

As the legacy of the Red Power occupations reminds us, property disobedience is not always just about specific claims to resources; it is also about persuasion—drawing upon the unique ability of property law as an institution to communicate particular claims to others.[8] Not all outlaw movements, however, are created equal in terms of their scope, aims, or effectiveness. Just as property law aims to enhance stability by establishing a system of clear and fixed rules, dividing public from private, it also crucially motivates cultural and political forces that contest and destabilize, creating chaos and confusion in the midst of seeming orderliness. Today, forty years after the activists first set foot on Alcatraz, we see this dialectic emerge time and time again in contemporary urban and rural environments, with respect to both tangible and intangible forms of property. Homelessness advocacy groups have helped groups of newly homeless families suffering from the economic downturn to squat in vacant, foreclosed properties.[9] The bike collective Critical Mass takes over the streets of metropolitan cities in order to reinvent the concept of public space; urban community gardeners take over vacant lots to beautify the city and create a sense of shared ecological responsibility; pirate microradio stations in the Bay Area and mashup artists interrupt everyday sonic worlds; cyberactivists like the Electronic Disturbance Theatre and others mount international electronic civil-disobedience campaigns.[10] And still, tribal members continue to occupy property, as a group of Mohawk protesters in Canada demonstrated in 2007 and 2008 when they successfully blockaded a contested area of land to stave off development.[11]

The debates that these movements spark continue to unfold.

In this book we will not pretend to decide, in each instance, whether the phenomenon of property disobedience is defensible or necessary. Our goal instead is merely to identify some of the ways in which this pervasive phenomenon has, intentionally or not, spurred legal innovation, perhaps even strengthening the rule of law. In the process, we hope to shed new light on this important engine of legal change.

We could not have completed this project without the people and institutions who have generously assisted and supported us. We are grateful to the Fordham and Cornell law schools for generous research funding while we worked on this book. In addition, we thank the Hastings and Yale law schools for serving as homes away from our home institutions during significant periods of research and writing. We are also particularly indebted to research librarians at Fordham, Cornell and Yale. Paul Miller, of the Fordham law library, was especially helpful, performing the invaluable task of tracking down letters to the editor from the time of the Greensboro sit-ins.

We also owe an enormous debt to a wide variety of friends, colleagues, and family members who read various portions of the manuscript and offered us helpful criticism, commentary, suggestions, and encouragement. In particular, we would like to thank Bruce Ackerman, Greg Alexander, Graeme Austin, Ann Bartow, Barton Beebe, Rick Bierschbach, Scott Baker, Richard Brooks, Dan Burk, Kristen Carpenter, Michael Carrier, Andrew Chin, Julie Cohen, Adrienne Davis, Reza Dibadj, Graeme Dinwoodie, Eddie, Christine Farley, Robin Feldman, Lee Fennell, Matthew Fletcher, Brett Frischmann, Nicole Garnett, Wendy Gordon, Stuart Green, Richard Gruner, Drew Hansen, Hugh Hansen, Tim Holbrooke, Justin Hughes, Dan Kahan, Sital Kalantry, Amy Kapczynski, Neal Katyal, Harold Krent, Sudhir Krishnaswamy, Roberta Kwall, Greg Lastowka,

Mark Lemley, Lawrence Liang, Esther Lucero, Jason Lujan, Michael Madison, Kunal Malhotra, Michael Maurer, Thomas McSweeney, Jim Pope, Achal Prabhala, Margaret Jane Radin, Joel Reidenberg, Ryan Red Corn, Angela Riley, Darren Rosenblum, Caroline Shapiro, Jessica Silbey, Joe Singer, Henry Smith, Pamela Samuelson, Katherine Strandburg, Christine Tan, Rebecca Tushnet, Laura Underkuffler, Siva Vaidhyanathan, Andre Van der Walt, and Fred von Lohmann, as well as participants in workshops at Boston University, Chicago-Kent College of Law, John Marshall Law School, Harvard Law School, Queensland University of Technology, Rutgers (Camden) Law School, Syracuse Law School, and the University of North Carolina Law School. Portions of chapters 1, 3, 4, 8, and 9 previously appeared in the *University of Pennsylvania Law Review*. We are grateful to the editors of that publication.

We would like to acknowledge the excellent editorial assistance of Christian Stenti and Luke Davin, in addition to the superb research assistance provided by John Alan Farmer, Allison Schilling, Ru Bhatt, Genevieve Blake, Jana Checa Chong, Michelle Ekanemesang, Laura Jereski, Ellen Loeb, Emily Wash, Ethan Notkin, Ilana Ofgang, Robert Pierson, Paul Riley, and Genan Zilkha.

Finally, we would like to dedicate this book to our families.

INTRODUCTION

At 4:30 p.m. on Monday, February 1, 1960, Ezell Blair Jr., Franklin McCain, Joseph McNeil, and David Richmond—all freshmen at the North Carolina Agricultural and Technical State University (North Carolina A&T)—walked into the cafeteria at the Woolworth's store in downtown Greensboro, North Carolina. They sat down at the counter and quietly waited for service. They received none. Blair, McCain, McNeil, and Richmond were black, and Woolworth's, like all the department stores and restaurants in Greensboro, followed the local "custom" of refusing to allow black patrons to sit down to eat at the lunch counter. Although they received no service, the four men sat quietly and without incident. When the store closed at 5:30 that day, they left.

The next morning, at 10:30, the four young men returned to Woolworth's, along with sixteen other students from North Carolina A&T. They each purchased a small item from the store's lunch counter, which was willing to sell black customers food but not to allow them to sit down at the counter to eat it. As seats opened up at the lunch counter, the young men and women sat down in violation of the store's customary policy. Some students spoke quietly among themselves; others studied. In the meantime, white customers continued to come and go, puzzled at what they were witnessing. When the students finally left, shortly after lunchtime, they promised to return the next day in even greater numbers. McCain and Blair, acting as spokesmen for the group, said that they would continue to sit at the lunch counter for "several days, several weeks," until Woolworth's changed its racist policy. The students were careful to note that they were not planning to boycott the store. "We like to spend our money here," McCain said, "but we want to spend it at the lunch counter."[1]

By Thursday morning, the group had swelled to over sixty protesters and now included students from nearby Bennett College. They occupied virtually every seat at the lunch counter, and service came to a standstill as waitresses—in accordance with Woolworth's policy—refused to serve them. North Carolina's attorney general, Malcolm Seawell, commented on the situation, noting that North Carolina had no law against serving members of both races at a lunch counter, but also observing that there was no law that required a private business to serve anyone it did not wish to serve. His implication was clear. By sitting at the lunch counter against the wishes of the store's owners or managers, the students were engaging in a criminal violation of private property rights. Despite the attorney general's implicit threat, the sit-down protests continued on Friday and Saturday. White youths confronted the growing group of black college students, hurling insults at them. After a bomb threat on Saturday, February 6, Woolworth's decided to close its lunch counter indefinitely.

By the middle of the following week, copycat sit-down protests had sprung up in Winston-Salem and Charlotte. And lunch counters at Woolworth's and other department stores in those cities closed down as well. Joseph Jones, a black student at Johnson C. Smith University and a leader of the Charlotte sit-ins, commented, "I have no malice, no jealousy, no hatred, no envy. All I want is to come in and place my order and be served and leave a tip if I feel like it."[2]

By the end of the month, similar sit-down protests were occurring throughout the South. As the movement grew in strength, the department stores began to change their tactics. At first, the stores had responded to the protesters by ignoring them or closing the lunch counters entirely, perhaps in hope that the students would quickly lose interest. But as the protests persisted, and even grew, the stores began to assert their private property rights more forcefully.

Under the laws of most states at that time, owners of private businesses could refuse to serve anyone for any reason, and a person who failed to leave a store after being asked to do so by its proprietor was guilty of criminal trespass. When the protests showed no signs of abating, store owners began to flex these legal muscles, and the arrests began. On February 22, thirty-four students were arrested for criminal trespass in Richmond, Virginia, when they refused to leave the lunch counter at a large downtown department store. Over the succeeding days and months, hundreds more students were arrested in North Carolina, Virginia, and throughout the South for refusing to honor the racially discriminatory exercise of private property rights by the owners of lunch counters.

Forty-five years, to the day, after the four Greensboro college freshmen sparked a national movement to end private discrimination in stores and restaurants, Downhill Battle, an anticopyright activist group, organized a massive nationwide screening of the acclaimed 1987 documentary *Eyes on the Prize*—a film that had been shown to generations for its valuable historical footage of the civil rights movement.[3] As various Internet and print news sources, and Downhill Battle's own Web site, reported, the film, billed as the "most important civil rights documentary ever," had languished since 1995 because of expired copyright licenses for the photographs and other archival footage used in the film. Some of the footage in the documentary had been licensed for only five years, and the film's producer, Henry Hampton, had passed away before the rights were renewed. Things had changed since the film was first created—licenses had become far more costly to procure, and the vast archival material included in the film made them prohibitively expensive. Blackside, the production company that had inherited the rights to the film, could not afford to renew the licenses. As a result, the film could not be rereleased until new licenses were procured. By the mid-1990s, the film had become, for all practical purposes, unavailable to the general public—a few rare VHS copies occasionally surfaced on eBay for as much as $1,500.[4]

Ironically, many of the sources used in the film would have fallen into the public domain, or been close to doing so, had Congress not retroactively extended the length of copyright protection by twenty years in the 1998 Copyright Term Extension Act. For example, in one poignant scene, Martin Luther King Jr.'s staff is shown singing the song "Happy Birthday," a song that would have entered the public domain in 2010 had the law not been passed. Because of the Copyright Extension Act, however, the song will not enter the public domain until 2030, and the cost of a license has grown dramatically since the film was made. According to some Warner Brothers executives, the song currently commands licensing fees between $3,000 and $5,000 for a single use in a film.[5]

Eyes on the Prize had, in a sense, become a victim of its own high standards for documentary production: because it relied on such an exhaustive array of research and sources, it became too costly to rerelease after the original licenses had expired. And without the proper licenses, any public display of the film risked infringing the rights to the panoply of material that was still protected. The high cost of relicensing the material made the film a captive of its content, barring its general distribution to the viewing public. As a result, this important and revered film could no longer be shown in public.

For many civil rights advocates, particularly educators and historians, this was a tragic turn of events. After a few news articles reported on the film's unavailability, Downhill Battle decided to organize a public protest to coincide with Black History Month in order to draw attention to the effect of copyright law on *Eyes on the Prize* in particular and the circulation of information in general. The only way to do this, the group reasoned, was to simply *show* the film—in other words, to defy the restrictions of copyright protection in order to demonstrate the cost of the law itself. One civil rights leader, Lawrence Guyot, proclaimed, "'Eyes on the Prize' is one of the most effective documentaries ever put together that dealt with civic engagement. . . . This [absence of license renewal] is analogous to stopping the circulation of all the books about Martin Luther King, stopping the circulation of all the books about Malcolm X, stopping the circulation of books about the founding of America. . . . I would call upon everyone who has access to 'Eyes on the Prize' to openly violate any and all laws regarding its showing."[6] Just as earlier generations of civil rights activists challenged property laws, through sit-ins and other forms of everyday resistance, in order to articulate their demands for equal access to lunch counters and other places of public accommodation, Guyot called for similar challenges to existing intellectual property rights in the name of greater access to information.

So Downhill Battle organized a massive day of digital disobedience. Its announcement read: "Eyes on the Prize is the most renowned civil rights documentary of all time; for many people, it is how they first learned about the Civil Rights Movement. . . . But this film has not been available on video or television for the past 10 years simply because of expired copyright licenses. We cannot allow copyright red tape to keep this film from the public any longer. So today we are making digital versions of the film available for download."[7]

Downhill Battle's method of protest was simple: the group digitized the first three episodes of the documentary and posted them online, where the episodes could be downloaded for free using peer-to-peer software, like Bit-Torrent. Then, Downhill Battle encouraged people to copy and distribute the files in order to raise awareness of copyright's effect on the circulation of information. Downhill Battle dubbed their protest "Eyes on the Screen" and coordinated hundreds of public showings of the movie at universities and in private homes throughout the country. The organizers believed that their activities fell squarely within the "fair use" protections of the Copyright Act. "We're talking about a cultural and national icon," Guyot explained in a telephone interview to the *Boston Globe*. "There's never been a more key time to revitalize our faith in our ability to impact on every level. I'm not doing anything illegal, I'm persuading people to buy copies and those who have copies to share them, to facilitate as many showings as possible."[8]

The protest, however, was short lived. Downhill Battle's efforts, though nationally visible, were ultimately curtailed—because of Blackside's own intervention. Even though Downhill Battle planned to digitize and post the remaining episodes on peer-to-peer networks, it was forced to take them down after Blackside contacted its copyright lawyers, who concluded that the protest not only violated the filmmaker's copyright but might also irritate the various license holders whose works were used in the film. Tony Pierce, one of Blackside's lawyers, strongly disagreed with the protesters' belief that their activities were legal, calling their fair use defense "warped." Pierce continued, "Their activities were blatantly illegal, and I think they knew they were when they did them." Other Blackside lawyers were more moderate in their assessment. "We appreciate and are very glad that people are interested in 'Eyes,' but I think the way Downhill Battle is going about it is unacceptable and illegal," said another Blackside lawyer, Sandy Forman from the law firm of Akin Gump Strauss Hauer & Feld. "We don't like that Downhill Battle would illegally digitize copies and then encourage people to illegally download them and encourage people to exhibit them without the rights to do so."[9]

A similar perspective was offered by another Blackside representative on a widely read blog. "This protest might be a good thing, as far as copyright goes, but as far as *Eyes* goes, it's really not." The representative pointed out that Downhill Battle's calls to illegally copy and distribute the film made negotiations with the copyright holders even more difficult. "Whatever the motives," he added, "the counter-copyright crew are essentially hijacking someone else's life's work and appropriating its power and recognition for their own purposes. In the process, they are potentially diminishing and damaging its own effectiveness. . . . They invoke Henry Hampton's name and legacy on their page, where they advocate downloading and illegally distributing his works. Henry Hampton may have made documentaries, but that doesn't mean he worked for free. . . . So trying to invoke his name while you encourage everyone to trample on the rights granted his works strikes me as extremely hypocritical."[10]

The critical comments generated a firestorm of discussion about the relative merits of the "Eyes on the Screen" protest—for copyright law, for the future of civil rights education, and for the intersection between the two areas. In the end, Blackside received several hundred thousand dollars in grants from the Ford Foundation and private philanthropists to purchase the rights to use the images in the film. Even with this infusion of money, however, the expense of licensing the songs used in the original film was thought to be too expensive, and Blackside expected that it would have to drop some of them in order to stay within budget. By 2006, however, the film was once again being shown on PBS.

At first glance, the four college freshmen who launched the 1960 sit-down movement at the Woolworth's in Greensboro, North Carolina, and the intellectual property activists at Downhill Battle may not appear to share a great deal. The Greensboro protests were aimed at defending the fundamental human dignity of black Americans, a dignity that had been under assault for centuries. The intellectual property activists at Downhill Battle are focused on helping people get access to information that is, for the most part, already available to them, albeit for a price. Even if we focus on the fight over *Eyes on the Prize,* an important repository of documentary material about the most important social movement of the twentieth century, we must recognize that there is a stark difference between fighting for civil rights and fighting for access to a *film* about civil rights.

We should not, however, let hindsight distort our assessment of either effort. At the time of their sit-down protests, the Greensboro protesters were maligned as threatening sacred rights of private property and the rule of law in pursuit of what many commentators considered a trivial interest in access to lunch-counter service. Such criticism did not come just from conservatives and segregationists. Thurgood Marshall railed against the sit-down protests, and a black minister in Charlotte, North Carolina, lambasted the students' actions as "uncalled for, unnecessary, ill-advised and inexpedient."[11] Conversely, some contemporary observers viewed Downhill Battle's efforts to provide access to *Eyes on the Prize* as vital to the future of our democracy. One former staff member of the Southern Christian Leadership Conference (Martin Luther King Jr.'s organization), Bruce Hartford, explained his efforts to organize an illicit screening of the film by noting the similarities between the fight for civil rights and the fight for access to information. "I think probably the issue of the 20th century was race. The issue of the 21st century is going to be access to information. . . . Without access to information," he observed, "democracy is a myth."[12]

Whatever one thinks of the relative merits of the two protests, they share a great deal. The most obvious commonality operates on the level of tactics. Both the Greensboro protesters and the information activists relied on a readiness to trample on entrenched property rights in order to draw attention to their demands for political change. And in so doing, both movements demonstrated a flair for the dramatic and for attracting the media attention that politically motivated property disobedience generates.

Whether the Greensboro students or Downhill Battle knew it or not, in violating property rights as they did, they were tapping into a long tradition within the history of American property law. For as long as there has been private ownership, it seems, there have been people who have sought to challenge the prerogatives of ownership in search of a more just social order. Sometimes they have succeeded. More often, they have not. But the pervasive influence of these outlaw tactics on the development of American property doctrine cannot be denied. In this book we hope to explore in some depth the phenomenon of property disobedience, in its various forms, and the role that it plays both as a challenge to and as an essential component of our system of private ownership.

Imagine that scientists invented a machine capable of costlessly detecting every crime, no matter how trivial, and identifying its perpetrator. If such a machine were possible, should the state build it? Set aside concerns about privacy. Suppose that the machine would not detect or record any noncriminal activities, whether conducted in public or private. It would not, for example, involve videotaping and then evaluating the activities of innocent people as they went about their business on the streets or in their homes. Burglaries, assaults, thefts, and criminal trespass would all be detected and recorded in the system's database.

To some readers, entertaining any doubt about the desirability of the goal of perfect law enforcement might be the sign of some moral or intellectual defect, particularly coming from two professors of law. If a society, especially a democratic society, has enacted criminal statutes, established a system of private property and contract, and defined duties of care that its members owe to one another, then surely the perfect enforcement of those norms would be an unmitigated good and ought always to be preferred to a situation in which some people violate those norms with impunity. As long as it did not run afoul of *other* legal norms (such as privacy rights) or cost too much, anything that might improve the effectiveness of legal enforcement should be welcomed without hesitation. The machine must be built. Right?

As alluring as the idea of perfect law enforcement might appear at first glance, some doubts very quickly begin to spring to mind. The question whether to build the machine would seem to be an impossible one to answer without first knowing a number of different facts, both about the society that is proposing to build the machine and about the specific acts (and actors) that the machine detects. How just, for example, are the laws defining specific actions as "criminal"? Are the society's criminal punishments excessive? Are its property rights wisely defined and fairly distributed? Even if an act meets the definition of a legal violation, can the machine always correctly assess whether the person who engaged in that criminal act was justified in doing so? If the person committed an assault, for example, was she acting in self-defense? If he stole some bread, was he driven by hunger or by avarice? Even if a specified illegal act was not justified, was it the consequence of circumstancés that mitigate our moral condemnation such that we think its perpetrator ought to be wholly or partially excused from sanctions?

We are obviously not breaking any new ground by raising these questions. Most legal theories make some provision for at least some categories of justified lawbreaking, such as conscientious disobedience of unjust laws or apparently unlawful behavior necessitated by the exigencies of a natural disaster. On the other hand, the precise contours of these exceptions and the application of these exceptions in the evaluation of unlawful behavior are often controversial and have been hotly debated. Some, for example, have argued that taking a person's life, even in self-defense, is never permissible. Others have argued that economic need, no matter how great or blameless, cannot justify taking someone else's property.

In this book we cannot hope to recount the full scope of these debates, or even join many of them—at least not in any comprehensive way. Instead, we intend to focus on the phenomena of property disobedience and on the role, if any, it appropriately plays in the construction and design of a system of private ownership. Moreover, we come to the discussion of disobedience not as criminal lawyers or philosophers but rather as specialists in property and intellectual property, respectively. What does our project exclude? Primarily, any discussion of crimes and other legal wrongs that implicate a person's body. Removing from the conversation actions that violate people's physical integrity, either negligently or intentionally, will (we hope) limit the scope of controversy in ways that will permit a richer consideration and discussion of the topics that remain. Our narrow focus on property violations is not an arbitrary effort to dodge hard cases. We believe that such a focus is justified not simply on account of our own particular intellectual interests, but because, as we will argue at greater length in chapter 1, violations of property rights differ in morally significant respects from other sorts of legal wrongs. As the Model Penal Code affirms, an action that implicates a person's body is both more serious and more irrevocable in its consequences than one that implicates a person's property rights. This is not to say that there are not borderline cases, that there might not be violations of property rights that implicate interests whose importance rivals a person's bodily integrity—as might happen, for example, where the property in question is so closely bound up with a person's bodily security as to render a violation of property rights tantamount to a violation of the person. Home invasion is an example of such a borderline case. Close cases might also arise where the owner's relationship with the property is so intimate that a violation of that relationship is felt by the owner to be as intense and irrevocable as a physical assault. Such liminal cases are interesting, and we address them at various points throughout the book. But we do not believe that their existence vitiates the fundamental validity of the broad distinction we are drawing at the outset between violations of property rights and violations of the body.

So let us assume that our hypothetical law-enforcement machine is only capable of detecting violations of property rights. The question we hope to address at length in this book is whether it would be wise for a government to purchase it and turn it on. Why wouldn't it be? After all, the image that most of us have of the person who intentionally flouts property laws is not a particularly favorable one. The *Oxford English Dictionary*, for example, defines a trespasser as a "transgressor, a law-breaker; a wrong-doer, sinner, offender."[13] In early modern England, landowners frequently left "man traps" and "spring guns" along boundary lines to discourage trespass on their lands.[14] Indeed, in rural areas of the United States, it is, even today, not uncommon to come across signs warning that "trespassers will be shot."[15] The overridingly negative view of property lawbreakers in popular consciousness comports with the status of property rights within our characteristically individualist, capitalist, political culture.

The dim view of property lawbreakers is shared to a large degree by scholars of property law and intellectual property law alike, who recognize the important role that property plays in maintaining social order through a stable system of private ownership. The apparent threat to that order and stability posed by property lawbreakers is underscored by the importance attached to exclusivity within contemporary theories of property. Both courts and commentators have placed this right at the conceptual center of private ownership.[16]

One of the key purposes of property law, as Abraham Bell and Gideon Parchomovsky have correctly argued, is to provide stability, both for owners and for those who would engage in transactions with them.[17] Property law achieves this stability in a variety of ways. One crucial way is through the criminal enforcement of existing property entitlements. Laws of criminal trespass protect the boundaries around real property established through market transactions. Laws prohibiting larceny, fraud, robbery, burglary, and the piracy of intellectual property similarly wrap private entitlements within the safety of the publicly enforced criminal law. The law protects the stability of property rights of all sorts with civil remedies as well, through the use of injunctive remedies and supracompensatory damages.

In contrast to this familiar story, in this book we hope to cast some doubt on the value of stability by retelling the story from a different angle. Our aim is to broaden the focus so that the discussion is not just about property's stability, but also about its need for dynamism, its ability to change and to fluctuate according to shifting norms, values, and social realities. In other words, we seek to supplement the dominant focus on the importance of property's stability by highlighting the powerful, and at times ironic, role of selective disobedience in the process of fostering the necessary evolution of property. We believe that the apparent stability and order provided by property law owes much to the destabilizing role of the lawbreaker in occasionally forcing needed reform and in generating a series of important legal shifts along the way. A more balanced portrayal of the lawbreaker than the one offered by an exclusive focus on the value of stability offers a richer and much more accurate picture of the dynamics behind the evolution of property laws and the forces that drive them.

Our goal in this book is therefore to discuss some reasons why the perfect property law-enforcement machine might not be such a great idea. We do not seek to applaud lawlessness in general, but rather to highlight some specific cases in which property disobedience has positively influenced the direction of the law. In the process, we hope to rehabilitate, at least to a certain extent, the image of the intentional property outlaw, and to show how this figure has repeatedly played an integral role in producing our system of property and intellectual property. We also hope to shed light on a complex and subtle tension: although property seems to be so stable and orderly, it also masks a latent instability stemming from the persistence of transgression. Far from universally undermining the value of property, however, this underlying instability is frequently constructive and indeed necessary to prevent the entire edifice from becoming outdated.[18]

We are not the first property scholars to notice these dynamic tensions within property law. Jeremy Waldron, for example, has observed that the central function of a system of private property is to resolve what might otherwise become intractable and violent conflict over access to and control over scarce material resources.[19] But property law's resolution of these latent conflicts is always somewhat tentative, and property remains the site of recurring conflict as competing camps state and restate their claims to particular contested resources. This dialogic (or, perhaps, dialectic) vision of property law extends to other areas of law as well. Indeed, it parallels in many ways recent discussions within constitutional theory that have privileged a popular bottom-up conception of lawmaking over the more traditional focus on official organs of lawmaking. Thus, Stanford Law School professor and dean Larry Kramer has described the important role played by lawbreaking and mob action in the early republic's popular constitutional legal culture.[20] And Rutgers law professor Jim Pope has discussed the importance of worker lawbreaking for the development of constitutional doctrine during the New Deal era.[21]

These many discussions of the venerable American tradition of popular lawmaking help render our own discussion of the value of property lawbreaking less radical or less threatening than it might otherwise seem. In addition, our task is made easier by the fact that, despite the broadly negative view of property lawbreakers that prevails among lawyers and lay people alike, our popular culture has also simultaneously embraced a more favorable view of outlaws. Even while we condemn theft and trespass, we celebrate the exploits of Robin Hood and the bravery of the 1960s civil rights protesters. We know that, although lawbreaking is by and large undesirable and even dangerous to social stability, property outlaws have repeatedly played a powerful role as catalysts for needed legal reform. Time and again, groups of people have intentionally violated property laws, and in a number of important cases, the law of property has responded by shifting to accommodate their demands, in the process bringing those groups back within the fold of the law-abiding community. At other times, the legal ambiguity of their activities has offered the law the opportunity to refine itself in response to their challenge. This is particularly true in the case of intellectual property law, which has long relied on the contributions of individuals who have exploited legally ambiguous technologies to spur innovation and new business models. Whatever one thinks of the merits of any individual case, there can be no doubt that—considered as a whole—these legally dubious activities have been important engines for legal change. As a consequence of this ambiguity, a diverse group of people disenfranchised by or disenchanted with the existing property system, from the squatters on the nineteenth-century American frontier to the Native American and civil rights protesters of the 1960s to the urban squatters of the 1970s and 1980s to file sharers and patent activists of the new millennium, have flouted property laws in hopes of achieving their diverse goals.

In most cases, they have been rebuffed. But in many important cases, they have succeeded. And yet the useful role repeatedly played by these challengers in forcing change has been mostly ignored by legal scholars. The failure is attributable, at least in part, to a larger tendency among scholars writing about property to focus their attention on questions concerning the initial emergence of regimes of private ownership, either from systems of common property or from open-access systems. Here, scholars have focused their inquiries mostly on why private property rights emerged over time. In addition, a growing number of scholars have explored the role of social norms and private ordering in the informal adjustment of formal property entitlements.

These discussions have no doubt provided substantial insight. Property theorists have paid less attention, however, to the equally interesting question of *how* formal regimes of private ownership evolve from one particular bundle of ownership rights to another. What accounts for key shifts in ownership and access over time? As history often reveals, once a robust system of private property has been established, the precise content of that standard bundle of rights changes over time in response to varying pressures and incentives, both internal and external to the institution of ownership. Indeed, a focus on the mechanisms of legal evolution within existing private property regimes is all the more important and interesting in an advanced capitalist society like ours, where, for large swaths of resources, the nearly complete "enclosure" of commons and open-access resources has already been accomplished.[22] Even in the intellectual property context, the pervasive growth of copyright control mechanisms may have drastic effects on the access to cultural and technological resources that might otherwise fall within the public domain.

Some scholars have taken up the question of legal transitions within existing property regimes. Many have done so by focusing on incentives to litigate as an explanation for patterns of change within the law.[23] Others have focused on the means by which interest groups band together to influence legislative change, both in the arena of property, intellectual property, and elsewhere.[24] But these officially sanctioned mechanisms of legal change provide only part of the picture, particularly within the law of property. Certain categories of nonowners, after all, are likely to be reluctant, or simply financially unable, to initiate costly civil litigation or to assert effective political pressure to stake their claims.

Almost by definition, intentional lawbreaking as a mechanism for legal change is a strategy employed by those who cannot afford to file civil suits or whose voice in the legislative process is too weak to attract the attention of lawmakers in order to wrest a change in property relations, whether de facto or de jure, from existing entitlements.[25] In other words, intentional lawbreaking is typically (though not always) a tool of the have-nots. And in many cases, as we shall show, an initial transgression of a property entitlement is an essential event in provoking a shift in the law. It should therefore come as no surprise that some of the most significant judicial opinions in the common law development of property law have come on the criminal side of the docket.[26] And even in the context of intellectual property, courts and legislatures have often been moved to enact civil safe harbors or to extend the concept of fair use to protect previously "disobedient" behavior. Moreover, protracted lawbreaking, as in the case of the civil rights protesters of the 1960s, may catalyze a favorable legal response by shifting public opinion and inviting legislative intervention. Given the tactic's appeal to the powerless and marginal, it is unsurprising that many of the stories of property change on which we focus have an undercurrent of concern about distributive justice.

We are under no illusions that property outlaws will always pursue ends that we consider good or worthy. Intentional lawbreaking has been used in the defense of oppression and discrimination just as it has been used to foster liberation and equality. The nature of property lawbreaking suggests that it will be used by nonowners more than owners and by those isolated from the majoritarian process more than by those well connected to the levers of power. But this does not guarantee that it will be directed toward progressive ends. Nineteenth-century squatters, for example, frequently dispossessed Native Americans of their land even as they clamored for recognition of their own informal property rights.[27] Similarly, racist property owners continue to break the law and exclude people from public accommodations on the basis of race, just as the civil rights protesters dissented from the status quo by forcing themselves onto segregationist property in violation of trespass laws. Although our own political commitments lead us to view civil rights lawbreaking more sympathetically than segregationist lawbreaking, we believe that both lawbreakers qualify as "property outlaws," and our discussion attempts to encompass actors whose ends we share as well as those whose ends we find reprehensible. The legal responses we discuss in part 3, however, will likely have different impacts on different sorts of property outlaws, given differences in the objective circumstances and aims of the outlaws and in the democratic response to their activities.

We do not pretend to provide a general theory of shifts in legal regimes, or even in property law. Instead, we hope to explore just one interesting facet of this larger issue by focusing on the role of disobedience as a mechanism that, time and again, has played a key role in fostering both symbolic and substantive evolution within the law of private ownership in both the property and intellectual property contexts. In so doing, we hope to draw increased attention both to the general question of change within property rights and, in particular, to the crucial function frequently performed by outlaws within that process.

Recognizing this recurrent cycle of productive disobedience and legal reform yields a variety of interesting conceptual, descriptive, and normative conclusions. To the extent that those on the outside of the property system frequently bring about a change in the content of property rights by flouting established property rules, the story we tell in this book offers a view of property law as a dynamic institution that is broadly reflective of evolving community values as opposed to a fixed set of natural entitlements. Our discussion therefore contributes to the growing body of literature emphasizing the dialogic and social nature of property law and rejecting the frequently static, individualist conception of property rights favored by many property libertarians. More normatively, however, we argue that lawbreakers have repeatedly played integral roles in spurring the evolution of property law. Their stories argue in favor of a careful consideration of the ways in which legal processes can be shaped to isolate the productive contributions of property outlaws from their less desirable effects.

Part 1 lays some conceptual foundations for the remainder of the book. In chapter 1 we ask why it is worth focusing on the law of *property*, whether tangible or intellectual, in our discussion of outlaw tactics for legal change. We argue that, despite the generalized nature of disobedience as a tool for reform, there are reasons to think that it will play a particularly important role within the evolution of property and intellectual property. Property law has a greater tendency than many other areas of law to become ossified and out of date, and therefore has a greater need for occasional "shocks" to the system. Although we do not dispute the value of stability in property entitlements, both for the individual and the market as a whole, the long-term health of this system depends on its ability to respond dynamically to changing economic and social conditions. Property outlaws have repeatedly played a crucial role in drawing attention to the need for reform. In chapter 2 we discuss the broad contours of intellectual property regulation, with particular attention to those areas that relate to our study of disobedience. We highlight how the considerations at work within intellectual property law differ from those that operate within the law of tangible property.

With those preliminaries out of the way, in part 2 we begin our discussion of outlaws in earnest, elaborating two broad categories of intentional lawbreaking that are particularly relevant to our discussion. For ease of discussion, we posit that intentional lawbreaking falls somewhere along a continuum ranging from self-regarding appropriative violations of property rights, at one end, to more other-regarding, expressive violations of property rights, at the other end. On the basis of this observation, we offer two broad categories of lawbreaking: "acquisitive" and "expressive." These examples are not meant to be exhaustive or even representative of the sheer variety of property disobedience that exists. Rather, they are simply meant to serve as illustrations of one possible typology of the disobedience that frequently reappears within the history of property and intellectual property law.

Expressive disobedience, which corresponds loosely though imperfectly to the category traditionally called "civil disobedience,"[28] is not primarily acquisitive in nature, but seeks instead to send a strong message about the perceived injustice of existing property arrangements. The 1960 civil rights lunch-counter protests, to which we return again in chapter 4, are a strong reminder of the power of expressive lawbreaking and its vital role within the process of democratic deliberation. Acquisitive disobedience, in contrast, involves actions that are oriented primarily toward direct appropriation. For acquisitive outlaws, the dominant motivating factor might be to gain immediate access to a certain good or property interest presently in the hands of another party (whether the government or a private party), as opposed to making a general statement about the appropriate scope of property rights. Like the expressive disobedience of the civil rights protests, acquisitive disobedience has a long (though more ambiguous) pedigree in our nation's history. In chapter 3 we describe the persistent lawbreaking of the squatting communities on the nineteenth-century frontier and the dramatic impact they had on the development of American land law.

The key difference between the acquisitive and expressive categories is the distinction between intentional lawbreaking that generates immediate and substantial benefits for the lawbreaker and lawbreaking that generates no such *immediate* benefits but that instead self-consciously aims to achieve (or generate support for) a larger legal goal. Of course, in drawing this distinction we recognize that self-interest and expression can often seem like inseparable halves of the same whole; nevertheless, we think that it is appropriate to draw some descriptive and normative distinctions between the two, recognizing, of course, the need for caveats and the presence of borderline cases.

Even though unauthorized activity takes place in both the property and the intellectual property contexts, intellectual property law, particularly copyright, has tended to tolerate more gray areas than other types of property regulation. To take one example, the copyright doctrine of fair use, about which we will have more to say later, is notoriously indeterminate. Rather than establishing clear rules, the fair use test sets forth a series of factors that courts are to weigh in determining whether a particular use is lawful or infringing. The consequence of this for copyright is that, unlike in the case of the squatter or the sit-down trespasser, both of whom violated clearly established legal norms, for an enormous number of uses of copyrighted material, it is often difficult to say *ex ante* whether the user is an "outlaw." For this reason, and as we discuss in more detail in chapter 5, it is frequently more accurate in the intellectual property context to speak of "altlaws" rather than "outlaws." Because of the cloudiness of many intellectual property doctrines, intellectual property altlaws are more likely to be able to claim that their particular interpretation of the law is consistent with existing law than are property outlaws. In chapters 6 and 7 we discuss two stories of disobedience—one that focuses on the realm of patent disobedience in the global movement toward access to HIV medicines, and another that focuses on the significance of citizen journalism in the face of copyright restrictions. Both stories highlight the same expressive and acquisitive trajectories of real property disobedience that we explore in earlier chapters, but they also offer a much wider arena for contemplating whether the language of illegality properly attaches to such behaviors and whether the differences between intellectual property and real property require us to use different lenses altogether.

In part 3 we apply the theoretical and normative implications of our analysis to offer a series of suggestions concerning how the law should respond to property outlaws and altlaws. Here, we recognize that some forms (indeed most) of lawbreaking are unproductive. For this reason, our analysis does not aim to offer a categorical defense of the practice. Instead, we argue at the most general level that, in light of the importance of property outlaws to the evolution of property doctrine, the state's response to outlaws should be structured in specific ways to ensure that people are not overdeterred from (or unjustly punished for) challenging existing property regimes. The value of at least certain categories of property lawbreaking is twofold. First, there may in certain situations be value in the outlaw's directly redistributive conduct. That is, there may be circumstances under which we determine that the lawbreaker's decision to take someone else's property, either for him- or herself or for another, is itself defensible. We refer to this phenomenon as the lawbreaker's creation of "redistributive value." Second, in cases of persistent, widespread lawbreaking, citizen behavior may communicate useful information to property owners and to the state, indicating that some element of property law, or some dimension of the owners' use of property, may be out of date or unjust. We refer to this signaling function provided by outlaw conduct as its "informational value." If property lawbreaking is perfectly deterred, either through draconian penalties or certain enforcement, each of these categories of potential value stands to be eliminated.

There are some indications that we might be headed toward overdeterrence, at least in certain areas. Although a far cry from our hypothetical law-enforcement machine, advances in the technology of property-rights enforcement have the potential to reduce the expected rewards of property lawbreaking to such an extent that any redistributive and informational value of such lawbreaking would be eliminated. This is particularly true in the arena of intellectual property, where the rise of digital technology, in combination with the Internet, has increased the ability of intellectual property owners to monitor and control how ordinary citizens use their products.

In light of these implications, we propose a set of policy responses that lawmakers and law enforcers can use to balance property's dual role as a source of stability and a locus of recurrent conflict and to preserve space for the possibility of productive forms of disobedience while discouraging its more destructive forms. Because the implications of our discussion differ somewhat for tangible and intellectual property, we address the two areas separately. In chapter 9 we focus on tangible property. Our proposals in this area are relatively modest, largely because the law of tangible property already contains within it a number of venerable doctrines that, in our view, acknowledge the value of a significant amount of lawbreaking. The doctrines of adverse possession and necessity, for example, provide mechanisms for nonconsensual transfers of property under certain constrained conditions. Although there have been some efforts in recent years to roll these doctrines back, or limit their application, we favor preserving them and even expanding them in a number of respects.

In chapters 10 through 12 we turn our attention toward intellectual property. When altlaws successfully defy the wishes of intellectual property owners, they can generate substantial redistributive value by shifting legal entitlements away from owners. Similarly, their conduct generates potentially valuable information about the popular conception of (or rejection of) the intellectual property owner's version of the law, and provides an important opportunity for decision makers to clarify or revise official legal norms defining the intellectual property owner's rights. Although we draw on the similarities between outlaw and altlaw conduct in our exploration of how the law might respond, we also draw on a series of special considerations that focus on preserving innovation in the face of the complex legal challenges presented by the altlaw.

It is important to note, at the outset, that this book is not meant to be construed as a repudiation of the power and importance of the rule of law. That would be an unduly simplistic account of what property disobedience actually comprises. Instead, our project emerges from a strong faith in the rule of law, but one that embraces the occasional productive instability introduced by the forces of disobedience and that, in doing so, hopes to gain important insights into the law's proper response to the challenge posed by outlaws. Our goal, therefore, is not to undermine the institution of private property but to better understand its complexity and dynamism and, in the process, to spark new conversations about the direction that property and intellectual property law should take in the future.

1

WHY <u>PROPERTY</u> OUTLAWS?

We are not the first to observe the role of intentional lawbreaking in fostering valuable legal change. Legal theorists have long left some space for the occasional disorder created by conscientious civil disobedience. Two aspects of this literature, however, are of particular interest to us. First, these discussions typically fail to distinguish among the various substantive areas of law on which the mechanisms of intentional lawbreaking might operate. Second, with a few notable exceptions, they tend to disfavor or condemn what we are calling "acquisitive" disobedience. In this chapter we address the first of these issues. Later in the book we address, among other things, the significance (and at times insignificance) of the outlaw's goals in evaluating the proper legal response to lawbreakers.

Within the Western legal tradition, theorists have for centuries taken the position that citizens are not obliged to obey unjust laws. Saint Augustine, for example, famously said that "a law that is unjust seems to be no law at all."[1] Thomas Aquinas adopted and refined the Augustinian position in his own natural law jurisprudence. Unjust laws are not laws, Aquinas said, but rather acts of violence.[2] Frequently misunderstood (and misconstrued), the essence of Aquinas's position is that an unjust law does not compel obedience of its own moral force, although one may be obligated to obey unjust laws in order to avoid creating even worse consequences, such as social disorder or demoralization.[3] Although Aquinas's concern with the consequences of legal disobedience substantially qualifies his endorsement of unlawful behavior by citizens confronting unjust laws, Thomistic legal theory leaves ample room for justified disobedience. Thus, it was not at all inappropriate that, in defending the morality of his own campaign of civil disobedience against racial injustice in his famous "Letter from a Birmingham Jail," Martin Luther King Jr. relied heavily on this Augustinian-Thomistic natural law tradition.

More recently, Ronald Dworkin has made a powerful argument for the (limited) legitimacy of civil disobedience, an argument rooted in the dignity and power of individual conscience. Dworkin argues that lawbreaking can sometimes be justified when it is undertaken to protect a person's sense of integrity, as when the law requires people to perform acts that they view as deeply immoral, or when lawbreaking is employed as a means of expressing views about the injustice of an existing law. He distinguishes these two motives for lawbreaking from conduct aimed at merely expressing or hindering the foolishness of a particular law, which he considers more difficult to justify. Moreover, he distinguishes all three sorts of conscientious lawbreaking from "ordinary criminal activity motivated by selfishness or anger or cruelty or madness," which he says is always wrong.[4] Distinctions like Dworkin's have also been drawn by John Rawls (who argues that disobedience could not be based on group or self-interest alone) and Michael Walzer (who contrasts justifiable civil disobedience with "frivolous or criminal disobedience" not based on "morally serious" objections).[5]

In contrast to the justice-centered account of the natural law tradition and the focus on individual conscience within Dworkin's theory of justified disobedience, the work of some scholars has focused on the instrumental role of disobedience as a tool to challenge the inertia of the political system that impedes the realization of majority sentiment. In a recent essay in the *Yale Law Journal*, Daniel Markovits sets forth a more expansive justification of disobedience than Dworkin's, a justification based not on the governing role of individual conscience but on the nature of governance itself. His paper valuably highlights the institutional role of intentional lawbreaking as a tool for exposing and overcoming inertia within democratic processes. Markovits views inertia as an inescapable feature of democracy, one that is necessary for the cultivation and reproduction of democratic engagement. He argues that through the practice he terms "democratic disobedience," civil disobedients can overcome that inertia by using disobedience to bring outmoded laws dramatically to the attention of lawmakers and the electorate, forcing onto the agenda issues that might otherwise go undetected.[6]

Finally, in his classic *Harvard Law Review* foreword "*Nomos* and Narrative," Robert Cover takes an even broader approach, describing some lawbreaking as part of a process of decentralized legal interpretation through which dissenting groups pursue their own normative visions by structuring their lives around their own particular legal understandings. According to Cover, the private legal conceptions of these dissenting groups are, at least as an initial matter, no less "law" than the official legal understandings enshrined in the formal law of the dominant community. It is possible, Cover argues, that lawbreakers and judges alike "are all engaged in the task of constitutional understanding," and their distinctive perspectives "make us realize that we cannot pretend to a unitary law."[7] In contrast to conceptions of civil disobedience that view lawbreaking as an exceptional case of justified deviation from official versions of the law, and to Markovits's discussion of disobedience as a mechanism for vindicating subsumed majoritarian impulses, Cover's pluralistic approach views conscientious disobedience as an example of faithful commitment to a dissenting minority's own understanding of law.

Applying this conception, Cover describes the Greensboro protesters we discussed in the opening pages of this book not as lawbreakers so much as a group of people aligning their actions with their own reading of the Constitution. According to Cover, that behavior does not occur in a vacuum. By choosing to honor their commitment to an unofficial version of law, the lunch-counter protesters remained true to their legal vision while communicating to those in officialdom a forceful message of dissent. Equally important, in a manner not possible through any other means of legal discourse, they forced public officials to examine the strength of their own commitments to the official legal status quo—and some officials answered by embracing the protesters' legal interpretation.[8]

These four approaches we have been describing offer valuable insights into the legitimate role of legal disobedience in a democratic society. They have not, however, taken account of the possibility that there might be a special relationship between disobedient dissent and the law of property, understood broadly to include both tangible and intellectual property. We seek to add texture to these broader philosophical discussions of disobedience by focusing on the special significance that *property* lawbreaking has for private citizens who are disenfranchised from institutionalized structures. Outlaws and altlaws have played a uniquely important role by repeatedly vindicating rights and overcoming democratic inertia. By creating an informal space for actively reevaluating and challenging dominant legal understandings, they have helped catalyze deliberation about the degree to which the law may be based on outdated assumptions or has otherwise failed to give due regard to the rights or interests of some segment of the community.

In focusing on the particular value of lawbreaking for the development of property law, however, we do not deny that disobedience can be (and has been) used effectively to express political dissent about any number of questions. Our argument for the special significance of *property* lawbreaking proceeds in four stages: (1) first, we observe the (subjective and objective) importance of property in people's day-to-day lives; (2) next, for reasons related to its importance, we argue that property doctrines and distributions have a particularly strong tendency toward inertia and ossification; (3) somewhat paradoxically, however, despite its apparent stability, violations of property laws are typically seen as less culpable than other categories of unlawful acts; and (4) because of property's blend of importance, stability, and violability, property lawbreaking acquires a unique communicative power to reimagine our relationships with the material world and with each other and to provide an informal forum for airing conflicts over resources between owners and nonowners, which the law can eventually shift to accommodate.

The Important Role of Property in People's Lives

Tangible- and intangible-property laws play a vital role in shaping people's lives. Hegelian thinkers, such as Margaret Jane Radin, have thoughtfully elaborated theories asserting that property ownership is uniquely essential to the construction of personal identity and personhood.[9] These theorists argue that the control we enjoy over our property develops our capacity to act as autonomous beings. Moreover, our public exhibition of such control permits us to communicate that autonomy to our fellow citizens.[10]

One need not fully embrace Hegel's *Philosophy of Right,* or go as far as Radin in asserting a connection between property and identity, to appreciate the unique value of property in the construction and experience of our social reality. Ownership of land and the structures attached to land provide the spaces and places in which we carry out our social existence and clarify the divisions of labor, responsibility, and authority necessary for the very conduct of human society. We form and communicate our identities as individuals or members of groups by wrapping ourselves in personal or cultural property. Likewise, our contemporary popular culture is embodied in expressions and innovations that are increasingly protected by intellectual property. Accordingly, property rights and the social norms that accompany (and are often reinforced by) ownership play a vital role in ordering our interactions with other human beings. As the Canadian geographer Nicholas Blomley has put it, "the environment of the everyday is . . . propertied, divided into both thine and mine and more generally into public and private domains, all of which depend upon and presuppose the internalization of subtle and diverse property rules that enjoin comportment, movement, and action."[11]

The importance of property for human beings points in several directions at once. On the one hand, it suggests a need to protect existing property entitlements forcefully. On the other hand, the centrality of property to the satisfaction of fundamental human needs in turn creates a strong impetus for those excluded from participation in the system of ownership to challenge both existing property rules and established allocations of entitlements.[12]

For example, those who lack access to the social benefits of private ownership, such as the very poor and the homeless, find themselves extraordinarily isolated from much of the social and commercial activity that most of us take for granted.[13] This social isolation, rooted ultimately in our system of property distribution, can cause enormous psychological, and even physical, harm.[14] The isolating and disabling effects of *exclusion* from participation in a property system, however, mean that those on the outside looking in will often have few means to communicate their dissent beyond the simple act of taking or occupying.

This duality of stability and conflict is further complicated by the simultaneous over- and underinclusiveness of ownership as the crucial link between property and identity. Not all property owners feel the same expressive and interactive link between property, ownership, and identity, a factor that directly implicates the productive role of the lawbreaker in shifting entitlements. Vast numbers of property owners (publicly traded corporations and their shareholders, for example) feel no essential connection to a great deal of their owned properties. Conversely, many nonowners feel strong connections to many things they do not own but come into intimate contact with for any number of reasons.

The possibility of such a mismatch was, for example, the basis on which sit-down strikers in 1936 and 1937 defended their occupation of tire and automobile factories in an effort to force manufacturers to recognize workers' rights under federal law to unionize and bargain collectively. In 1937 alone, roughly 400,000 workers participated in nearly 500 sit-down strikes. At the height of the sit-down movement, industrial employment in Detroit slumped by a third as a result of the strikes. The largest of these strikes, the famous occupation of the General Motors facilities in Flint, Michigan, which involved tens of thousands of GM workers, began in the last days of 1936 and was resolved (favorably to the workers) just as the Supreme Court was hearing oral arguments in the pivotal *NLRB v. Jones & Laughlin Steel Corp.* case (the case that gave us the so-called "switch in time" in which the Court reversed its earlier opposition to the New Deal, averting a confrontation with the Roosevelt administration and a possible constitutional crisis).[15]

Employers responded to the sudden explosion of factory occupations by appealing to the sanctity of private property rights. According to Jim Pope, when GM initially refused to negotiate with sit-down strikers, it "claimed to be fighting for the rights of every car manufacturer, business, and even homeowner, for the sit-down strike was 'striking at the very heart of the right of possession of private property.'"[16] Employees, however, scoffed at the attempts by industrial employers to compare the nature of their ownership rights with those of homeowners. "Corporate property," they argued, "can be no one's 'castle' because the exclusion of others would render it useless."[17] To the contrary, the workers argued, their contribution to the production of corporate wealth gave them a property right of sorts in their relationship to the company, one that rivaled or exceeded the property rights of shareholder-owners. Robert

Morss Lovett, a GM shareholder writing for the *Nation,* agreed. He provocatively posed the question: "Who has the better human and natural right to call the Fisher plant his—I, whose connection with General Motors is determined by the price recorded on the New York Stock Exchange, or the worker whose life and livelihood are bound up in the operation of making cars?"[18] It is precisely this imperfect fit between formal ownership and perceived moral entitlement that underlies the ambiguous role of the property outlaw and sets the stage for potentially productive disobedience.

Property's Conservatism and Stability

In part because of its importance, property law is unusually resistant to change. Indeed, central to the ability of the institution of property to carry out its functions are the stability and predictability that it fosters for both owners and nonowners alike. As Abraham Bell and Gideon Parchomovsky have argued, "the institution of property is designed to create and defend the value that inheres in *stable* ownership."[19] Further, fixed, stable property rules, Thomas Merrill and Henry Smith have suggested, provide informational benefits not just for the owner but also for the entire community that orders itself around those entitlements.[20] In addition, as Radin has observed, stable property rights help individuals develop their identities and carry out their life plans.[21]

Almost by definition, then, property law resists changes to its contours for the very reason that change, as such, strikes at one of its core values. Indeed, American property law is full of doctrines whose principal purpose appears to be the hindrance of nonconsensual alterations in existing property allocations and entitlements. Laws governing contract, fraud, theft, and trespass wrap existing property entitlements in a blanket of public and private legal protection. And the law of the Fifth Amendment's takings clause, particularly the doctrine of regulatory takings, makes it more difficult for the government to rearrange or redefine existing property rights. A regulatory taking can only be found when there has been some change in property law.[22] By requiring government to compensate property owners for certain—particularly severe—changes, regulatory takings law serves as a check on political property reform, a function that has endeared it to libertarians as a legal vehicle for hindering activist government.

Similarly, both property and intellectual property doctrines demonstrate a pervasive tendency to favor first-in-time property users. When two litigants have more or less equivalent claims, property law almost reflexively favors the prior user, appropriator, or occupant.[23] Likewise, the conclusion that a plaintiff has "come to a nuisance," although not an ironclad defense, often makes it harder (or at least more expensive) for that plaintiff to obtain relief.[24] Within trademark law, which protects brands and logos, the law almost always favors the senior user of a mark, even if a junior user has made strong claims of investment. These choices have the collective effect of providing a legal endorsement for preexisting property uses.

Finally, although not a legal protection, the so-called endowment effects and status quo biases described by behavioral economists suggest that people, in general, are willing to sacrifice more to avoid parting with property in their possession than to acquire new property.[25] Applied to processes for change in property law and distributions, this insight suggests that, all things being equal, people who benefit from existing property regimes will tend to resist changes in that regime more forcefully than others will push for modifications. Endowment effects likely exert a conservative influence that helps make property law resistant to political change. As a result of these mutually reinforcing conservative tendencies, official property doctrine is especially unlikely to keep pace with the shifting conditions of society.

Property's (Relative) Violability

At the same time that property is considered so sacred, so revered, within our legal system, it is ironically also considered more violable than other sorts of laws. Even those who are conscientiously opposed to violence as a means of political expression are frequently willing to violate *property* laws in order to draw attention to their grievances and perceive no inconsistency in this combination of positions. Martin Luther King, Jr., for example, was a disciple of Gandhian nonviolence, but he was willing to nonviolently violate the laws of trespass to drive home the seriousness of his demand for racial justice. Other pacifist theorists have made similar distinctions between actions directed toward persons and property.[26] Like an effigy, property is an effective target of protest because of its visible, often physical, identification with the owner or the prevailing legal regime. But, occasional Hegelian hyperbole aside, property is decidedly *not* the person. Accordingly, *nonviolent* violations of property rights constitute a means of communicating strong moral disapproval that many people of high moral scruples deem acceptable. The sit-in and the picket are therefore favorite tools of those seeking nonviolently to change the behavior of the property owner or to draw attention to an important issue.

This tolerance of lawbreaking is even more pronounced in the area of intellectual property. As we are constantly reminded by the Motion Picture Association of America in the public service announcements that precede their movies on DVD, people who are otherwise law abiding seem more than willing to violate intellectual property laws by downloading a pirated copy of a film or song from a peer-to-peer network. The sheer volume of intellectual property infringement among otherwise law-abiding citizens powerfully demonstrates the widespread perception that, somehow, violating intellectual property laws is a less serious offense than breaking other sorts of laws.

The reduced social disapproval of property-rights violations is embraced by the criminal law itself. A hierarchy of values categorically placing bodily injury over harm to property forms the basis for the Model Penal Code's treatment of the criminal defense of necessity. As we discuss at length in later chapters, that doctrine justifies criminal law violations committed in order to avoid greater evils.[27] The doctrine therefore raises the crucial question of how to weigh various categories of harms. In discussing necessity, for example, the commentary to the Model Penal Code makes clear that harm to persons should always be given more weight than harm to property. Property might be harmed to avoid death or bodily injury, but the opposite should not be permitted.

Finally, our moral intuitions make us more willing to excuse the hungry man who quietly sneaks a loaf of bread from a grocery store than someone faced with the same dilemma who satisfies his needs by threatening a passerby. Criminal laws affirm this intuition by treating simple theft as less serious than robbery. The reason lies in a broad consensus that the act of surreptitiously taking someone's property is less blameworthy than doing so in a way that threatens bodily harm. A related intuition may also underlie the common law definition of burglary, which requires that the defendant enter someone's dwelling at night with the intent to commit a felony. The twin requirements that the invaded structure be a dwelling and that the invasion occur at night may reflect efforts to isolate those invasions in which the occupant is probably present, confusion heightened, and bodily injury more likely to result.[28] In light of the apparent consensus that violations of property rights are less serious than bodily harm, it is not surprising that nonowners, disregarded by the political process but acutely aware of the shortcomings of the dominant legal regime, have frequently perceived property disobedience as an acceptable means for altering the status quo.

The Communicative Abilities of Property Lawbreaking

Property's combination of importance, rigidity, and violability gives property lawbreaking a unique communicative power. Property's importance and consequent rigidity mean that the law of property will frequently fall out of step with the values of the community it serves. But, paradoxically, its simultaneous importance and violability will also combine to encourage dissidents to resort to lawbreaking to register their strong dissent.

The power of this dissent is generated by two of its features. First, an actor's willingness to break the law signals the intensity of his or her dissenting position and creates a difficult choice for officials charged with enforcing the law. As Cover put it, "The community that disobeys the criminal law upon the authority of its own constitutional interpretation . . . forces the judge to choose between affirming his interpretation of the official law through violence against the protesters and permitting the polynomia of legal meaning to extend to the domain of social practice and control. The judge's commitment is tested as he is asked what he intends to be the meaning of his law and whether his hand will be part of the bridge that links the official vision . . . with the reality of people in jail."[29] Cover's observation focuses on the intensity signaled by a willingness to endure (or mete out) criminal punishment, but it overlooks a second, deeper source of lawbreaking's communicative power.

The intensity of the dissent communicated by the lawbreaker (or the commitment signaled by the law enforcer) is, of course, communicated whether the protester objects to the very law being broken or to some other law. But if legal dissidents are to perform the role of exposing unjust, inefficient, or outdated legal norms, they can sometimes do so most effectively by acting out their interpretations in practice rather than merely engaging in abstract discussion, even discussion that is accompanied by the exclamation mark of lawbreaking.

As one observer noted during the 1960 lunch-counter protests we discussed in the introduction, "no argument in a court of law could have dramatized the immorality and irrationality of [segregated lunch counters] as did the sit-ins."[30] There is a difference between talking about something and being confronted with an actual example of it. In a different context, John Hart Ely, quoting Alexander Bickel, hinted at the commonsense epistemological reasons for this difference between mere discussion and actual confrontation: "There are reasons for supposing that our moral sensors function *best* under the pressure of experience. Most of us did not fully wake up to the immorality of the war in Vietnam until we were shown pictures of Vietnamese children being scalded by American napalm. . . . The effect [of watching vicious white supremacists spewing racist epithets at black children] must have been something like what used to happen to individuals (the young Lincoln among them), at the sight of an actual slave auction."[31] As Bickel eloquently argues, our lived experience of law is deeply relevant to our own moral and legal interpretation of both justice and injustice, and the role of regulation in facilitating both ends.

Property law deals with tangible (and intangible) realms that touch on basic necessities and entitlements. In breaking property laws, outlaws are therefore able to offer a particularly concrete vision of their alternative conception of the law. The property outlaw provides the official decision maker with actual, rather than hypothetical, circumstances under which to evaluate his or her commitment to the status quo. Discussions *about* dissenting legal interpretations, even those backed by the forceful message of civil disobedience, leave much to the imagination. The relative violability of property laws means that property outlaws can sometimes actually live out their alternative conception of property relations by violating the law in the very way they would like to see it changed. Their actions can reverse the operation of status quo biases and force officials and members of the public to confront an actual instance (as opposed to an abstract concept). Both of these effects give property outlaws an exceptional ability to push those in power toward a different conclusion than might have been expected given the political currents that prevailed before they acted.[32]

The importance of being able to conjure a concrete vision of alternative legal possibilities through the violation of property laws should not be underestimated. It can be all too simple to reject or judge an abstraction. But our generalized ethical commitments are often incomplete or indeterminate. They may well be poor predictors of our actual moral judgments when we are confronted with specific instances of dissenting legal interpretations being lived out in their full human richness.[33]

Thus, whites in the 1960s South, who might have expressed opposition when abstractly questioned in advance about integrated lunch counters, sometimes reacted to the student sit-ins in ways that were unexpected, perhaps even to themselves. For example, in response to her observation of black students being turned away from a lunch counter in Raleigh, one "elderly white woman of the old school" said: "They have no business refusing such nice, polite young people."[34] Even the segregationist *Richmond News Leader* found its preconceived notions of black and white challenged by the protesters. The newspaper gave the following account of one of the sit-ins: "Here were the colored students, in coats, white shirts, ties, and one of them was reading Goethe and one was taking notes from a biology text. And here, on the sidewalk outside, was a gang of white boys come to heckle, a ragtail rabble, slack-jawed, black-jacketed, grinning fit to kill, and some of them, God save the mark, were waving the proud and honored flag of the Southern States in the last war fought by gentlemen. Eheu! It gives one pause."[35]

The concrete living out of an alternative legal conception by property outlaws can undermine opposition to reform that may be based on irrational prejudice and untested presuppositions. At the outset of the sit-in protests in the South, the *Wall Street Journal* editorial page warned readers of the evils of civil rights legislation that would go beyond the recognition of equal public rights and seek "to compel immediate social integration." The proposed legislation, it predicted, "is doomed to failure. . . . Such enforced togetherness amounts to regimentation, an invasion of individual rights."[36] It was not until black southerners simply took for themselves the right to sit at the same lunch counters as whites, forcing togetherness in the absence of legal protection (indeed, in direct opposition to the owners' legal right to exclude), that the segregationists' predictions of doom began to be debunked. In over one hundred cities across the South, lunch counters were desegregated in response to the sit-ins, three years prior to the passage of Title II of the Civil Rights Act of 1964, in many cases without the violent white reaction predicted by naysayers at the *Wall Street Journal* and elsewhere. The success of that experience likely helped smooth the path for the passage of Title II, which prohibited racial segregation in privately owned "places of public accommodation," and undermined arguments that "enforced togetherness" was doomed to failure.

2

PROPERTY AND INTELLECTUAL PROPERTY

In February 1996, in Davos, Switzerland, John Perry Barlow, a cattle rancher and former lyricist for the Grateful Dead, sat down to write A Declaration of the Independence of Cyberspace, largely in response to Congress's passage of the Telecommunications Act of 1996, one of the first major legislative attempts to govern the Internet. "Governments of the Industrial World, you weary giants of flesh and steel," he began, "I come from Cyberspace, the new home of Mind. On behalf of the future, I ask you of the past to leave us alone." "Governments derive their just powers from the consent of the governed. You have neither solicited nor received ours," Barlow explained, describing cyberspace as a world that transcended matter and materiality. "Your legal concepts of property, expression, identity, movement, and context do not apply to us," he argued. "Your increasingly obsolete information industries would perpetuate themselves by proposing laws, in America and elsewhere, that claim to own speech itself throughout the world. These laws would declare ideas to be another industrial product, no more noble than [a] pig iron. In our world, whatever the human mind may create can be reproduced and distributed infinitely at no cost." In his closing line, Barlow predicted, "We will create a civilization of the Mind in Cyberspace. May it be more humane and fair than the world your governments have made before."[1]

In later writings, Barlow waxed eloquently about the limits of intellectual property protections over digital property, arguing that we needed an entirely new set of methods to govern patent and copyright in cyberspace.

"Software piracy laws are so practically unenforceable and breaking them has become so socially acceptable," Barlow explained, "that only a thin minority appears compelled, either by fear or conscience, to obey them." Given the vast divergence between law and social practice, Barlow argued, we needed to unlearn the laws of intellectual property in order to grapple with the creation of a new world in cyberspace—a world that is based on relationships and interactivity rather than simple possession and tangible property.[2]

The gist of Barlow's observations, at the time, were also echoed by other prominent scholars such as Jessica Litman, Lawrence Lessig, and Siva Vaidhyanathan, who explored the limitations of copyright law in the modern world of digital technology.[3] Each of them focused on the concrete question of how copyright law should govern the challenges that digital technology posed to its structure, and how the law should relate to innovation in the world of cyberspace. Should law intrude on these worlds at all? And if so, how? If not, who would regulate them? Writing in 1994, Jessica Litman observed: "If we want ordinary people to look at unlicensed music, unlicensed software, and unlicensed digital reading material the same way they see stolen personal property, and to treat them accordingly, then we need to teach them the rules that govern intellectual property when we teach them the rules that govern other personal property, which is to say, in elementary school. . . . The problem, though, is that our current copyright statute could not be taught in elementary school, because elementary school students couldn't understand it. Indeed, their teachers couldn't understand it. Copyright lawyers don't understand it."[4] Relying on Litman, Professor John Logie writes that "to the extent that average American citizens engage with intellectual property laws, they understand them to be maddeningly complex, unfair, or insignificant, or some combination of all three."[5]

Every year, standing before students in intellectual property classes across the country, law professors ask their classes which will prevail: intellectual property law's efforts to regulate, or technology's potential to evade control.[6] At the turn of the millennium, the prediction of most students seemed clear: technology would win. Students regaled us with tales of their own experiences online, sharing files, posting files, and (sometimes) escaping the ire of their respective undergraduate institutions, many of which stood by haplessly as file sharing spread across peer-to-peer networks. Some of our students identified with the hacker movement, and others did not, but many expressed the feeling that intellectual property protections threatened to encroach on a dizzying array of activities that they once thought were outside the reach of regulation.

Over the past several years, however, we have noticed a shift. In response to the questions raised by Barlow's assertions, our students have increasingly begun to argue that the law will ultimately prevail over technology. They have stopped offering stories about their successes in evading the law and have begun more often to defend intellectual property owners' efforts to control the sharing of content. "It's their property," many of them now argue. "They have a right to control who has access to it." In many ways, their confident assertions belie a deep uncertainty in the law regarding whether this presumption holds true in the context of both tangible and intangible property. Is intellectual property just like any other form of property, or is it something else?

Information as a Public Good

Information, unlike tangible property, is characterized by nonrivalrous consumption. If one person possesses a tangible object, others cannot possess the very same good. But with information and ideas, as Thomas Jefferson and others famously noted, one person's possession does not exclude others. Because tangible property is composed of matter, it can only occupy one place at one time.[7] Once it has been created, however, intellectual property carries no such danger of scarcity. As several of the leading intellectual property scholars have pointed out, "in this state of nature, there is no danger of overuse, or overdistributing an idea, and no danger of fighting over who gets to use the idea without diminishing its value."[8] The nonrivalrous nature of the consumption of intellectual property means that more than one individual can share a single good simultaneously with others, and with no danger of depriving anyone else.

As a result, the law treats intellectual property rights differently from tangible property rights. Simply put, intellectual property law is preoccupied with preserving incentives to produce new information. The law of tangible property is also concerned with incentives to produce, but it adds to this a concern with questions of coordination and allocation, issues that are far less pressing in the informational context. Perhaps for these reasons, whereas the utility of tangible property often depends heavily on the law's clarity and predictability, intellectual property law is often perceived as its somewhat less stable cousin, a system characterized by imprecise boundaries, uncertain entitlements, and punctuated moments of legal change. In other words, because of their differences in subject matter, intellectual property law is not merely a subset of the law of tangible property, but rather comprises a distinct legal regime, albeit one that shares important similarities with the law of tangible property.[9]

In authorizing Congress to create intellectual property, the Constitution reflects intellectual property's focus on incentives to produce. Article I, Section 8 of the Constitution permits Congress to grant exclusive rights to authors and inventors for "limited times" in order "to promote the progress of science and useful arts." Thus, intellectual property rights are granted for a fixed period of time, are limited in scope, and are only awarded when they meet certain basic threshold requirements for protection. In other words, from the outset, intellectual property law's instrumentalist and (broadly) utilitarian outlook justifies the grant of exclusive rights to authors and inventors on the basis of the need to ensure proper incentives to innovate. This constitutional provision suggests a different form of governance for intellectual property than for real property, one that focuses more narrowly on questions of aggregative welfare.

As many authors have observed, Article I, Section 8's utilitarian calculus reflects an asserted balance between the need to protect incentives for the creation of new information and the desire to protect access to a resource whose consumption is nonrivalrous. As a result of the tension between these interests, intellectual property is governed not only by legal devices that focus on *ex ante* incentives that promote innovation, but also by devices that encourage the dissemination and the protection of information once it is created.[10] Intellectual property rights, though robust, are nonetheless frequently relativized by countervailing interests like freedom of expression,[11] freedom of imagination,[12] the right to innovate,[13] and other public-welfare considerations.[14]

Whereas the "thinglike" quality of tangible property facilitates the identification of relatively static and fixed boundaries, the boundaries are necessarily less clear in the context of intellectual property because of its intangible and nonrivalrous nature.[15] As Clarissa Long has aptly observed, because information is intangible, determining the protected borders of an intellectual good is far more complicated than simply surveying a piece of land.[16] Nonowners first must determine the qualitative aspects of a good to separate out protected from unprotected elements, an exercise that causes some degree of uncertainty and unpredictability.[17] This task is made more difficult by the very composition of intellectual property itself, which often reflects a combination of ideas, expressions, and innovations that build on publicly available material. Copyrighted works, for example, can sometimes comprise a mixture of original content and expression that the author takes out of the public domain. And patented inventions can build on prior innovations, many of which are themselves the subject of patent protection. Moreover, as Long notes: "The goods protected by intellectual property rights will usually not have accumulated a patina of social meaning that reduces information costs for observers. Intellectual goods, by their very nature, are new and original creations and will present particularly high information costs at the start of their term of protection. Whereas everyone knows what land is, observers must often learn about intellectual goods unaided by longstanding customary definitions, communal norms, or widespread social understandings about their meanings and boundaries."[18] Since there are so many different kinds of "things" that operate under the rubric of intellectual property, determining the boundaries of intellectual property generates enormous information costs for those attempting to move through the world without infringing on another person's rights.

Not only do nonowners need to understand precisely what constitutes the good itself, but they will also need to know what actions constitute infringement so that they can avoid "trespassing" on the owner's rights.[19] Whereas widespread familiarity with the concept of, for example, private land and (generally speaking) the rights that owners enjoy in it lowers information costs for nonowners and potential transaction partners, the law of intellectual property often demands a much higher degree of sophistication regarding both the attributes of a particular good and the definition of infringement.[20]

As a result of these complexities, in each of the areas covered by the term "intellectual property," we see a much larger role for the law in defining the boundaries of owned "things." For example, within the world of patents, which covers inventions, the law has set forth important limits regarding the subject matter susceptible to patent ownership, prohibiting the patenting of inventions that merely embody the laws of nature. In addition, protection is unavailable for natural substances and printed matter. The reason for this is to ensure the accessibility of basic "building blocks" of invention for everyone to use, and to reward only those inventors who have used their labor in the creation of new inventions. By drawing lines around protected and unprotected subject matter, the law ensures the continued accessibility of areas for others to use and build upon.

Similarly, in the context of copyrighted works, the law imposes a series of requirements that also attempt to draw lines around protected and unprotected subject matter: the law of copyright ensures that original literary, musical, dramatic, and artistic works are protected, and the law expressly limits the duration of protection in order to stimulate the eventual entry of works into the public domain. Moreover, the law contains two important limitations that carve out space for the needs of nonowners. One of these limitations is known as the "idea-expression dichotomy," under which, simply put, copyright protection applies to the expression of an idea but not to the idea itself. This limitation is similar to the subject-matter limitations in patent law: it carves out specific territory—ideas—that are free from proprietary restrictions. Another limitation involves the "fair use" provisions in copyright, which permit nonowners to use a work for the purposes of criticism, news reporting, teaching, or scholarship (among other uses). The fair use exception thus capitalizes on the nonrivalrous nature of intellectual property by enabling others to share in the work when there are important expressive issues at stake, a point that underscores the role of expressive disobedience in intellectual property.

Finally, trademark law, which protects brands, symbols, and logos, has a similar set of doctrines that carve out certain areas of expression, like parodies and comparative advertising, from the control of a trademark owner. The functional features of a product, in addition, are also not protected by trademark law. Because trademark rights are not limited in time, the functionality doctrine is important for protecting the ability of other products to compete in the marketplace. In addition, the law's protections for parodies and other types of expressive uses reconcile the interests of intellectual property enforcement with those of the First Amendment.

Doctrines restricting patentability, the idea-expression dichotomy, functionality, and, perhaps most of all, fair use, are subtle tools that make intellectual property rights far more complex for the average layperson to navigate than the more familiar world of tangible property. Whereas tangible property's "thinglike" character often defines and circumscribes the laws that govern property, the opposite is true in the context of intellectual property. The intangible nature of intellectual property means that the law has a great deal more latitude in defining intellectual assets and the structure of the rights that accompany them. The result, we argue, is an architecture that is typically prone to qualify the rights of owners at different points, particularly when there are First Amendment considerations at stake.

Distinguishing Intellectual Property from Real Property

At some points, the "exclusivity" of intellectual property rights conflicts with these larger social goals, and these conflicts often provide fertile ground for the emergence of disobedience. The differences between intellectual property and tangible property necessarily force us to consider their relevance for our discussions of disobedience. What does "disobedience" mean in the intellectual property context? Outright illegality? Unauthorized behavior? Unlicensed free riding? We discuss examples of all three in this book, though it is not always easy to tell the difference between them.

Most people who consider the relationship between intellectual property and property either enthusiastically embrace or emphatically reject the increasing tendency to treat intellectual property as "property" by deferring to the wishes of owners.[21] These two perspectives have both descriptive and normative facets. The first viewpoint celebrates the similarities between property and intellectual property, and generally favors greater propertization of intellectual property and stronger property-rule entitlements that honor an owner's gatekeeping right of exclusion. Underlying this view is an implicit presumption that disobedience and other types of free riding are undesirable, irrespective of the precise circumstances under which they occur.[22] According to this view, disobedience will cause property owners to refuse to invest sufficient resources in their property because the ability of others to copy or imitate intellectual works without incurring the costs of creation will prohibit original owners from reaping sufficient profits from their creative investments.[23]

The second perspective is the diametric opposite of the first—it rejects out of hand the analogy of intellectual property to traditional property and views intellectual property law as a far more regulatory regime than its tangible property counterpart, highlighting its similarity to other approaches like tort law, telecommunications and antitrust regulation.[24] Scholars in this latter group frequently emphasize the numerous exceptions to the right of owners to exclude in intellectual property law, offering the examples of compulsory licensing and limited exceptions for fair or experimental use.[25] Given the range of these exceptions, scholars within this latter group implicitly suggest the need for a limited tolerance toward free riding, arguing that owners need not necessarily control or reap all the benefits of their creation in order for the law to encourage future creation.[26]

Both perspectives, we think, tend to suggest oversimplified conceptions of both tangible property rights and the trajectories of disobedience. It is true, for example, that copyright law has a limited duration (in contrast to land ownership, which, conceptually speaking, lasts forever).[27] It is also true that landowners have broader exclusion rights—at least as compared with rights under copyright law.[28] But, at the same time, tangible property rights are far from absolute—a point that intellectual property scholars have more recently begun to emphasize.[29] Laws that govern land frequently operate to limit landowners' rights in particular circumstances. Nuisance law, civil rights protections, environmental regulations, and zoning laws restrict owners' freedom to do as they please with their land. These sorts of regulations emerge out of a recognition that constraints on owners' rights are necessary to protect the public interest in privately held land.

As Stewart Sterk has reminded us, analogies can be dangerous things in comparing real and intellectual property. Real property rights, he has explained, are often relied on to prevent breaches of the peace and the "tragedy of the commons."[30] But in the intellectual property context, rights are designed primarily to preserve the incentive to create. Unlike in the tangible property context, in which trespass or theft might completely or partially deprive an owner of his or her property, the nonrivalrous nature of intellectual property means that questions of deprivation play out differently and suggests that we need not stamp out all forms of disobedience as a result. Further, there is also a deeper reason why leaving room for free riding is important. As Mark Lemley and others have recognized, at least some of the free riding in question generates "technological spillovers" that turn out to be valuable forms of innovative activity.[31]

Part of the tendency in some quarters to excoriate the free rider flows from the largely unexamined view that private ownership is necessary to avoid the "tragedy of the commons."[32] This perspective is also historically linked to the emergence of tangible property rights and connected to the avoidance of negative externalities associated with overuse. Garrett Hardin's famous story of the degraded commons suggests that privatization is necessary in tangible resources because it helps to prevent the overuse of resources.[33] Hardin argued that if property owners were forced to internalize the costs as well as the benefits of their uses, owners would be more likely to take steps to prevent damage and overgrazing.

Extending this view, Harold Demsetz argued that private ownership discourages waste by helping the owner to internalize the consequences of her land-use decisions and facilitating the internalization of the externalities that remain by encouraging self-interested bargaining between neighboring owners. "Private ownership of land," he argued, "will internalize many of the external costs associated with communal ownership, for now an owner, by virtue of his power to exclude others, can generally count on realizing the rewards associated with husbanding the game and increasing the fertility of his land. This concentration of benefits and costs on owners creates incentives to utilize resources more efficiently."[34] Yet, as Lemley has pointed out, Demsetz's work and its progeny were concerned largely with the role of property rights as tools for internalizing *negative* externalities, not positive externalities: "At first glance, free riding seems to be the flip theory of the tragedy of the commons—one party benefits from another's use of land without compensating the other for that benefit. It does not follow, however, that because we are right to try to internalize negative externalities we should be similarly preoccupied with internalizing positive externalities. In a market economy, we are only concerned that producers make enough return to cover their costs, including a reasonable profit. So long as that cost is covered, the fact that consumers value the good for more than the price, or that others also benefit from the goods produced, is not considered a problem. Indeed, it is an endemic part of the market economy."[35] Positive externalities are common in the context of real property; Lemley offers the example of a private property owner who cannot be expected to internalize all the positive benefits from his garden as an example. It seems almost preposterous, he observes, to suggest that these benefits must be fully captured by the owner alone. Although it is important for real property owners to internalize negative externalities because of their impact on the autonomy of others, it is less important for owners to internalize all of the positive externalities unless generating these benefits requires substantial investment.[36]

Although the privatization thesis has certainly helped solve some problems of resource overuse in the context of real property, Lemley's analysis suggests that a robust right to exclude free riding seems far less necessary when the resources in question are nonrivalrous or unlimited in nature, as in the context of intellectual property, and where they fail to create negative externalities like pollution.[37] Since positive externalities predominate in intellectual property, justifications for privatization based on the need to internalize negative externalities have less salience.[38] Moreover, because creative activity is an iterative process, broad intellectual property rights run the risk of deterring the very innovation they are supposed to promote.[39]

Further, intellectual property rights, no less than rights in tangible property, are sticky. Once created, endowment effects, transaction costs, and political inertia combine to keep them in place. In many cases, some free riding may be essential to combat this inertia and force decision makers to consider altering the status quo. Within this dialectic between legal inertia and transgression, the free rider plays an integral role by exposing existing entitlements to a degree of instability and forcing either the parties, the judiciary, or the legislature to at least consider a reallocation of entitlements. Intellectual property law as a whole—far from always protecting the rights of the owner—thus serves as a means by which the expected entitlements of an owner can be tested against other, nonowner, interests. At times in this context, for example, disobedient conduct by a nonowner is often motivated not by a desire to acquire, or to own, but by a desire to share, or alternatively, by a demand for recognition that access to an intellectual good (like a patented medicine) is integral to the fulfillment of other important interests, such as life, liberty, culture, or health. Like real property, intellectual property touches on nearly every aspect of self-actualization and survival for nonowners and owners alike—patents deal with (among other things) pharmaceuticals that are essential for human survival; copyright governs expression, autonomy, and creativity for both authors and appropriators; trademarks protect both corporate and consumer interests in commerce; and trade secrets address basic entitlements to protect innovation for owners and those who seek to reverse engineer them. The weight of these sometimes conflicting interests provides a powerful set of reasons for considering carefully the role of disobedience in intellectual property's regulatory framework.

Piracy and Privatization

Intellectual property's basic architecture attempts to protect innovation and access simultaneously, both to secure expressive rights and to foster future follow-on inventions. Yet the advent of the digital age has drastically affected the law's efforts to pursue these two goals simultaneously. As Stacey Dogan has explained, the public-oriented goal of Article I, Section 8 justified many of the limitations that copyright law developed along the way—fair use, for example, functions, in part, to ensure a balance between preserving the incentive to create and permitting access by the consuming public. And throughout the development of copyright, it has become quite clear that unauthorized copying is an unwanted (at least from the perspective of owners), but persistent, reality. Even before the digital age began, Dogan explains, "a certain amount of unauthorized copying continued unchecked," largely because of the difficulty of controlling or regulating every use of a copyrighted work. Although the law promised a basic level of protection, it could not ensure that every single use of a copyrighted work was paid for. As a result, the common law of copyright accepted some leakage but stepped in to prevent "market-destroying floods."[40] Total recoupment was simply an impossible task.

Then came a technological revolution. New copying technologies introduced to the consuming public in the 1950s, 1960s, and 1970s—photocopiers, cassette recorders, and VCRs—shifted the balance in dramatic ways. With these new devices, people could make copies of copyrighted content in a matter of hours or minutes, and they could more easily share them with others.[41] Copyright owners faced two choices: either pursue individual violators, or target the equipment manufacturers themselves for inducing the infringing activities of their users. Given the difficulty of identifying the end users, the copyright industry chose to pursue the equipment manufacturers first, identifying theories of indirect, rather than direct, liability to shift the responsibility for infringement to the innovators who made the infringement possible.[42] In 1984, however, the copyright owners suffered a major setback with the Supreme Court's decision in *Sony Corp. of America v. Universal City Studios, Inc.*, which protected VCR manufacturers against copyright actions by the movie industry and which we discuss further in chapter 11. Ironically, the *Sony* decision encouraged the development of even more technologies—some to the benefit of copyright owners, who discovered a huge market for film consumption in the home.

Copyright has historically tolerated some forms of disobedience and unlicensed uses, but the digital age opened up two new trajectories of possibility for users and copyright owners, respectively. In the 1990s, for the first time, an end user could make, replicate, and distribute near-perfect copies of a copyrighted album—all in a few seconds.[43] As copying technologies spread, the music industry examined its options and decided to stamp out as many forms of disobedience as it could. As a result, another trajectory began to develop in response to the first. This trajectory, however, involved a much more expansive system of control and surveillance than copyright law had ever relied on to detect unauthorized activity. The recording industry began filing suit against both the creators of copying software and technologies and against the end users themselves, suing tens of thousands of individuals in the space of just a few years.

Together, these two trajectories have transformed the landscape of copyright law and have had a drastic impact on privacy, expression, and innovation. During this period of digital upheaval, copyright owners have managed to effect changes, both inside and outside the law, in order to protect their interests. Recent developments within intellectual property law have tended to strengthen proprietary boundaries at the expense of concerns with access.[44] The basic story of the expansion of intellectual property rights in the modern era is a complicated one, and we do not seek to comprehensively retell it here. Yet three factors—consolidation, privatization, and the rise of technological constraints—deserve mention because they collectively pose profound challenges to intellectual property's original, leaky architecture, enabling greater private ordering over owned products and, paradoxically, increasing the incidence of disobedience as a result.[45]

Consider, for example, the role of increased market consolidation in copyright law. As Neil Netanel and others have pointed out with respect to copyright, the vast majority of works are now becoming rapidly concentrated in the hands of a few owners.[46] Even had this not been accompanied by changes in the law, this development would have been sufficient to foster a speech hierarchy in which corporate entities hold vast inventories of expressive works, leaving a disproportionate burden on individuals to obtain permission to use them.[47]

This consolidation has been accompanied by a steady expansion of the very bundle of rights within intellectual property itself.[48] Today's copyright owners, for example, enjoy an increasingly robust right to exclude others from access,[49] longer terms of protection,[50] and a wider degree of ownership over derivative markets[51]—and copyright infringers face stiffer penalties for infringement. The rights of patentees have expanded through greater enforcement and a drastic enlargement of protected subject matter in the context of biotechnology, business methods, and computer software.[52] Similarly, trademark law has expanded beyond its original purpose of protecting the consumer from confusion and now exists as a powerful means of enabling corporations to protect the social meaning of brands from dilution. Meanwhile, the rights granted to nonowners to engage in unauthorized uses—fair use in the copyright context, compulsory licensing in the patent context, nominative uses in trademark law—are highly contested and case specific, often yielding little precedential value outside of identical circumstances and thus generating a great deal of uncertainty.[53] As Michael Carrier, an intellectual property professor at Rutgers, has argued, "IP [intellectual property] is quickly becoming property not only in the essentially unlimited scope and duration of its initial rights but also in the ubiquitous assertions that IP is absolute property."[54]

Finally, the precarious utilitarian balance between incentives and access that characterizes the governance of intellectual property is swiftly becoming overshadowed by an increasing tendency to rely on private forms of control through a combination of contract and technological surveillance. The advent of digital rights management (DRM) technologies and other types of "lock-out" systems, for example, promises to foreclose certain challenges to intellectual property from reaching the public arena. More and more, disputes tend to be resolved by the growing power of technology and contract. Consider four basic types of private ordering that now often take precedence over other intellectual property restrictions:

• *Contractual Enforcement:* A greater and greater number of disputes are now being resolved through "shrinkwrap" and "clickwrap" licenses that often require licensees to agree to forgo a variety of activities, including reverse engineering, that might fall within the contours of fair use protections. Courts have repeatedly enforced these agreements, finding that they are not preempted by the fair use protections within copyright law and are thus enforceable as a matter of state contract law.[55]

• *Technological Surveillance:* Today, a greater number of copyright owners are exploring ways to circumvent fair use protections through the growing power of DRM, which enables a host of technological restraints on a user's anonymous ability to shift, copy, and access content, irrespective of whether such activities fall within the purviews of fair use and other allowable exceptions. Even the realm of biotechnology has parallels: scholars have outlined the development of biological "lock-out" systems that, for example, physically prevent activities that go beyond the scope of a license, such as unlicensed seed production from genetically engineered crops.[56]

• *Private Dispute Resolution:* Particularly in the realms of trademark law and copyright, more and more private entities have become responsible for mediating proprietary conflicts over issues like freedom of speech, due process, and privacy. The best example is the Internet Corporation for Assigned Names and Numbers (ICANN), a private agency created to mediate trademark disputes in cyberspace. But concerns have also been raised about the Digital Millennium Copyright Act's (DMCA's) notice-and-takedown provision (section 512), which requires only a very low level of judicial oversight over potential copyright disputes and thus allows the private copyright owner to exercise a high degree of control over material placed on Web sites by third parties.

• *Anticircumvention:* Perhaps the strongest tool that content owners rely on is the DMCA's criminal prohibition against circumventing technological copy-protection measures. Under this provision, disabling a technical protection measure can create criminal liability. The act thereby gives content owners a "new right of technological access," enabling them to restrict access to content, even in cases of fair use.[57] The anticircumvention provisions essentially allow copyright owners to block access to uncopyrightable material, even material that is taken from the public domain or whose use almost certainly would have been protected by fair use defenses.[58] This development has led some commentators to use the term "paracopyright" to refer to these rights as a separate system that offers content owners an exclusive right not only to control access to technologically protected works but also to affect the development of ancillary technologies that might be related to content protection.[59]

As a result of these shifts toward consolidation, privatization, and technological control, owners have a much greater degree of authority to decide the composition of allowable uses and restraints on the intellectual property in question. As these forces expand, the owner's assertions of authority, instead of the relevant legal doctrines, increasingly define the boundaries of disobedience.[60] The public domain shrinks in contrast to the burgeoning world of privatized intellectual property, and property rights often take precedence over countervailing public values in freedom of speech, due process, and innovation.

As we discuss in part 4, this tug of war unwittingly produces a symbiotic relationship between disobedience and the architecture of intellectual property law. When the interests of nonowners are pervasively ignored within traditional democratic channels, as they arguably have been in the area of intellectual property law, nonowners typically resort to either litigation or disobedience to resolve their differences. Discussions of disobedience in the mainstream media, however, often short-circuit this process by casting the figure of the intellectual property owner as the sole legitimate actor, threatened by piracy, and fail to grasp the complex relationship between disobedience, enforcement, and the overall dynamism and long-term health of the intellectual property system. This tendency is even more damaging in the intellectual property context than it is in the domain of traditional property law because, in contrast to disobedience in the context of tangible property, where boundaries and doctrines are more settled, intellectual property challenges tend to center on the most unsettled areas of technological innovation—the uploading and downloading of protected content, for example, and the relevant intermediaries that enable the sharing of content. The law governing these actions—and the norms that accompany them—are rapidly changing. Precisely because the law is so unsettled, the occurrence of unauthorized behavior signals important information to the courts and legislatures about the purpose, intent, and effect of such activities and whether the law should shift to accommodate these interests by instituting forms of compulsory licensing or other means, as it has done in the past.

PART

PROPERTY OUTLAWS
AND INTELLECTUAL
PROPERTY ALTLAWS

3

ACQUISITIVE OUTLAWS: THE PIONEERS

Land for Revenue versus Land for Settlers

The history of land law in the nineteenth-century American West is, in part, one of protracted conflict between those who held legal title, whether Native American tribes, the federal government, or private land speculators, and white settlers who resided on the land, often without any formal legal entitlement. This story is well known and has been ably narrated by a series of historians.[1] Our purpose in this discussion is therefore not a comprehensive retelling. Instead, we hope simply to bring out the ways in which this struggle replicates a pattern of legal change instigated by property outlaws, one that that has been repeated throughout the history of Anglo-American property law in a variety of guises.

In this particular case, settlers created the impetus for legal change by running roughshod over established property laws and creating for themselves communities governed by their own, self-serving, conception of just property relations. Although their actions were initially met with condemnation by the legal establishment, their persistent lawbreaking ultimately paid off. Over the course of the nineteenth century, the law slowly but surely accommodated the reality the settlers created on the ground.

The nineteenth-century conflict between settlers and owners played out within the context of a larger policy debate between competing visions of how to dispose of the vast western territories acquired by the federal government. By 1803, more than 90 percent of the nation's territory consisted of sparsely populated wild lands, with large (and increasing) areas under public ownership.[2] Virtually all involved in the discussion agreed that the ultimate goal of government policy should be to expeditiously transfer public lands to private ownership and to encourage settlement of what was, from the perspective of everyone but the Native Americans who lived there, an unoccupied and unexploited continent.[3]

According to the historian Paul W. Gates, despite these shared long-term goals, policymakers differed over whether public lands should be used as a source of revenue to help pay off the national debt or as a reservoir of public largess with which to create a nation of Jeffersonian small-holding property owners. Policymakers who wanted to use public lands to generate revenue typically preferred to auction off large tracts of public lands to speculators at relatively high prices, with the understanding that the speculators would in turn divide the property into smaller parcels to sell or lease to settlers for a profit. Policymakers who favored direct distribution of public lands to settlers extolled the virtues of a nation of small property owners and warned of the consequences of widespread tenancy and concentrated absentee ownership. They therefore argued for the direct sale of public land to actual settlers at low, fixed prices or, even better, the free distribution of land to those willing to work it.[4]

Unsurprisingly, the sympathies of the settlers themselves were with the latter camp. Although their judgment was no doubt influenced by their own substantial financial interest in the outcome of the policy debates, settlers and their supporters tended to frame their views in strongly moral terms. Every citizen, they argued, is entitled to own land, and the claims of those who actually work the land should take precedence over the fungible interests of absentee land speculators.[5] Echoing John Locke's discussions of property in the *Second Treatise of Government*, settlers frequently argued that "possession was the best title" and that to obtain true ownership of the wilderness lands on the frontier, a putative owner "must not only claim it, but annex his labor to it, and make it more fit for the use of man; till this be done it remains in the common stock, and anyone who needs to improve it for his support, has a right."[6]

An 1861 editorial in the *Wisconsin State Register* was typical of settler sentiment on the western frontier: "The land policy of the general government has been a mistaken policy always. One of the great injuries done to the Lumbermen of the Pineries has been done by the selling of land to speculators. This never should have been done, either in the pineries or in the agricultural lands. The selling of land ought always to have been confined to the actual settler."[7] Settlers demanded that the government recognize a right of "preemption," which would entitle squatters on public land to purchase the land they improved at low, fixed prices or, at a minimum, to obtain the value of their improvements from those who purchased the land at auction.[8]

In the years following Independence, the center of national power was firmly planted in the already settled lands of the East. Consequently, the views of western settlers initially took a backseat to the views of those who favored using public land to raise revenue. Late-eighteenth- and early-nineteenth-century land law for the most part provided for the sale of public lands at auction with relatively high minimum prices and large minimum tract sizes. During the land boom of 1835–1837, for example, three of every four acres of public land sold by the federal government went to speculators.[9]

In order to make public lands as attractive as possible to those bidding in the auctions, the federal government attempted to keep squatters off public lands in advance of the sale. To that end, Congress enacted a series of laws criminalizing intrusion by settlers on federally owned land.[10] During the Jefferson administration, illegal settlers faced fines of up to $1,000 and imprisonment of up to one year.[11] From time to time, the military was called in to push squatters off federal lands. Despite all of this, settlers persisted in trespassing on and improving government land.

Faced with an official policy of hostility toward their presence and an inability to purchase land at an affordable price, squatters turned to extralegal means to obtain the land they occupied. They organized themselves into "settlers associations," which served as quasi governments that protected squatters' interests, both by lobbying state and federal governments and by threatening retribution against those who attempted to take title to squatter-occupied lands. According to Alfred Brunson, "if a speculator should bid on a settler's farm, he was knocked down & dragged out of the office, & if the striker was prosecuted & fined, the settlers paid the expense by common consent among themselves."[12] When things got out of hand, squatters could count on their friends and neighbors on the local jury to acquit. Groups of settlers attended land auctions in order to intimidate speculators' agents from bidding on squatter-occupied land. Settlers were frequently able to achieve what amounted to a de facto preemption right by flouting federal laws mandating competitive bidding.[13]

Legal Responses

Eastern politicians condemned the squatters' lawless "usurpation of public lands" and "audacious defiance" in the face of Congress's will, accusing squatters of being "greedy, lawless land grabbers who had no respect for law, order, absentee ownership of property, and Indian rights."[14] President James Madison issued a proclamation warning "uninformed or evil disposed persons . . . who have unlawfully taken possession of or made any settlement on the public lands . . . forthwith to remove therefrom" or face ejection by the army and criminal prosecution for trespass.[15] Even Kentucky senator Henry Clay, whose state contained a large number of untitled settlers, dismissed squatters as a "lawless rabble."[16]

The dim view of squatters held by the eastern establishment was not shared by residents of the West. Western public opinion, among squatters and legal settlers alike, favored squatters over absentee landlords, public and private.[17] Of course, many settlers were themselves also landlords and speculators, but westerners typically distinguished between resident and absentee speculators. As Paul W. Gates put it, resident speculators "paid their taxes more regularly, made some improvements perhaps, and used their profits for the development of the community, whereas the [absentee owners] took their profits elsewhere and did nothing for the community."[18]

Western residents voiced three broad objections to absentee land speculators: (1) they paid their property taxes grudgingly, if at all; (2) they urged their agents to resist local public expenditures, no matter how necessary; and (3) they failed to improve their land, preferring to wait until the improvements made by others enhanced the value of their own property.[19] This parasitic strategy meant that in areas where large areas of land were held by absentee speculators, settlement and development were hindered, producing what one observer at the time referred to as a "speculators' desert."[20] "Idle and unimproved land," Gates noted, "yielded little in taxes, contributed nothing to the aid of railroads, drainage or other local improvement schemes, and sometimes, by its very existence, blighted the reputation and future prospects of an area. Compact and orderly settlement was impossible where settlers were forced to scatter widely in their search for government land, and scattered settlement made it difficult and expensive to secure roads and schools."[21] Iowa senator George Jones made the case against absentee speculators in an 1851 statement:

> In Wisconsin, near where I now reside, an English capitalist did buy at the Government land office for that district a large tract of the most fertile and valuable land, for which he paid the minimum price in money. . . . That single case . . . had the most deleterious effect on the settlement and improvement of that part of the country. I know the country well, for I resided in it for some seventeen years, and know that it is one of the richest counties in America for fertility of soil, mineral resources, water power, timber, etc., and yet it has been kept back in population and wealth because of this monopoly, whilst less fertile and desirable districts, where no such obstruction existed, have become thickly settled. These lands were entered into in 1836–7 and are still held by the original purchaser, who many years ago . . . refused $5 per acre, and would not sell now for less than . . . ten or fifteen dollars. The consequence is that the emigrant has to push on still further to the westward, at the loss of time and money, and health, to get inferior land and a less desirable home.[22]

Kansas senator Jim Lane concurred. "No greater damage can be inflicted upon a State," he argued in the Senate in 1850, "than to have its lands held in large quantities by non-residents. I have travelled days over . . . Iowa without seeing a house, and on asking the reason, the answer was because the land belonged to non-residents."[23]

Absentee ownership had a significant impact on patterns of land tenure, and the consequences could persist for decades. Areas of Indiana purchased by large-scale land speculators ultimately yielded communities characterized by poorer tenant farmers, whereas areas originally settled by squatters resulted in more affluent communities of small-scale landowners. Moreover, as late as the mid-twentieth century, those tenant-occupied territories were associated with lower land values, poorer-quality homes, and less-cautious husbandry that led to more topsoil depletion relative to areas where smaller-scale owner-occupied landholdings dominated.[24]

Over time, squatters were able to leverage their support within settler communities to obtain the legal changes they demanded. In part, this victory grew out of local residents' and officials' sympathy for the squatters and the ability of those officials to use local property laws to undermine federal policy. It also reflected the general helplessness of the federal government in the face of a concerted refusal to obey the law. Failure by federal officials to recognize the reality of squatters' power threatened to undermine general respect for law on the frontier.[25] Ultimately, then, settlers' continued refusal to recognize the rights of absentee owners rendered the federal government's pro-speculator stance untenable.

Although local governments could not directly counter the federal policy of selling public lands to absentee speculators, they could support squatters by adapting local laws to make it easier for squatters to dispossess private absentee owners. According to the historian Henry Cohen, "a kind of guerrilla warfare against absentee landlords was endemic in the West."[26] For example, Cohen describes, local governments raised taxes on land to make it expensive for absentee landlords to hold land idle while they waited for land values to increase. Local law also sometimes required payment of taxes in specie while permitting rent to be paid in depreciated paper currency.

High taxes also made it relatively easy for local residents to obtain tax titles on absentee-owned property. This was particularly true when, as sometimes happened, local officials refused to accept tax payments from the agents of absentee owners.[27] The significance of tax title was enhanced by local laws, which often granted favorable treatment to squatters who occupied land with "color of title," a requirement that could be satisfied by purchasing tax-delinquent land at cut-rate prices at a government tax sale. In a move pioneered by Kentucky but imitated across the West, statutes also frequently required owners who succeeded in an ejectment action against squatters with color of title to reimburse the occupants for any increase in value due to improvements they had made. Because local juries were responsible for assessing the value of the land and improvements, they could be counted on to protect the interests of their untitled neighbors over the property rights of an absentee owner, and, unsurprisingly, they frequently found those improvements to exceed the value of the land itself. Combined with liberalized adverse-possession statutes in western states that shortened periods for transferring title from owners to occupiers and granted other sorts of favorable treatment for those claiming under color of title, tax titles constituted a powerful tool in the hands of squatters on private land.[28]

State courts likewise pitched in on behalf of squatters.[29] For example, in the 1820 case *Parker v. Stephens,* the Kentucky Court of Appeals, acting under the auspices of "equitable principles," extended to squatters having no color of title the statutory protection Kentucky offered to untitled settlers with color of title. When the U.S. Supreme Court invalidated that Kentucky statute in 1823 in *Green v. Biddle,* its decision was excoriated in the local press. For their part, local courts simply ignored the high court's ruling and continued to enforce the popular state law.[30]

The unwillingness of state courts in the West to act against the interest of settlers made good political sense. After all, as Gates noted, "the local judge, dependent upon popular support for re-election, could not afford to challenge the prevailing custom[s]."[31] Accordingly, as several property scholars have observed, over the course of the nineteenth century, local courts transformed state property law in ways that favored the actual occupants of land over absentee owners.[32] John Sprankling has, in a series of articles, documented the variety of ways in which nineteenth-century state courts modified the common law in order to encourage intensive uses of wild lands, uses that also favored the interests of local residents over those of distant speculators.[33] Most significantly, in the context of adverse possession, Sprankling has argued, courts loosened the requirements for the intensity of the activity on the basis of which possessors could assert ownership. As applied to wilderness land, these changes eviscerated the requirement that a possessor's activity be sufficiently permanent and visible so as to put the true owner on notice that someone else was making use of his or her property.

The liberalized approach to adverse possession was a powerful tool in the hands of squatters in the nineteenth-century American West, particularly because the American law of adverse possession has not traditionally inquired into the subjective state of mind of adverse possessors.[34] Indeed, when jurisdictions have deviated from this general stance, they have often done so to *rule out* adverse possession on the basis of a good-faith mistake about one's ownership. This counterintuitive approach, embodied in the so-called Maine rule, at one time enjoyed "considerable support" but has more recently fallen from grace.[35] The Maine rule has the effect of favoring claims by squatters who knowingly trespass on absentee-owned land, but makes it virtually impossible for unintended boundary encroachments—the sort most likely to arise between neighbors—to mature into adverse possession. Such a rule made some sense for Maine, where settlers had a long tradition of resistance against absentee proprietors. Squatters were a significant political force in the state after its break from Massachusetts in 1820. Until that time, Massachusetts had, like the federal government in the West, used its Maine lands as a source of state revenue, preferring to sell the land in large lots to speculators.[36] Consequently, Maine had its own absentee-owner problem and struggled during the middle decades of the nineteenth century to attract and retain settlers lured by the western frontier. In appeals that were the mirror image of Horace Greeley's famous advice (quoting John Soule) to go West, editorials in Maine papers urged residents to "Stay at Home!"[37]

The adoption of local legal innovations favoring squatters explains why easterners at the time tended to regard frontier settlers as "having no respect for private property and as being ever ready to strain and distort the law to strike at nonresidents."[38] Nevertheless, confronted with an utter inability to protect absentee owners or to enforce prohibitions against squatting on federal land, the federal government slowly but surely began to alter its policies during the middle decades of the nineteenth century, shifting from the use of public land for revenue and toward the direct distribution of land to actual settlers.

The first federal concessions to illegal squatters were a series of retroactive preemption laws passed repeatedly during the first half of the nineteenth century. Perhaps more significantly, however, the tone of federal policy began to shift markedly under the Jackson administration in the 1830s. Andrew Jackson himself called absentee ownership—or, as he put it, "non-resident proprietorship"—"one of the greatest obstacles to the advancement of a new country."[39] In his 1836 Specie Circular, he sought to deter speculation in federal lands by requiring payment for the purchase of those lands in specie only. The last paragraph of the circular stated that the action was being taken "to withhold any countenance of facilities in the power of the Government from the monopoly of public lands in the hands of speculators and capitalists, to the injury of the actual settlers in the new States."[40] President Martin Van Buren reaffirmed this shift in policy in his first annual message to Congress, when he observed that "selling [public] lands for the greatest possible sum of money without regard to higher considerations" was not the proper goal of federal land policy.[41]

But a more significant victory for squatters came in 1841, when Congress, in the Act of September 4, 1841, enacted the first generally applicable and prospective preemption statute for surveyed federal lands. In creating such a right, the federal government in effect abandoned its long-standing (though increasingly empty) position that squatting on public lands was illegal and should be discouraged or punished. Over the subsequent years, the 1841 preemption statute was steadily expanded to cover both surveyed and unsurveyed land (see, for example, the Act of June 2, 1862). The federal embrace of squatters' rights reached its apogee with the 1862 Homestead Act, which provided for the free acquisition of federal land by those who met the statute's five-year residency and improvement requirements.

The transformation of the image of squatters from the shameless law-breakers and usurpers reviled by eastern elites to the revered pioneers of American mythology is nothing if not ironic. But squatters' influence on American land law and on patterns of land tenure in the United States is undeniable. Their persistent and acquisitive lawbreaking raised the political profile of conflicts over how to dispose of the massive quantities of public land acquired by the U.S. government during the first half of the nineteenth century and ultimately led to the resolution of the conflict in their favor.

4

EXPRESSIVE OUTLAWS: CIVIL RIGHTS SIT-INS

The Lunch-Counter Sit-In Movement

Prior to the 1960s, the civil rights movement was focused largely on achieving legal change through a sophisticated litigation program in the federal courts directed by the NAACP. Congressman John Lewis, who made his start in public life as a student leader of sit-ins in Nashville, characterized the NAACP-led strategy as relying on "a handful of lawyers [working] in a closed courtroom."[1] Students in Greensboro, North Carolina, however, dramatically shifted the focus of the movement when they began sitting in at segregated lunch counters in February 1960—protests that were quickly replicated by student groups across the South.[2] Within weeks, students were trespassing at segregated lunch counters in copycat actions in nearly three dozen southern cities; they were well organized, nonviolent, and persistent.[3]

The sit-in movement we first described in the introduction falls squarely within our category of intentional property lawbreaking intended to bring about larger changes in existing property laws. Throughout the South, the segregation of privately owned places of public accommodation, such as the Woolworth's lunch counters targeted by the Greensboro students, was not accomplished by mandate of state or local law, as is sometimes suggested.[4] Instead, black patrons were typically excluded as a matter of local "custom," that is, through owners' private exercise of their common law property right to exclude.[5] By disobeying store owners' instructions to leave the premises, the black students participating in lunch-counter sit-ins were, like the squatters in the American West, intentionally disregarding the very property rights they sought to change.

That the sit-ins were primarily expressive can hardly be questioned. The goals of the sit-in participants would not have been satisfied had they simply been allowed to eat at the lunch counters where they were sitting, without larger changes prohibiting the maintenance of segregated lunch counters more generally. Instead, the sit-ins were aimed at achieving a broad legal transformation of the social meaning of public accommodation, a transformation that would permanently rearrange the property rights of all owners, for the benefit of *all* black citizens—whether or not they had participated in the sit-ins.

The expressive nature of the sit-ins is further illustrated by the symbolic force participants attributed to the act of lawbreaking itself. Many of the participants in the sit-ins spoke about the deep significance of their protests, independent of any legal change they might ultimately have been instrumental in bringing about. One Greensboro demonstrator, for example, later said of the first day of the sit-ins: "I probably felt better that day than I've ever felt in my life. I felt as though I had gained my manhood."[6] Unsurprisingly, then, historians have described the protests in plainly expressive terms. William Chafe, for example, describes the protests as "a new language," adding, "The language communicated a message different from that which had been heard before. A direct connection existed between style and content. In an almost visceral way, the sit-ins expressed the dissatisfaction and anger of the black community toward white indifference."[7]

The initial reaction to the sit-ins among mainstream civil rights leaders and elites within the black community was largely one of disapproval. Some black professionals, put off by the protesters' disregard for the law —a tactic that they thought likely to prove counterproductive—were "slow to support the students."[8] And the NAACP, which was, as a general matter, "hostile to mass action, and especially to breaking the law," initially refused to support the sit-in movement.[9] After hearing about the Greensboro sit-ins, Thurgood Marshall "stormed around the room proclaiming . . . that he did not care what anyone said, he was not going to represent a bunch of crazy colored students who violated the sacred property rights of white folks by going into their stores or lunch counters and refusing to leave when ordered to do so."[10]

Reaction among many southern whites, who had long believed and insisted that southern blacks were content with the segregated status quo, was even more hostile. Governor Luther Hodges of North Carolina, for example, called the sit-ins "counterproductive and a threat to law and order."[11] "I have no sympathy whatsoever," he declared, "for any group of people who deliberately engage in activities which any reasonable person can see will result in a breakdown of law and order, as well as interference with the normal and proper operation of a private business."[12] Governor Ernest F. Hollings of South Carolina lashed out at the protesters, who, he said, "think they can violate any law, especially if they have a Bible in their hands."[13]

In Washington, D.C., southern politicians denounced the conduct of the sit-in protesters on the floor of both the House and the Senate. Georgia congressman Elijah Lewis Forrester, for example, condemned the tactic, arguing that the protests had "caused fights, riots, and near riots."[14] Arkansas senator John McClellan argued that the sit-in demonstrators were "stirring up bad feeling and tension and hatred between the races."[15] He relied on the protestors' actions as his stated reason for opposing the Civil Rights Act of 1960.

In countless letters to the editor, southern whites deplored the sit-in participants as lawless violators of property rights.[16] As one letter (characteristically) put it, "those who invaded private property in violation of the regulations of the owners are the violators of our oldest and most time-honored laws and should be dealt with as lawbreakers. . . . Those who want to make a protest against the regulations of the owners have a perfect right to do so, but such protests should be made through the proper channels and within the law."[17]

White moderates in the South, though expressing sympathy with the protester's goals, likewise disapproved of their violation of property rights and called for the protesters to express their grievances by less confrontational means. The moderate *Greensboro Daily News,* for example, attempted to weave a middle path, disapproving of the sit-in participants' unlawful tactics while criticizing business owners who welcomed black shoppers throughout their stores only to exclude them from lunch-counter service.[18] "The right to private property is a precious one," the newspaper's editors warned in an April 1960 editorial. "It ought not to be chipped away, even in what may be considered a righteous cause. Once weakened in one area, it becomes subject to attack in others, and precedents designed for good purposes may later be used for objectionable or evil ones. This newspaper has joined Governor Leroy Collins and other thoughtful Southerners in questioning the fairness of inviting the Negro into variety stores and soliciting his trade, and when he has bought his merchandise then declining to let him sit down on a stool for a cup of coffee. But we have also recognized, with the courts, that a private business has, and ought to have under our laws, the right to operate as it sees fit, in a discriminatory fashion or otherwise."[19]

Former president Harry Truman, using more colorful language, concurred, observing that "if anyone came into my store and tried to stop business, I'd throw him out. The Negro should behave himself and show he's a good citizen."[20] Asked about the protests during a news conference at the height of the sit-ins, President Dwight D. Eisenhower equivocated, saying that although he sympathized "with the efforts of any group to enjoy the rights . . . of equality that they are guaranteed by the Constitution," equality should be pursued only "in a perfectly legal way."[21]

Legal Responses

Hundreds of students who participated in the sit-ins were arrested and charged, typically with criminal trespass.[22] In some jurisdictions, such as Georgia and Virginia, where applicable criminal statutes did not exist, legislatures quickly enacted laws making it a crime "to refuse to leave an establishment when requested to do so by its operator."[23] The new laws were described as efforts to protect property rights against the depredations of the sit-in protesters. Courts also used their power to issue injunctions backed by contempt sanctions to supplement existing laws. And in the Deep South, protesters frequently were brutalized, both by police and by counterprotesters.[24]

Despite this predictable legal (and extralegal) opposition, the sit-ins accomplished a variety of things. First, a number of merchants in cities affected by the sit-ins, and by the consumer boycotts they often inspired

among sympathizers, responded by voluntarily ending the practice of segregated lunch counters. The sit-ins put particular pressure on national
companies, such as Woolworth's, which, despite their willingness to serve
blacks at their lunch counters in northern states, acquiesced in segregationist norms at their stores in the South, even in the absence of any legal compulsion to do so.[25] After seven months of protests, Woolworth's
shifted away from a policy of blind deference to "local custom" and became one of the first lunch counters in Greensboro to offer integrated service.

Other businesses followed suit. "By September 1961, restaurants in 108
southern or border cities had ended racial segregation, as a result of the sit-
ins."[26] Typical in this regard was Winston-Salem, North Carolina, where
merchants voted unanimously on May 23, 1960, to integrate their lunch
counters. Even retailers in segregationist strongholds like Birmingham,
Alabama, proved susceptible to the pressure of the sit-in tactic, agreeing to
desegregate their facilities months before the passage of the 1964 Civil
Rights Act.[27]

Second, the sit-ins helped disabuse white southerners of the view that
blacks were satisfied with the segregated status quo.[28] Confronted with
the sit-ins, many white southerners initially continued to doubt that blacks
were dissatisfied, arguing instead that the protests were surely the work of
outside agitators.[29] But as the protests spread and gained strength, the
truth of black anger at their second-class treatment became undeniable. In
a letter to the editor, one white southerner explained how the protracted
protests had opened his eyes to the injustice of commercial segregation:
"For many years, while working every day in downtown Greensboro, I
have enjoyed the privilege of eating a well-balanced mid-day meal in one
of the lunch counters or restaurants in the business district. . . . The term
'have enjoyed' is used advisedly. The pleasure of dining in my accustomed
manner has recently been much diminished. That is because the lunch
counter sit-down protests have brought to my attention in sharp focus an
injustice that I formerly thought of, when at all, only vaguely. . . . If there
is anything Christ-like, charitable or just about prohibiting a fellow man to
eat, publicly, in any other than a vertical position, I challenge the most avid
of segregationists to point it out."[30]

By the same token, prior to the protests, many white politicians overestimated white enthusiasm for segregated facilities.[31] Despite predictions of doom from some quarters, the *Greensboro Daily News* reported that the introduction of integrated lunch-counter service in Winston-Salem, North Carolina, in May 1960 "took place quietly." On the first day of integrated service, "business appeared to be about normal . . . on a warm day when shoppers must have welcomed a convenient cool drink."[32] By 1964, it was increasingly difficult to hold on to the illusion of black acquiescence in or of widespread white insistence on segregated dining facilities, and, as a consequence, Miles Wolff said, "many white southerners were getting an entirely new picture of the Negro."[33]

Third, by refusing to be bound by property laws that ostensibly permitted merchants to exclude them on the basis of race, the protesting students demonstrated to local authorities the need for black cooperation in the preservation of private property rights. The disruption that a few hundred students were able to produce illustrated how even a small number of persistently uncooperative people excluded by the allocation of private ownership rights could substantially undermine the ability of the most determined state to enforce established law. In his memoirs, John Lewis describes how Nashville police were overwhelmed by the student protesters. "They couldn't deal with the numbers they were facing," he writes, "and there was no more room at the jail."[34] Aldon Morris tells a similar story about Martin Luther King Jr.'s 1963 Birmingham campaign: "Bull Connor and his political officials also felt pressure, because the jails were filling up."[35] Retailers across the South complained about the effects of the sit-ins on their bottom lines, due both to the boycotts organized by the protesters and their sympathizers and to the hesitance of white shoppers to frequent the stores for fear of disorder.

Finally, by taking the fight for civil rights out of the professionalized realm of civil litigation, the students succeeded in making it into a mass movement, thrusting the civil rights question to the top of the nation's political agenda. As Clifford Lytle put it, "the sit-ins marked the beginning of an era in which civil rights became the foremost issue of the day. The newspapers, television, radio, all media of communications became preoccupied with the problem. It was no longer necessary to keep racial abuses before the eyes of the public. The movement was becoming perpetuated by its own momentum. . . . The nation was beginning to see, and having seen, was becoming concerned. The invisible world of discrimination was no longer invisible."[36]

Whereas President Eisenhower distanced himself from the protesters' lawbreaking, presidential candidate John F. Kennedy gave them his support, a move that injected civil rights into the heart of the 1960 presidential election and set the stage for the passage, after Kennedy's assassination, of the Civil Rights Act of 1964.[37] Title II of that law prohibits discrimination on the basis of race in "any place of public accommodation," which the act defines broadly to include everything from hotels to movie theaters to neighborhood hamburger joints.[38] Although opponents criticized it, both before and after its passage, as a violation of private property rights, the statute reflected a broad endorsement by the American polity of the demands of the 1960 sit-in protestors. As Lytle put it, "the public had needed an awakening, and within the span of a few brief years, a cluster of militant interest groups had responded to this need" by taking the civil rights struggle out of the courtrooms and "in[to] the streets."[39] The result was a substantial curtailment of the common law right of business owners to exclude on whatever ground they saw fit.[40]

5

PROPERTY OUTLAWS AND PROPERTY ALTLAWS

In September 1999, Jon Johansen, a teenager from Norway, grew frustrated that he couldn't watch DVDs on his computer. Johansen's computer was running on the Linux operating system, which had not been licensed by the motion-picture industry to play DVDs.[1] To protect their movies from piracy, the studios relied on a digital rights management system called a Content Scramble System (CSS), an encryption algorithm that scrambled the data on a DVD and used a system of "keys" for decryption and authentication, thus enabling a user in possession of the "keys" to "unlock" the contents of a DVD. The studios licensed the use of their master key sets to a select number of DVD-player manufacturers, requiring them to keep the information confidential. Since computers running on the Linux system had no access to the keys, there was no way to enable them to play DVDs.

Johansen, with the help of a few others, managed to reverse engineer the CSS algorithm and access the keys.[2] His new program, simply put, descrambled the DVD's encryption software, enabling the user to play the DVD on an unauthorized device. Johansen called his program, appropriately, "DeCSS," and posted an executable version on his Web site.

A short time afterward, he received a letter from the Motion Picture Association of America (MPAA) demanding that he remove the DeCSS program from his Web site.[3] Once Johansen had posted DeCSS on his Web site, however, the program quickly became widely available online in various forms.[4] Fearful of this possibility, in the month of November 1999 alone, the MPAA sent out sixty-six cease and desist letters to various Web sites.[5] The response it received was not cooperative. Consider this excerpt from Slashdot, a Web site popular among computer programmers: "This code was released before anyone checked into the legal end of things. . . . Get it spread around as widely as possible. It may not be able to be used legally when all is said and done, but at least it will be out there for others to work with."[6]

Eric Corley, a journalist, decided to write an article about the DeCSS phenomenon for the Web site 2600.com, related to the print magazine *2600: The Hacker Quarterly*. The article described the process of developing DeCSS and also detailed the motion-picture industry's attempts to block access to the code. At the end of the article, Corley made a key decision—he posted the source and object code for DeCSS, later explaining, "In a journalistic world, . . . [y]ou have to show your evidence . . . and particularly in the magazine that I work for, people want to see specifically what it is that we are referring to." According to Corley's testimony in court, writing about DeCSS without actually posting the code would have been like "printing a story about a picture and not printing the picture."[7]

The motion-picture industry, of course, was understandably concerned about the flood of sites that had posted the DeCSS code and even more disconcerted that its letters were having only a minimal effect. So they adopted three separate legal strategies—one employing copyright law, one involving trade-secret law, and another using criminal law. (This last strategy, undertaken in Norway, sought to employ Norwegian criminal law against Johansen himself.)

On the East Coast of the United States, the motion-picture industry turned to federal copyright law to prevent Corley and others from linking to sites that posted DeCSS. The industry argued that the circulation of the code violated the anticircumvention and antitrafficking provisions of the Digital Millennium Copyright Act (DMCA).[8] The defendants responded by challenging the constitutionality of the DMCA itself, arguing that the studios' attempt to use the DMCA to regulate the posting of computer code violated the First Amendment and imposed substantial burdens on the exercise of fair use entitlements.

In California, the motion-picture industry turned to trade-secret law instead, and filed suits against every infringing Web site it could identify, ar-

guing that the Web site posters had misappropriated confidential proprietary information by posting the DeCSS code. The industry noted that
there were about 118 sites, spread across approximately eleven states and
eleven different countries, that had posted the information, and time was
running short: "If the court does not immediately enjoin the posting of
this proprietary information, the Plaintiff's right to protect this information as secret will surely be lost, given the current power of the Internet to
disseminate information and the Defendants' stated determination to do
so," the trial court observed in granting an initial preliminary injunction
against the posting of the information.[9]

Despite their best efforts, however, the industry's approach ultimately
backfired. The more that the MPAA tried to squelch the code, the more the
code continued to spread. One California court observed that after the suits
were filed, "a campaign of civil disobedience arose by which its proponents
tried to spread the DeCSS code as widely as possible before trial." As the
court explained, "Some of the defendants simply refused to take their postings down. Some people appeared at the courthouse on December 28, 1999
to pass out diskettes and written fliers that supposedly contained the DeCSS
code. They made and distributed T-shirts with parts of the code printed on
the back. There were even contests encouraging people to submit ideas
about how to disseminate the information as widely as possible."[10]

What could possibly justify such defiance? To these defendants, the
answer was simple: information was meant to be free, not subject to the
restrictive confines of property ownership. For many, the DeCSS code—
and freeing the code—implicated the heart of First Amendment protections. Although some defendants complied with the preliminary injunction, others continued to post links to other Web sites that carried
DeCSS. Under the heading "Stop the MPAA," Corley himself even
urged other Web sites to post the code, lest "we . . . be forced into submission."[11] Carnegie Mellon professor David Touretzky put together a
"DeCSS Gallery of Descramblers," which showed a variety of the artistic
and creative ways in which people posted and published the confidential
code. Some published it in mathematical proofs or on T-shirts and ties;
some used the code in songs for square dancing; and others found ways to
integrate the code into haikus. One person used the code in an animated
film. Another used the code to make an image with a DVD logo on the

front. Yahoo! even entered the fray, offering an electronic greeting card with the source code as the message (along with a coupon for a Slurpee). The code was, in short, available pretty much everywhere.[12]

Given the rapidly developing facts on the ground—the motion-picture industry playing the role of the hapless victim of teenage hackers, journalists, T-shirt makers, and computer geeks—it is perhaps unsurprising that courts reached wildly different outcomes in response to each of the industry's strategies. The copyright case in federal court—which implicated the balance between First Amendment and intellectual property interests—went in favor of the motion-picture industry, to the surprise of many legal scholars and commentators. The federal trial court issued an injunction that barred the defendants from posting or linking to DeCSS. In its opinion, the court noted that it hoped that the decision would "contribute to a climate of appropriate respect for intellectual property rights in an age in which the excitement of ready access to untold quantities of information has blurred in some minds the fact that taking what is not yours and not freely offered to you is stealing."[13]

On appeal, to the consternation of free-speech advocates, the U.S. Court of Appeals for the Second Circuit upheld the injunction. Even though computer code might be a protected form of speech, the court reasoned, the injunction did not violate the protections of the First Amendment because the DMCA was content neutral and targeted only the functional components of the DeCSS postings in question. The appeals court observed that it was forced to choose between two unattractive options: "either tolerate some impairment of communication in order to permit Congress to prohibit decryption that may lawfully be prevented, or tolerate some decryption in order to avoid some impairment of communication."[14] Given the alternatives, the court opted for the former but noted that it was "mindful that it is not for us to resolve the issues of public policy implications by the choice we have identified," suggesting that it was best for Congress to undertake that task.

Given the outcome, it may seem as though the forces of copyright prevailed. But the industry's victory was hollow. Even though the court prevented Corley from posting the information, the information had already become so widely disseminated that there was no way to keep it out of public hands. Moreover, as a result of the controversy that accompanied the case, many more individuals had become concerned about copyright's newfound tendency to muzzle the commentary of journalists, bloggers, and technology aficionados.[15] Despite the ruling, DeCSS remained ubiquitous on the Web.

Things took a different turn before the California state courts. There, contrary to the predictions of many legal commentators, the defendants (those who posted the code) won, though only after a long journey through the courts. The defendants initially lost in the trial court, which issued an injunction prohibiting others from posting the code. Then, one of the Web site posters, Andrew Bunner, appealed, claiming that his First Amendment rights had been violated.[16] Although the state Supreme Court upheld the preliminary injunction against the free-speech challenge, just as the Second Circuit had, it remanded the case to the lower court, directing it to examine whether the initial injunction was even warranted on trade secret grounds.[17]

In this issue, surprisingly, Bunner had the last word. On remand, the California Court of Appeal concluded that the injunction was invalid because the trade secret had already been destroyed by the time the initial injunction was issued. "If the allegedly proprietary information contained in DeCSS was already public knowledge when [the defendant in that case] posted the program to his Web site," the California court wrote, a Web site poster "could not be liable for misappropriation by republishing it because he would not have been disclosing a trade secret."[18] Given that the information was already so widely circulated, the court found that CSS had already lost its status as a trade secret when the case began.

The outcomes of both cases highlight an important and ironic reality in the relationship between intellectual property law and digital technology: the technology moves so quickly that facts can often change very dramatically while the judicial wheels slowly turn. Consequently, legal outcomes are only part of the story, and frequently not the most significant part. The DeCSS code is as ubiquitous today as if the cases had never been filed at all. In fact, as the California trade-secret case demonstrates, the Web site posters—and the journalists that followed them—were, in the end, far more successful in freeing the code than the motion-picture industry had expected.

And what about the third strategy, the criminal complaint filed against

Johansen himself? That too turned out to be unsuccessful. After two criminal trials in Norway, Johansen was acquitted on all counts. Since Johansen
reverse engineered the software in order to watch DVDs on his home
computer, and he made no infringing copies, the court found no evidence
that Johansen had used the decryption code for illegal purposes. Nor was
there any evidence that Johansen intended to contribute to illegal copying
since it was not illegal to use the DeCSS code to watch DVD films obtained by legal means. At the time, the decision was heralded as a "huge
win" for consumers because it suggested the existence of a sphere of protection for activities like reverse engineering.[19]

We begin with this example because it aptly demonstrates the difficulty
of discerning what constitutes disobedience in the intellectual property
context. A single act—posting computer code or linking to sites that post
the code—might have implications for copyright law, trade-secret law, or
First Amendment principles, but courts may reach different conclusions in
those three areas. In light of the uncertainty of legal outcomes, although
the DeCSS posters' actions reflected an unwillingness to back down in the
face of legal threats, it was impossible to determine how lawyers, activists,
and journalists should plan for the future. Is an outlaw someone who
defies the law, or someone who defies the wishes of a copyright owner, or
both? Sometimes the law is just too blurry. At times, the decision to violate
intellectual property rights crosses a perfectly clear line between legal and
illegal conduct, making the "outlaw" moniker appropriate. In many cases,
however, and as the DeCSS example (as well as the other intellectual property stories we will be recounting in this part) illustrates, the boundaries of
intellectual property rights are unclear, leaving the illegality of seemingly
transgressive actions open to dispute. If the conduct is not clearly illegal, in
what sense does a story like Johansen's constitute an example of property
"disobedience"?

It is admittedly difficult to come up with a definition that fits every case.
Accordingly, and to avoid confusion, we introduce the more neutral term
"altlaw" for the purposes of our discussion of the phenomenon of intellectual property transgression. We use the term "altlaw" to highlight two
alternative distinctions. First, we use it to distinguish between those who
understand their conduct to violate clearly established legal norms (outlaws) and those who have a plausible claim that their conduct fits within

the boundaries of existing law (altlaws). Second, alternatively, we use the term to distinguish roughly between those who reject the notion of intellectual property in a fairly categorical way (outlaws) and those who, broadly speaking, accept the idea that certain information can legitimately be subject to the constraints of ownership in order to encourage innovation (altlaws). Accordingly, the "altlaw" will be one whose conduct at least arguably falls within the boundaries of legality and, at the same time, who does not reject out of hand the concept of intellectual property.

The Altlaw and Legal Uncertainty

Although owners are often eager to label all such behavior "illegal" and to refer to their adversaries as outlaws or pirates, the murkiness of intellectual property rights will often make it very difficult—in the absence of protracted litigation—to determine conclusively that the behavior in question is actually contrary to the law. Those who engage in intellectual property disobedience are therefore often in a position to counter that their actions are perfectly lawful under, for example, expansive conceptions of constitutional rights of free speech or of the fair use doctrine. Or they may be able to argue that the law has not yet developed a cohesive viewpoint on the activity. As Robert Cover said, "The transformation of interpretation into legal meaning begins when someone accepts the demands of interpretation and, through the personal act of commitment, affirms the position taken."[20] Property altlaws are engaged in precisely this attempt to convert legal interpretation into legal meaning.

In contrast to property outlaws, property altlaws skirt the boundaries of property legality and can often make an objectively plausible argument that, although in a sense they are rebelling against the property status quo, their conduct actually falls within the boundaries of legal permissibility. For example, Johansen argued (successfully) that the law protected his reverse engineering; Corley argued (unsuccessfully, but plausibly) that the First Amendment protected his journalistic reporting. Successive posters of the DeCSS code believed (and the California court agreed) that the trade-secret protection that attached to CSS had already been extinguished. Each might have rightfully believed that the law, *ex ante,* protected the challenged activities. Thus, whether or not the conduct we are describing clearly violates laws of intellectual property, the stories we tell in the next two chapters involve actions taken without the authorization (and at times in the face of explicit hostility) of the intellectual property owners.

Even though unauthorized activity takes place in both the property and intellectual property contexts, intellectual property law, as we have already argued, has tended to tolerate more legal "gray" areas than other types of property regulation, particularly in the domain of copyright. There are several reasons for this. One stems from the formal dynamism and complexity typical of intellectual property regulation. Another related reason is the murkiness of the extralegal social and cultural norms that govern authorized uses, particularly in the areas of copyright and trademark. These extralegal intellectual property norms are frequently far less robust than the norms of the law governing tangible property. Consider, for example, the number of times that many individuals have copied, shared, or distributed copyrighted music without acquiring permission. Were these acts of sharing always illegal?

Where social norms are undefined, the law has to do more of the heavy lifting in establishing the precise scope of property rights. For intellectual property law, however, the work of formal legal definition has not (yet) been done comprehensively. In the context of tangible property, we have a decent idea of the boundaries of the owned object and the content of the legal rights conferred by ownership. But in the intellectual property context, as Mark Lemley writes, the boundaries are not always so clear, and it is thus more difficult to tell whether a person is trespassing upon another's intellectual property right. In the patent context, for example, it is often very hard to determine the scope of the patent right. These problems are exacerbated in other contexts as well: trade secrets (because they are secret) do not even require legal definition before a court, and copyright law's boundaries are often porous and obscure since a work can reflect a combination of copyrightable and uncopyrightable material.[21]

Because the boundaries of intellectual property are often ill-defined, crafting defenses to infringement can be difficult. To take one obvious example, the copyright doctrine of fair use, about which we will have more to say later, is notoriously indeterminate. Instead of establishing clear rules regarding which uses of copyrighted material are permitted and which are not, the fair use test sets forth a series of factors that courts are to weigh in determining whether a particular use is lawful or infringing. As a consequence, the fair use test offers prospective users little guidance in determining how far they can go without crossing the boundary between lawful fair use and unlawful infringement. Unlike in the case of the squatter or the sit-in protester, who has violated clearly established legal norms, in an enormous number of copyright cases, it may be genuinely impossible to say, *ex ante,* whether the user is an "outlaw."

Given the ambiguity that pervades much of intellectual property law, those making unauthorized use of protected information will often be able to make at least a colorable claim that they believed their activities were lawful. Should the issue ultimately come before a court, the intellectual property altlaw's argument is likely to be that the law already allows such conduct rather than that a new legal rule should be created to protect or ratify (after the fact) the challenged behavior. That is, intellectual property altlaws are more likely to be able to claim that their particular interpretation of the law is consistent with the "official" law as it already exists than are property outlaws, who typically understand the official law to be against them, as much as they would like to see it change.

We do not want to overstate the clarity of the distinction between outlaws and altlaws. In the intellectual property context, there are obviously some legal rules whose boundaries are clear enough. Even in the murky domain of copyright, for example, a great deal of the music file sharing over peer-to-peer networks cannot now arguably be claimed as fair use. So there certainly is such a thing as an intellectual property "outlaw." But the domain of uncertainty is larger in the intellectual property context, and as a consequence, the greatest potential for creative disobedience (with "disobedience" here understood by reference to the desires of intellectual property owners) has tended to arise in less determinate areas of intellectual property law.

Nor do we want to exaggerate the clarity of the law of tangible property. An argument might be made, and indeed was made, that the 1960 lunch-counter protests were in fact lawful acts, or at least were acts whose unlawfulness was open to question in the way that many purportedly fair uses of copyrighted material are. In the course of defending several protesters, for example, the NAACP argued that their actions were actually legal because any attempt by owners to exclude them from places of public accommodation solely on the basis of their race was unconstitutional state action under a broad reading of *Shelley v. Kraemer,* the case holding racially restrictive private covenants to be unconstitutional.[22] We think that there are reasons to question such a characterization of the 1960 protests. By 1960, *Shelley* had been read so narrowly that the NAACP's argument had very little chance of success.[23] More importantly, though, this interpretation of the sit-ins is inconsistent with the protesters' own understanding of their actions. To the extent that they saw their actions as lawful, sit-in protesters were typically appealing to a higher moral (that is, natural) law, not to positive (even constitutional) law.[24] But the point remains that, as in the intellectual property context, uncertainty regarding the scope of certain rules of tangible property means that at least some property "outlaws" might plausibly be described as property "altlaws." So the line between the two categories is somewhat indistinct. Nonetheless, we think that the distinction between disobedience that is self-consciously illegal (the outlaw) and disobedience that falls within a zone of legal uncertainty (the altlaw) remains a meaningful one and that the latter sort of disobedience is far more prominent in the intellectual property context.

In addition to the legal distinction we have been drawing, there are also differences in outlook and social meaning that correspond with the distinction between the outlaw and the altlaw. These differences, however, are also typically matters of degree. Altlaws, for example, will have a range of views about the likelihood that their activity is actually (or will, at the end of the day, be deemed) legal. Someone who thinks that there is only a 10 percent chance that a use of copyrighted material will be deemed "fair" probably has a perspective concerning the legality of such behavior that is not all that different from the attitude of an outlaw. For the same reasons, the social meaning of altlaw behavior will shade into outlaw territory as the likelihood that the altlaw behavior will ultimately be deemed legal decreases.[25]

In other words, the boundary between the altlaw and the outlaw can be an uncertain and porous one. This is increasingly the case as the law of intellectual property shapes itself around the claims of intellectual property owners. Given their enormous resources, and the legislative influence that those resources purchase, intellectual property owners are increasingly able to convert into legislative reality their characterizations of certain sorts of borderline conduct as "illegal." And in the meantime, intellectual property owners can shape the public perception of what "the law" is through their expansive access to the means of mass communication. Even if the courts would ultimately conclude, for example, that space shifting (that is, moving content from device to device) constituted fair use, for example, the recording industry can subject us to a protracted media campaign to convince us otherwise. These efforts by intellectual property owners have the power to push the altlaw's status much closer to that of the outlaw.

Another (related) factor that helps blur the line between the outlaw and the altlaw is the asymmetric impact of litigation when the legal status of conduct is uncertain. The cost of vindicating uncertain rights through litigation can easily eat through the net worth of even wealthy individuals while barely making a dent in the litigation budget of large-scale intellectual property owners. Without breaking a sweat, the recording industry, for example, can bring families to the verge of bankruptcy, putting enormous pressure on them to forfeit what might well be legitimate legal defenses in order to avoid the crippling cost of protracted litigation. Given the risk of a pervasive inequality of power and access to enforcement, the expansive legal claims of intellectual property owners tend to take on the force of law, even in the absence of an objective legal basis for those claims. From the point of view of the intellectual property consumer or the small-scale creator, disobeying the commands of entrenched owners can feel just like (and have precisely the same consequences as) violating a clearly established legal norm.

Further, although we tip our hats to the distinction between the outlaw and the altlaw, we do not want to ascribe too much significance to it. For both the property outlaw and the intellectual property altlaw, the reform process necessarily begins with an action in defiance of the property owner's assertions of legal right. This action generates substantial risk for the outlaw or altlaw. For the outlaw, the risk is that of being caught and having the law (which we are, for the purposes of our discussion, assuming to be a clearly established legal norm) enforced against him or her. In the altlaw context, where the state of the law is less clear, the risk is that of getting caught and having the property owner (or the state) attempt to use the coercive power of the law to enforce the property owner's conception of his or her legal right, a process that, by itself, can be so costly as to constitute its own form of punishment. In addition, the altlaw bears the risk that the relevant authoritative legal interpreters (most likely the courts, but perhaps an arbitrator or an administrative agency) will adopt the owner's legal interpretation as the correct (that is, the official) one and therefore treat the altlaw as if the conduct were illegal all along.

Except where the law provides different sanctions for bad-faith violations (and even there only when the altlaw can convince the relevant authorities that he or she acted in good faith), once the legal question is decided against the altlaw, the consequences are largely the same as if the altlaw had been wrong from the beginning. In both contexts, if the *ex ante* risk of loss is great enough, the deterrent effect might be sufficiently strong that the process of challenging the intellectual property owners' asserted rights never gets off the ground, and the opportunity for legal reform (or clarification) is correspondingly diminished. As a consequence, the altlaw —the one willing to disobey the owner's wishes under color of a plausible assertion of legal privilege—on closer examination comes to look more like an outlaw, for all practical purposes. And, as we will discuss at greater length, altlaws come to play a role with respect to intellectual property that resembles in many ways that of outlaws in the context of tangible property—overcoming the ossification within the law that results from owners' disproportionate role in defining the law and from the inertia within the lawmaking process itself.

At the end of the day, then, we do not want to overstate the significance of the distinction between outlaws and altlaws, though it is meaningful and (at times) useful. Both outlaws and altlaws can generate important redistributive and informational benefits. And, for both outlaws and altlaws, our analysis suggests the importance of the initial act of transgression in generating the possibility of legal reform (or in the case of altlaws, legal clarification). Finally, for both groups, our analysis suggests a need to avoid overdeterrence in order to avoid closing off this path of legal change and to reduce the risk of legal ossification.

Ideology, the Altlaw, and the Outlaw

Globally, as the Indian copyright scholar Lawrence Liang has observed, the worlds of illicit cultural production appear to be moving in two divergent directions. One is characterized by the virtue of creative remixing of content, and another is characterized by the shadowy activity of piracy. Prominent intellectual property scholars, notably Lawrence Lessig among them, celebrate the transformative potential of the former while decrying the illegal nature of the latter. Consider this statement from Lessig: "All across the world, but especially in Asia and Eastern Europe, there are businesses that do nothing but take other people's copyrighted content, copy it, and sell it—all without the permission of a copyright owner. The recording industry estimates that it loses about $4.6 billion every year to physical piracy. . . . This piracy is wrong. . . . Asian law does protect foreign copyrights, and the actions of the copy shops violate that law. So the wrong of piracy that they engage in is not just a moral wrong, but a legal wrong, and not just an internationally legal wrong, but a locally legal wrong as well."[26] This type of piracy is often portrayed as imbued with a parasitic, "immoral" character—irrespective of whether the copied material pops up in corner stores throughout Asia, Europe, or even in an American teenager's bedroom. Lessig is certainly correct that piracy is a problem. But his observations obscure the complexity of defining piracy in the first instance.

According to scholars like Ravi Sundaram and Lawrence Liang, both of whom live, work, and write in Asia, the existence of piracy in places Lessig is discussing is a far more complicated phenomenon than it may seem. As both authors point out, the specter of "piracy" in such areas often reflects the proliferation of informal economies that exist largely in the shadow of the tenuous rule of law (and often with the tacit approval of intellectual property owners and law enforcement).[27] "While we would deny that practices of piracy are exclusive to economically marginalized people and nations," Liang writes, responding to Lessig, "or that they should be navigated with an alternative moral compass when located in the South," copyright scholars should recognize that the stereotypes behind the ideas of "the pirate" (the embodiment of evil) and "the creative artist" (the personification of fair use) often prevent a much more rigorous examination of how we construct notions of disobedience in the context of intellectual property. Others have similarly noted the ambiguity of piracy in the developing world. The Indian artists' group Raqs Media Collective reminds us that the "illegal emigrant, the urban encroacher, the electronic pirate,

[and] the hacker . . . are not really the most glamorous images of embodied resistance," because they act out of self-interest, rather than a desire to "resist" or to transform the world.[28] But, in their own way, these figures destabilize and undermine the worlds of intellectual property, forcing us to look back on our faith in the rule of law and to ask how the notion of disobedience gets constructed and disseminated within the uncertain boundaries of intellectual property law.

Thus, we would suggest that the pirate, understood as an "outlaw," is a more complicated figure than Lessig's discussion seems to allow. A great deal of this ambiguity arises as a result of the nonrivalrous nature of information consumption. Does the pirate represent a substantial threat to intellectual property owners if copied DVDs or books are of inferior quality and circulate primarily in the developing world, where pervasive and crippling poverty means that markets for the original expression were limited to begin with? Or is such a pirate actually helping consumers obtain access to cultural and intellectual resources that might otherwise be out of reach? Indeed, does such a pirate plausibly help owners by providing a low-cost, low-quality product that extends the reach of the intellectual property owner's brand but whose defects are not blamed on the owner itself? As Liang points out, "the figure of illegality poses fundamental questions to our neat categories of the liberal public sphere . . . [demanding] that we ask fundamentally different questions of the relationship between law, legality, property (tangible and intangible) and that which we call the public domain."[29]

Nevertheless, as the phenomenon of piracy reminds us, there are, of course, "outlaws" in intellectual property, some of whom celebrate their status outside the boundaries of law. In addition to distinguishing between the outlaw and the altlaw on the basis of the ultimate legality of their conduct, we can also make a parallel distinction that operates at the cultural or ideological level. Most literature that discusses intellectual property disobedience tends to conflate all types of transgressions without recognizing their varying gradations of skepticism about the validity of intellectual property rights. Within the domain of intellectual property, at the most system-threatening end of this spectrum lies the ideologically motivated intellectual property outlaw—the "hacker"—who may exhibit a fundamental (and frequently Marxian) discomfort with the entire notion that information can be property. This philosophy is aptly summarized by the Proud-honian conclusion that "property is theft."[30] For some hackers, evidence of the truth of the Proudhonian epithet lies in the pervasive sequestration of information.[31] In contrast, in most cases, the altlaw does not disagree with the existence of intellectual property protections, only with how they may be applied to specific circumstances. Whereas an outlaw might disagree with the concept of intellectual property altogether, an altlaw might seek simply to expand privileges like fair use in order to allow more access to nonowners. For some, clear intellectual property rules present no more of a moral barrier than the murky boundaries of fair use, and as a consequence, a greater proportion of their conduct is likely to fall comfortably within the "outlaw" category.

A concrete example of the ambiguity of the legal status, self-understanding, and social meaning of outlaws and altlaws is provided by the notion of "hacktivism."[32] In some, but not all cases, hacktivists would seem to fall within the outlaw camp. Consider a description of the "hacker ethic" from Steven Levy:

> All information should be free.
> - Mistrust authority—promote decentralization.
> - Hackers should be judged by their hacking, not bogus criteria such as degrees, age, race or position.
> - You can create art and beauty on a computer.
> - Computers can change your life for the better.[33]

Other definitions of the same term, however, are less clearly hostile to intellectual property rights and seem to straddle the boundary between outlaw and altlaw. Dorothy Denning, for example, describes hacktivism more broadly than Levy, calling it a hybrid between computer hacking and political activism.[34] Others define it in terms of any kind of computer-generated "grassroots political protest"; and still others require some element of illegal or legally ambiguous character.[35] Finally, some conceptions seem to fit more unambiguously within the altlaw category, such as those that distinguish hacktivism from "cracking." The latter encompasses activity that is more clearly illegal or destructive, like Web site defacements, redirects, denial-of-service attacks, and sabotage.[36]

According to McKenzie Wark, one proponent of the hacker worldview, the hacker is categorically opposed to the notion of information as property. Wark, for example, argues that the very idea of "intellectual property" is in and of itself a legal abstraction, a Marxian dystopia, wherein a class of creators labor in service of a ruling class of owners, who have attained near-absolute control over intellectual property through aggressive strategies of command and control.[37] As a result of these structures, Wark argues, information becomes privatized, and institutions of privatized ownership become a "dominant, rather than a subsidiary, aspect of commodified life."[38] "To make something property," Wark writes, "is to separate it from a continuum, to mark it or bound it, to represent it as something finite."[39]

The conflict between "fixed" legal theories of ownership and the fluid and free-flowing nature of information generates a critical conflict between those who seek to own information and those who seek to free it from its legal moorings. For this reason, the rise of intellectual property, Wark argues, also engenders a sustained and thoughtful oppositional force. From the legal abstraction of intellectual property emerges the "hacker class," which Wark describes as follows: "The hacker class arises out of the transformation of information into property, in the form of intellectual property. . . . The hacker class is the class with the capacity to create not only new kinds of object and subject in the world, not only new kinds of property form in which they may be represented, but new kinds of relation, with unforeseen properties, which question the property form itself."[40] In this way, the very creation of the institution of property is intimately bound up with the creation of an opposing outsider class of individuals, who are paradoxically bound to further the creation of intellectual property, just as they are the very forces who philosophically oppose its existence. They labor under the abstraction of intellectual property but, ironically, seek liberation from it as well. The central theme of the hacker, therefore, is the liberation of information. "What may be free from the commodity form altogether," Wark writes, "is not land, not capital, but information."[41]

In a similar vein, Brian Martin, in his recent book *Information Liberation,* sketches out a series of reasons for rejecting the institution of intellectual property, arguing that it impedes innovation, exploits less developed countries, and aggravates inequality. To remedy these problems,

Martin advocates a strategy of complete information nonownership in which everyone has access to ideas and information. Martin has called for a campaign of "openly refus[ing] to cooperate with intellectual property," embracing a variety of nonviolent tactics, such as noncooperation, boycotts, and the creation of alternative institutions. Martin advocates a program of "being principled in opposition, and being willing to accept penalties for civil disobedience to laws," predicting that the use of harsh penalties against conscientious objectors to intellectual property might provoke a backlash against the laws themselves.[42]

Partly as a consequence of the different way that these property outlaws understand the legal status of their own actions, the activities of the outlaw may also have a distinct social and cultural valence. Because their conduct is more clearly and self-consciously illegal, property outlaws arguably represent a more direct and serious challenge to the legal order than do altlaws. In contrast, to the extent that an altlaw believes certain behavior to be legal (and aims to so demonstrate), the altlaw fundamentally affirms the rule of law, whereas an outlaw challenges it more fundamentally.

Consider a parting example. In 2003, a Swedish programmer named Gottfrid Svartholm volunteered to assist a file-sharing advocacy group called Piratbyrån ("The Bureau of Piracy") in setting up a BitTorrent tracker that would enable individuals to share and search for files online. At the time, the site was unapologetic about its purpose and intent: the founders named the site Pirate Bay in order "to make clear what the site was there for: no shame, no subtlety," a *Wired* journalist reported. Based in Sweden, a country with weak copyright laws and where 1.2 out of 9 million citizens claimed to engage in file sharing, Pirate Bay quickly became "the most popular and hunted piracy site in the world." It boasted over a million visitors a day. They shared movies, songs, conversations about hacking and cracking copy-protected software, and other information.[43]

The impetus for the name Pirate Bay, along with its activities, was a curious mixture of distaste for the laws of intellectual property and an almost willful blindness to the rule of law. Commenting on Pirate Bay, one *Wired* journalist reported that "these people were pirates. They believed the existing copyright regime was a broken artifact of a pre-digital age, the gristle of a rotting business model that poisoned culture and creativity. The Pirate Bay didn't respect intellectual property law, and they'd say it publicly."

As the site grew more popular however, it received cease-and-desist letters, and the group soon decided to create a gallery of the scanned letters alongside its mocking replies. "They [the cease and desist letters] are rude in a polite way," the group's legal adviser claimed. "We are rude in a rude way back at them."[44]

The gallery highlighted Pirate Bay's transformation from an engine that facilitated the sharing of material to an international political movement that expressly and completely disagreed with the politics and theory behind the concept of information ownership. Whereas other peer-to-peer services first faltered and then finally fell into oblivion because of an onslaught of legal threats, Pirate Bay remained a "lone civil dissenter," using its trademark brand of humor, geekiness, and outright defiance to capture the sympathies of a public whose file-sharing behavior was clearly out of step with the laws that regulated them. Mikael Viborg, one of the founders of Pirate Bay, even helped found a Swedish political party, the Pirate Party, whose platform focuses on the reform of intellectual property laws.[45]

The Web site was finally raided in 2006, much to the satisfaction of content owners (the MPAA triumphantly celebrated its downfall, claiming that the raid "serve[d] as a reminder to pirates all over the world that there are no safe harbors for internet copyright thieves"[46]). The police took away tons of computer equipment, arrested a few individuals, and believed that they had won. But just three days later, Pirate Bay relaunched itself in the Netherlands, through a new Web site address, hey.mpaa.and.apd.bite .my.shiny.metal.ass.thepiratebay.org, and continued on as before. In fact, the attention generated by the raid created a new flush of fans for the site: traffic increased dramatically, and orders for T-shirts with its logo numbered in the thousands, forcing employees to work day and night.[47]

In early 2008, Swedish prosecutors filed criminal charges against three of Pirate Bay's administrators, Hans Fredrik Neij, Gottfrid Svartholm Warg, and Peter Sunde, as well as Carl Lundstrom, a far-right-wing activist and early investor in Pirate Bay. On April 17, 2009, the four were convicted, sentenced to a year in prison, and ordered to pay $3.6 million in damages to various entertainment companies.[48] The conviction had no immediate impact on Pirate Bay's operations. The company remained defiant. A message on its Web site called the verdict "crazy." "As in all good movies, the heroes lose in the beginning but have an epic victory in the end anyhow," the Web site read. "That's the only thing Hollywood ever taught us."[49]

Although these various outlaw approaches are both practically and theoretically rich, the categorical rejection of the notion of intellectual property often yields a vision of a sort of information anarchy—a world where information circulates freely but is owned by no one and governed by few legal limitations. The categorical rejection of the notion of intellectual property itself within hacker and electronic civil-disobedience circles often lends itself to an unqualified valorization of generalized intellectual property lawbreaking. As we argue in the chapters to come, this view is overly simplistic and ultimately fails to give sufficient credit to the role of intellectual property protections in fostering innovation. Nor does it take into account the complexity and variety of the social norms of individuals and communities—hackers and nonhackers alike—in relation to intellectual property.

Despite the often blurry line separating the outlaw from the altlaw, however, our analysis of intellectual property disobedience (in contrast with our discussion of tangible property) concentrates largely on the altlaw—the person who challenges intellectual property protections but who broadly accepts the notion of intellectual property and whose behavior may itself be consistent with intellectual property law. That is, our focus is on actors whose perspective is distinct from that of the people running Pirate Bay and of the proponents of other types of computer-based malfeasance like cracking and cyberterrorism.[50] Although we have a broad interest in the phenomenon of intellectual property disobedience, the broadest and most radical anti-intellectual property programs raise distinct normative and empirical questions with implications that deserve much fuller analysis than we can hope to provide in this book. At the same time, however, the sustained proliferation (on a mass scale) of far less radical forms of intellectual property disobedience calls out for discussion. Some of our conclusions will be of interest to proponents of the anti–intellectual property hacker worldview, but our goal in this book is to discuss the role that intellectual property disobedience can play even for those who accept the notion of an established system of intellectual property protection.

6

ACQUISITIVE ALTLAWS: THE TREATMENT ACTION CAMPAIGN, PATENTS, AND PUBLIC HEALTH

Patents, like copyrighted works, occupy a delicate intersection between public and private property interests. But, in addition to the utilitarian bent of much of intellectual property law, at least part of the justifications for frequently offered patent protections stem from Lockean theories that focus on the desire to reward inventors: the law establishes a proprietary system of protection, giving the patent holder a quasi-monopoly right to price the invention, which, in turn enables him or her to exclude others from using the same invention for a limited period. Perhaps as a result, our system of patent protection is robust: patent holders are entitled to prevent others from making, using, or selling their invention. Unlike copyright, which has substantial exceptions, such as fair use, built into its architecture, patent law has far fewer exceptions protecting unlicensed use: only a very narrow allowance for "experimental use" and very few other exceptions that limit the owner's scope of control.

Yet we must be careful not to overstate the private nature of this entitlement; James Gathii reminds us that at the heart of our patent system is a commitment to public welfare and progress.[1] The Supreme Court in *Brenner v. Manson* clearly articulated the utilitarian justification for patent protection, observing that "the basic quid pro quo contemplated by the Constitution and the Congress for granting a patent monopoly is the benefit derived by the public from an invention with substantial utility."[2] This balance between private and public interests is always shifting, and the boundaries of protection are constantly redrawn in response to challenges.

Nevertheless, the result of this robust system of patent rights generates some predictable economic consequences. Unlike other kinds of goods, which face competition from similar products in the marketplace that forces owners to charge competitive prices, patent owners enjoy monopoly rights over their inventions for a period of time. This monopoly power allows owners to charge prices that are significantly higher than the marginal costs of production, a factor that can contribute to substantial wealth transfers from consumer to producer.[3] Such monopoly pricing also excludes consumers who might be willing or able to purchase the good at a price somewhere above the marginal cost of production but who cannot afford the price demanded by the monopolist.[4] These individuals find themselves unable to purchase or license patented goods under the terms set by the owner. In most cases, these outcomes are unavoidable because of the practical difficulty of charging different consumers different prices according to their ability and willingness to pay (a practice known as "price discrimination"). Strong property rights afforded to the patent owner and the difficulty of price discrimination combine to prevent competitors from entering a market and selling the good at a lower price (a price that would be closer to its marginal cost of production).

Despite the costs associated with monopoly pricing, there is obviously a strong case for granting inventors exclusive property rights in their inventions. Without the incentives afforded by the grant of a patent monopoly, inventors would be hard pressed to invest the necessary resources in developing an invention. For example, the development life cycle of a pharmaceutical drug is typically eight to ten years. It is unlikely that inventors would be able to recoup such development costs if competitors could simply step in after all the work has been done, copy the invention, and sell it on the open market at competitive prices. At the same time, however, the interests of those who are excluded by the prohibitive cost of an invention are often left without much consideration.

Until now, this dilemma played out relatively peaceably, leaving the architecture of the patent system virtually untouched except in rare cases. In most cases, the divide between those who can purchase the good and those who cannot is a reality of life in a market economy that most consumers are willing to accept. In the case of patented pharmaceuticals, however, the gravity of the interests at stake for potential consumers has spurred an important debate about the impact of intellectual property rights on public health. Today, at least in the area of patented pharmaceuticals, many governments have been forced to confront a critical conflict between the two interests and the difficult question whether the right to property and the right to health are drawn in stark opposition to one another.

Nothing has forced these questions into the public eye more than HIV and AIDS. Ironically, at the same time that the world faced the ravages of the global AIDS epidemic in the 1990s, a number of developing countries also faced substantial international pressure to sign the Agreement on Trade-Related Aspects of Intellectual Property (TRIPS), which created a more harmonized system of patent protection and, in some cases, instituted systems of patent protection for pharmaceuticals in developing countries. In attempting to integrate themselves within the international system by enacting robust patent laws, many nations also risked creating substantial obstacles to protecting the public health of their communities.

Some scholars have suggested that the right to health must come before patent protections, contending that intellectual property is not an inalienable right, like dignity or the right to adequate health.[5] This assertion raises an important question: How should countries balance the immediate demands of public health against the incentives generated by intellectual property interests, incentives that are necessary for future lifesaving innovation? On this question, the TRIPS agreement failed to provide a substantive answer until the AIDS epidemic demanded a response. The tragic confluence of a global epidemic coupled with the intense pressure faced by developing countries hit hardest by that epidemic to join these international trade agreements created a controversy that captured global headlines and, in doing so, actually altered the public's views on patent protection and the role of disobedience.

Indeed, as the scholar Deborah Halbert has explained, the TRIPS agreement marked a central moment in the formation of resistance to globalized systems of intellectual property.[6] Halbert writes, "Ironically, expanding protection of intellectual property meant educating people on what exactly intellectual property was, which created an opportunity to critique the notion of expansive intellectual property rights and who benefits from them."[7] Modern history has revealed that the very conditions for the patent system's success have also, ironically, sown the seeds of resistance and disobedience, particularly where lifesaving medicines are concerned. These complex dialectics between the public and private nature of patented inventions and between property protection and property disobedience are well illustrated by the experiences of developing countries, like Brazil, South Africa, and Thailand, who have long been faced with tremendous challenges in obtaining antiretroviral medicines for their citizens—and who turned toward selective disobedience of intellectual property rights as a result.

South Africa and the Struggle for Affordable HIV Treatment

In 1997, South Africa passed a law that attempted "to provide for measures for the supply of more affordable medicines in certain circumstances."[8] The law was passed partly in recognition of the fact that the country's constitution granted everyone the right to health care. The law had a variety of objectives, the most important of which stemmed from the government's recognition that the cost of lifesaving medications had become prohibitive for those who needed them. Proponents of the law hoped that permitting the government to purchase, import, or license generic substitutes of costly patented medicines would lead to wider access to medication for those affected by HIV/AIDS. The new law gave the minister of health discretion to provide for generic substitution, among other regulatory schemes, to ensure greater supply and distribution.[9] As one scholar explained: "The social theory behind the amendments was that the high cost of HIV/AIDS drugs—protected by patent rights held by major pharmaceutical companies—put them beyond the reach of many infected people relying on public health services. The government of South Africa could not afford the task of subsidizing those drugs to its needy population, and given that five of the leading pharmaceutical multinational corporations involved . . . had global sales tripling South Africa's entire national budget, they had to share in the distributive burden."[10]

Almost immediately, the world took South Africa's action to mean that the country intended a full-scale assault on patent protections.[11] "If the Health Minister thought it was in the interest of public health that those

$10,000 AIDS cocktails be cheaper, she could just rip off the patents and set up a factory in Cape Town to make them," complained an unnamed Western diplomat to a *New York Times* reporter. "And if the Minister of Health says this is O.K., then the Minister of Education will be able to say, 'Well, affordable computers are in the interest of public education, but Windows is just too darn expensive, so we're going to buy knockoff copies.'"[12] Criticism from the pharmaceutical community was equally harsh. Merck canceled a planned $10 million investment in South Africa, and Bristol-Myers Squibb, Pharmacia & Upjohn, and Eli Lilly closed their South African factories, attributing their decisions to the passage of the new law.[13]

South Africa, now in the global public eye, insisted that it had no interest in abrogating patent rights for drug companies and pointed out that it fully intended to support the patent system required under the TRIPS agreement.[14] "The minister has said constantly that we have no intention of abrogating patent rights," explained a British consultant who worked on the 1997 law.[15] Yet the South African law undeniably crafted dramatic exceptions to the patent system that the country had agreed to put in place under TRIPS.

The ensuing discussion thus focused on two key strategies.[16] The first of these, compulsory licensing, would have permitted South Africa to force a pharmaceutical company to grant the use of its patent to the state or other companies, in exchange for a royalty fixed by the government. A compulsory license enables the government to produce the drug on its own by peremptorily granting a license to third parties who can then make, use, or sell the invention for a fixed period of time. This is done without the consent of the patent owner, upon the payment of a royalty that is usually less than what the company would have demanded on its own. Because compulsory licensing eliminates one of the key incentives for seeking patents—monopoly pricing—it is meant to be used only in rare situations. Most countries, including the United States, have provisions in place for the use of compulsory licensing to remedy anticompetitive practices or in cases of national emergency.[17] Another solution, parallel importing, also raised significant legal questions. Under a parallel-importing program, a country imports a medication from a third country, usually one that permits the manufacture of generic versions of patented drugs and their sale at a lesser price.[18] Like compulsory licensing, this solution meant that a drug manufacturer would no longer enjoy monopoly power in South Africa and would have to compete with other manufacturers.

By putting these tactics on the table, the new law clearly had the potential to limit the scope of intellectual property rights in the face of national public-health crises. But was South Africa actually violating TRIPS? It was hard to tell. Although the TRIPS agreement included provisions allowing compulsory licensing in situations of national emergency, other circumstances of extreme urgency, or in cases of public noncommercial use, the provisions had never been used and were understood by many to have extremely narrow applications. One relevant article in the TRIPS agreement, which is hardly a model of clarity, permits members to "adopt measures necessary to protect public health and nutrition, and to promote the public interest in sectors of vital importance to their socio-economic and technological development."[19] On the other hand, the South African act lacked many of the limiting provisions and restrictions included in the compulsory-licensing provisions of the TRIPS agreement, which led some to question the act's legality.[20] Pharmaceutical companies feared that the law granted the South African government an open-ended license to seize a patent on whatever it wanted. But even in the absence of such a sensationalized fear, each of the proposed measures involved some limitations on the scope of the rights patent owners had previously enjoyed and relied on. Because the measures being considered by the South African government would have forced the pharmaceutical companies to grant licenses or compete with third parties who could manufacture the drug at a cheaper price, they dramatically undercut the monopoly power that a patent owner expected to enjoy.

The adoption of either of these two measures—compulsory licensing or parallel importing—suggested, at the very least, that pharmaceutical manufacturers might lose their foothold on the immense market for HIV drugs in developing countries. For these reasons, the new South African law—at least in the eyes of the pharmaceutical industry—seemed to challenge the very foundations of the TRIPS agreement, which had promised to harmonize and strengthen patent protections. Thus, even if South Africa's law did not clearly violate international law, the actions that the government considered taking would have limited a patent holder's control over pricing and distribution of pharmaceuticals, and would have relied for their legality on a gray area in international law that had not really been tested. The South African law therefore set the stage for a protracted struggle between property rights, public health, and the need for an accommodation between the two.

The United States, at least in the beginning, seemed to think that South Africa was openly flouting its international obligations. At first, the State Department issued a report claiming that the South African law was "inconsistent" with its obligations under the TRIPS agreement[21] and placed South Africa on a special watch list of trade violators.[22] Forty-seven members of Congress signed a letter asking the United States to "pursue all appropriate action" against South Africa.[23] The United States refused to grant preferential trade treatment to South Africa, maintaining that the U.S. government had "been engaged in an assiduous, concerted campaign" to convince the South African government to withdraw or modify the new law because of its potential conflict with the TRIPS agreement.[24] The European Union, for its part, warned that the new law would "negatively affect the interests of the European pharmaceutical industry."[25]

Fearful of the implications of the South African law, thirty-nine pharmaceutical companies filed suit in South Africa, claiming that the law conflicted with the patent rights they enjoyed.[26] The pharmaceutical companies argued that the legislation authorized the health minister to take measures that could eviscerate the patent system. The companies argued, in short, that the new law was far too broad because it could potentially allow much more than just the parallel importation of pharmaceuticals—it could extend to a number of other activities that might further compromise the patent protection they enjoyed.[27] They argued further that the act constituted an unconstitutional delegation of legislative power to the executive branch.[28]

At the same time that these companies criticized South Africa, they faced growing global criticism for their steadfast defense of intellectual property rights.[29] Three years passed between the filing of the lawsuit in 1998 and the opening arguments in the case. During that time, the world witnessed a dramatic shift in favor of limiting intellectual property rights in pharmaceuticals, a shift that owed a great deal to the patent disobedience that the AIDS epidemic encouraged. During the period the lawsuit was pending, a massive campaign erupted in the human-rights and public-health communities to persuade the pharmaceutical companies to drop their litigation. Indeed, in 1999, the United States backed away from its request to pursue trade sanctions against South Africa after AIDS activists disrupted several of then vice president Al Gore's speeches, just as he was launching his candidacy for president.

That same year, the Office of the U.S. Trade Representative proudly announced that it had reached a compromise: South Africa assured the United States that it intended to comply with the TRIPS agreement (a position South Africa had advanced from the very beginning), and the United States dropped its request for sanctions.[30] Then, on May 10, 2000, President Bill Clinton signed Executive Order 13155, which expressly provided that the U.S. government would not seek to challenge any intellectual property laws governing HIV/AIDS pharmaceuticals so long as the policy or law was consistent with the TRIPS agreement. In the end, the United States had totally reversed its position. (The *New York Times* claimed that the group ACT UP's persistent heckling of Vice President Gore was the "catalyst" for the shift in the Clinton administration's position.)[31]

The Treatment Action Campaign

Despite the fact that it had enacted a law permitting the government to license or import generic versions of patented antiretroviral drugs, the South African government received its share of criticism from AIDS activists for failing to take more concrete steps to actually make those drugs more available. The Treatment Action Campaign (TAC) was launched in South Africa on International Human Rights Day, December 10, 1998, to campaign for greater access to HIV treatments. The campaign was founded by Zackie Achmat, himself HIV positive, and a small group of other activists after a prominent gay civil rights activist, Simon Nkoli, died from AIDS even though antiretroviral therapy was readily available in South Africa at the time of his death. TAC quickly grew into a national— indeed global—social movement. Its campaigns drew support from South Africa's constitutional guarantee of the right to health care and employed strategies both within and outside the law, relying on a combination of litigation and civil disobedience, when necessary. In 1999, Achmat gained worldwide attention when he declared that he would not take antiretrovirals: "I will not take expensive treatment until all ordinary South Africans can get it on the public-health system," he declared. "That probably means I will die a horrible death, even though medical science has made it unnecessary." [32]

That same year, Eric Goemaere, a Belgian doctor, came to Johannesburg with the hope of setting up a drug therapy program with the help of government officials. South African officials had previously refused to help, explaining that antiretrovirals were simply unaffordable.[33] Disappointed, Goemaere was about to head home, but then, just before he left, he decided to meet with Achmat, who told him of an ongoing underground insurrection. Apparently, a group of African National Congress officials, in defiance of government instructions, had decided to administer AZT secretly to pregnant mothers. Shortly thereafter, and buoyed by their efforts, Goemaere decided to take over a clinic, even though the government eventually suspended officials who had furtively supplied antiretrovirals to their patients.[34]

In quietly cooperating with insurgent officials, Goemaere became only the first example in a strategy calculated to call worldwide attention to the need for antiretrovirals. In addition to employing the sorts of dramatic and ultimately symbolic gestures that had drawn attention to Western groups like ACT UP, TAC sought to achieve more concrete results by defying both patent law and other controls over drugs to actively provide medications directly to the public. In short, the group's actions comprised much more than a simple protest—TAC engaged in a stark defiance and an appropriation, both literally and figuratively, of the patents protecting antiretroviral medications in an effort to provide those medications to the public.

All of this, of course, did not take place in a vacuum. The pharmaceutical industry was understandably concerned that public opinion had crystallized against its position, and companies tried to ameliorate the situation by offering more and more price concessions to appease their critics. TAC, however, drew attention to the pernicious consequences of the strings attached to the pharmaceutical industry's carefully constructed "generosity" by setting the stage for even more disobedience. For example, in early March 2000, in response to a worldwide activist campaign against the company in eighteen countries, Pfizer announced that it would give away Diflucan (fluconazole) in South Africa.[35] The drug was used to treat patients with systemic thrush and meningitis. However, Pfizer's "offer" was limited only to patients with meningitis. Patients with systemic thrush—the more common of the two diseases—were excluded and would have to pay for their medicines.

Enraged by this exclusion, TAC announced the "Defiance Campaign against Patent Abuse."[36] The campaign was named after a TAC member, Christopher Moraka, who suffered from systemic thrush, a painful, widespread fungus that covered his tongue, chest, and pelvis, and prevented him from eating or swallowing. Even though Moraka had received a prescription for the drug, he could not afford it, and he died in July 2000, just two months after he testified before the parliament on this issue. To commemorate his passing, his TAC friends, after burying their friend, led a march to protest his unnecessary death. And then they decided to start a drug-smuggling operation in his memory.[37] Achmat explained: "Our patience had run out. The government had not responded to a TAC request to issue a compulsory license against the company and Pfizer announced record profits. In the interim, thousands of people continued to die."[38]

The Defiance Campaign against Patent Abuse began in earnest in October 2000. It had three objectives: "to save lives where possible, to draw public attention to patent abuse, and to set a moral example for the government to follow."[39] The campaign planned to import patented medicines in clear and direct defiance of the intellectual property protections enjoyed by the pharmaceutical companies. It began to assemble a network of doctors and pharmacists who were willing to prescribe low-cost generic drugs imported from Thailand and Brazil, and TAC, for its part, openly challenged Pfizer and others to take action against them.[40]

The activists drew heavily from South Africa's own rich history of protest. Defiance campaigns had been used in the 1950s during South Africa's antiapartheid struggle against the infamous pass laws, which confined black people to townships.[41] In fact, in the 1980s, when a union leader advocated restarting the campaign to challenge segregated facilities, then South African president P. W. Botha opted to abolish the pass laws entirely.

Achmat asserted that TAC actively sought to link its own actions to that tradition, pointing out that South Africa "would not be a democracy had Nelson Mandela [and others] obeyed the pass laws and other unjust legislation." He explained: "The liberation movement's moral tradition of disobeying unjust laws mobilized millions of people to constitute a force for democracy and social justice. Defiance of unjust laws also exposed the forces of inequality, privilege, and minority rule."[42]

The press release detailing the particulars of the defiance campaign announced that TAC planned to travel to Thailand, where the World Trade Organization (WTO) rules regarding patents were not yet being enforced, and to purchase essential medicines in clear defiance of Pfizer's patent, in order to provide them to patients in South Africa. The drug fluconazole cost around twenty-eight cents per capsule in Thailand, where it was sold under the label Biozole, whereas Pfizer sold the patented version, Diflucan, for as much as eighteen dollars in South Africa.[43] The price of Thailand's pill was less than 2 percent of the brand-name price.[44] TAC explained: "TAC will stop defying the unjust trade laws with fluconazole once Pfizer has lowered the price . . . and its 'donation' is implemented with no restrictions. . . . We are calling on civil society organizations in South Africa and everywhere to join TAC's campaign and to defy patent laws. These laws prevent people from enjoying their right to health. They amount to discrimination on the grounds of poverty. We ask you to publicly endorse the defiance of laws that place profit before people, and condemn millions to death from preventable and treatable illnesses."[45] The campaign was embraced by thousands of doctors, nurses, AIDS organizations, and children's rights organizations throughout the country—hundreds of doctors said that they planned to distribute the generic drugs with or without government permission.[46] "People were dying across the country and doctors were saying that they could not afford to prescribe the right medicines," Achmat explained. "We wanted to set a moral example and put the right to health and life before profit. We don't want to be smugglers—this is the government's job to do."[47]

In Thailand, Achmat purchased five thousand generic tablets of fluconazole and brought them back to South Africa, where he was promptly arrested for drug smuggling.[48] The health minister refused to condone Achmat's activity, explaining that "she understood the frustration of people with HIV/AIDS but could not condone unlawful actions," and initiated an investigation, calling Achmat's actions "criminal" and "unsafe" even though the tests on bioequivalence had proved otherwise.[49] "The choice is clear," Achmat stated as he entered a Cape Town police station. "The right to life and access to health care are non-negotiable. Profiteering, at the expense of life, even when protected by law, is not a right."[50]

TAC's efforts were very effective. Largely because of the ensuing public outcry, the government allowed a small number of clinics to dispense generic versions of the drug in clear defiance of the patent laws that ostensibly protected Pfizer.[51] A few weeks later, two South African actors, Morne Visser and Carolyn Lewis, brought back more generic medicines from Thailand. This is how one South African newspaper described the actors' arrival:

> "My wife and I could hear the singing as we were coming through customs," he said. "She thought it might be a new exercise to welcome tourists, but I said 'No, I think it's for us.'"
>
> When he finally made it into the arrivals hall, Visser was lifted into the air by delighted supporters, many of them HIV-positive activists who could benefit from the drugs. "People were hugging me and kissing me. And when I handed over the tablets, well, that was fantastic. I can't describe how I felt. It was the first time I realized what this was really about."[52]

Faced with such strong criticism and the prospect of losing the South African market to a generic competitor, Pfizer relented and announced its intention to distribute Diflucan free of charge in local clinics.[53] A few months later, Achmat was selected as *Time* magazine's "Person of the Week."[54] Flush with its success, the TAC's defiance campaign planned to expand its movement to challenge "without advance warning" patents on other AIDS drugs, including those patented by GlaxoSmithKline, Bristol-Myers Squibb, Boehringer Ingelheim, Merck, Abbott Laboratories, and Roche.[55]

By 2001, when the pharmaceutical companies' case against the South African government finally began in earnest, TAC argued that the limitation of patent rights was justified because there was a greater public good at stake—namely, the right to health care.[56] Shortly after the case began, an Indian manufacturer, Cipla, stepped in and offered to sell its generic AIDS treatments for a dramatically reduced price if compulsory licensing were introduced.[57] Just a few weeks later, worried about the prospects of success for the lawsuit, Merck slashed its prices for its own drugs, and Bristol Myers Squibb followed suit.[58] And then, one month later, under tremendous global pressure, the pharmaceutical companies reluctantly dropped their lawsuit against the government.[59] TAC, in short, had won.

Despite the victory in court, TAC continued to put pressure on both the pharmaceutical industry and the South African government to provide greater access to AIDS drugs. In 2002, three members of TAC, along with help from Médecins Sans Frontières and Oxfam, traveled to South Africa from Brazil carrying three types of generic drugs for use in one of its clinics.[60] Again, TAC announced that it was consciously infringing the patents for the drugs to demonstrate the need for compulsory licensing rather than donations, which the group viewed as ultimately counterproductive. TAC also argued that its actions were consistent with the South African Constitution, which protects the right to life and dignity.[61] "Today we have decided to openly break the patent right of the pharmaceutical companies . . . because we have decided that the life of a patient cannot be put under the patent right," said Goemaere.[62]

Brazil and Selective Disobedience

In 1996, Brazil became an international model in the global fight against AIDS when President Fernando Henrique Cardoso signed a law guaranteeing free distribution of drugs for individuals living with HIV/AIDS.[63] In Brazil, access to health services, including basic medicines, is considered a constitutional right.[64] That same year, however, Brazil also enacted legislation to amend its patent laws in order to bring them into compliance with international standards under the TRIPS agreement. Brazil's decision to enter into the TRIPS agreement marked a tremendous shift in its previous approaches to patentability, which had historically denied any protection for the patentability of chemical products and processes.[65] Brazil had relied on its system of generic production for its pharmaceuticals.[66] Brazil's decision to allow these types of patents was met with widespread public disapproval.[67]

But Brazil made a choice that suggested a compromise between its historical refusal to protect patented pharmaceuticals and its obligations under the TRIPS agreement: it decided to continue to produce generic versions of HIV drugs, which fell under an exception for locally produced drugs, and to import other drugs from outside the country.[68] For other drugs, however, Brazil threatened to invoke compulsory licensing, in stark defiance of the patent protections it had agreed to enforce.

The ambiguity of the language on compulsory licensing in the TRIPS agreement permitted Brazil to adopt the strategy, on several occasions, of threatening to invoke compulsory licensing to extract more favorable terms in its negotiations with the drug companies. In 1999, the president of Brazil drafted an order that established a set of rules for compulsory licensing.[69] Two years later, in August 2001, Brazil rejected Roche's discounted offer on the drug Nelfinavir, and the minister of health announced a plan to produce the medicine domestically, threatening to invoke compulsory licensing.[70] The legality of Brazil's threat, like South Africa's, was uncertain. The government's decision was, to say the least, unpopular among pharmaceutical companies and their allies. Brazil tried to put the best face on its actions, explaining that "local production of many of the drugs used in the fight against AIDS does not represent a declaration of war against the pharmaceutical industry. It is simply a way to fight for life."[71]

Others came to Brazil's defense, pointing out that in the same month, in the wake of anthrax threats, both the United States and the European Union had granted compulsory licenses for medications to protect the public against biological attacks. A joint statement of nongovernmental organizations pointedly observed a double standard in the reports that surround compulsory licensing: "When the United States issues a compulsory license, it is defending consumer interests. When Brazil does it, it is demonized, risks legal sanction and trade sanctions," an Oxfam coordinator observed.[72]

Given the country's history of generic production, Brazil's threat was taken to be very credible.[73] Brazil's decision to invoke compulsory licensing was met with profound opposition from the Bush administration, which largely defended the position of pharmaceutical companies in arguing that such activities gravely affected their ability to conduct research and development by reducing their economic returns. The United States promptly initiated action against Brazil with the WTO, requesting economic sanctions.

At the same time, fearing the precedent of a compulsory license, the pharmaceutical industry tried to broker a compromise. Roche offered to lower the price of Nelfinavir by 13 percent.[74] When Brazil rejected the offer and continued to make preparations for compulsory licensing, authorizing a state-owned laboratory to produce the drug, Roche offered to cut the price of Nelfinavir even more, by one-third.[75] While these discussions continued, Merck offered deep discounts on two key HIV/AIDS drugs of its own.[76]

The parties ultimately reached agreement. But, even though its legal status remains uncertain, the threat of compulsory licensing continues to serve as a powerful bargaining tool for countries hit hardest by the AIDS epidemic. In the six years since its first agreement with the pharmaceutical companies, Brazil has been ready to challenge the scope of patent protections and has willingly invoked its compulsory-licensing provisions on a number of occasions.[77] In July 2005, in a move that made global headlines, Brazil threatened to suspend the patent on a crucial HIV antiretroviral drug, Kaletra, if the owner to the patent, Abbott Labs, did not significantly reduce the price of the drug.[78] (Brazil explained that the cost of Kaletra, along with two other drugs, constituted 67 percent of its annual budget for imported AIDS drugs.)

As before, Brazil's threat sparked a worldwide debate. One member of the U.S. House of Representatives argued before Congress that Brazil's decision to invoke compulsory licensing amounted to "wholesale theft of American technology for another country's commercial gain" and recommended that the United States retaliate if Brazil proceeded with its plan.[79] The president of a group named Defenders of Property Rights, Nancie Marzulla, said that Brazil should not be able to invoke the TRIPS agreement's compulsory-licensing provisions, since it did not have a strong enough case for a national health emergency.[80] In an op-ed published by the *Wall Street Journal,* another author warned that such short-term solutions posed severe risks to long-term investments in research and development, concluding that Brazil was "cutting its own throat" in flouting patent rights in pharmaceuticals because of the erosion of research and development funds that would follow its decision.[81]

Brazil has certainly not been alone in facing criticism for its willingness to weaken patent protection. But its efforts have made drugs more accessible for its citizens, and inspired others. In the spring of 2007, tensions erupted once again when both Thailand and Brazil announced their intention to authorize compulsory licensing for two key antiretrovirals, Merck's Efavirenz (Brazil) and Abbott Labs' Kaletra (Thailand).[82] During roughly the same period, the Public Health Ministry of Thailand issued a white paper describing compulsory licensing as "a form of social movement that aims at improving access to essential medicines and the health of people" and declaring that the "public health interest . . . must come before commercial interest."[83]

Criticism, particularly in the United States, has continued. The *Wall Street Journal,* in an editorial deeply critical of the World Health Organization's role, complained of Thailand's "greed," declaring that AIDS was not a "national emergency," since only a little over 1 percent of the population was infected. The editorial also criticized Abbott's own reversal of its withdrawal, complaining that it set a bad precedent for global property rights.[84] In another op-ed, a health-care policy analyst called Thailand's tactics "patent theft" designed "to strong-arm pharmaceutical companies."[85] The *Chicago Tribune* reached similar conclusions, predicting, "If the Abbotts of the world can't protect their intellectual property, Thailand likely won't have as much opportunity to violate it in the future: Some other new drugs won't even be developed."[86] The United States placed Thailand on a list of intellectual property violators, and Abbott responded to the threat by withdrawing all its applications to market new pharmaceuticals in Thailand, much to the dismay of nongovernmental organizations like Oxfam and Doctors Without Borders.[87] Ultimately, the World Health Organization intervened and was able to broker a negotiated deal.

Patents and the Effect of the Property Altlaw

In each of the episodes we have described, we see the same basic pattern unfolding. A property owner seeks a monopoly price for its product through patent protection, a price that many people in the host country are unable to afford. The host country then threatens to set aside the patent rights, arguably in violation of international intellectual property norms. In the shadow of this threat, the parties reach a compromise solution: the pharmaceutical industry capitulates and provides the drug at a lower cost, enabling a wider distribution of lifesaving HIV medications, but in so doing it is able to avoid establishing a definitive precedent confirming the desirability of compulsory licensing. The scope of compulsory licensing remains largely untested, a state of affairs that, over the long run, may reinforce global intellectual property norms and, as a consequence, benefit pharmaceutical patent holders in ways that more than compensate them for the losses they have sustained in South Africa, Brazil, and Thailand.

Our purpose here is not to suggest that intellectual property rights are of no moment or that all patents, even all pharmaceutical patents, should be challenged in the way that patents on HIV/AIDS drugs have been challenged. But these stories highlight a crucial intersection between the concerns that animate the law of tangible property and intellectual property. Like the squatters and adverse possessors we described in chapter 3, who slowly forged communities that were collectively able to successfully challenge settled property law, activists and government actors in Brazil, South Africa, and Thailand have been able to use the tool of acquisitive property transgression to garner allies in the international system and eventually win significant concessions from the pharmaceutical industry.[88]

The success of this strategy has had both short- and long-term effects. Most significantly, it has redefined the debate over pharmaceutical patents, transforming the public's perception of them from privately owned property into entitlements deeply suffused with public implications.[89] This revised view has become particularly prominent in the press discussions of compulsory licensing and has spurred an important transition from public enactment of patent rights to private capitulation due to global health concerns.[90]

Nothing exemplifies this shift more powerfully than the dramatic shifts in the United States' own position. The Clinton administration was initially a strong opponent of compulsory licensing but then shifted its position in 1999. The Bush administration followed the same pattern. In January 2001, the United States formally filed a dispute with the WTO Dispute Settlement Body, challenging the Brazilian law that allowed compulsory licensing in a limited number of situations.[91] The United States' action backfired, however. Shortly after the United States filed the dispute, in a show of support for Brazil, the U.N. Human Rights Commission approved a resolution establishing access to medicine during a pandemic as a basic human right.[92] Just four months later, and perhaps in response, the United States abruptly withdrew its WTO claim.[93]

Somewhat ironically, as a result of a public scare over anthrax attacks shortly after the September 11 attacks, America found itself in the same position it had once criticized. When the public demanded access to the antibiotic Cipro, the U.S. government threatened compulsory licensing to pressure Bayer AG, the holder of the Cipro patent, to lower its price. On October 16, 2001, Senator Charles Schumer of New York asked the secretary of the Department of Health and Human Services to issue compulsory licenses to generic manufacturers.[94] Shortly thereafter, Bayer capitulated and agreed to lower the price of the drug and triple its production.

In the end, the efforts of Brazil and South Africa, coupled with the work of AIDS activists and journalists across the world, managed to broker a profound global shift toward compulsory licensing. Faced with their own concerns over public health, in November 2001 the United States and other WTO members unanimously approved the Doha declaration on the TRIPS agreement, which at the time marked a watershed in recognizing the importance of access to medicines in a time of public-health crisis.[95] The declaration clearly stated that the WTO members recognized the gravity of various public-health problems, not just HIV/AIDS, and the members expressly agreed that "the TRIPS Agreement does not and should not prevent Members from taking measures to protect public health. Accordingly, while reiterating our commitment to the TRIPS Agreement, we affirm that the Agreement can and should be interpreted and implemented in a manner supportive of WTO Members' right to protect public health and, in particular, to promote access to medicines for all."[96] The Doha declaration further recognized that each member had the right to grant compulsory licenses and the freedom to determine the grounds upon which the licenses would be granted, and that they enjoyed the right to determine what constituted a "national emergency or other circumstances of extreme urgency," expressly recognizing that diseases other than HIV could present similar concerns.[97] Later, on August 30, 2003, two years after Doha, the WTO adopted new rules that broadened

the Doha declaration by permitting countries without the ability to produce generic versions to import them from another country.[98]

Later, Malaysia and India issued compulsory licenses enabling Malaysia
to procure generic AIDS drugs from India—although the licenses were
for a limited period of time and for government use alone.[99] As of March
2008, compulsory licenses have been issued by Cameroon, Eritrea, Ghana,
Indonesia, Malaysia, Mozambique, the Philippines, and Zambia; and in
many other cases, pharmaceutical companies have agreed to offer drugs at
significantly lower prices to fend off the threat of such licenses.[100] Na-
mibia, Uganda, and Ethiopia are said to be moving forward with plans to
produce generic versions of HIV/AIDS drugs domestically.

Despite—or perhaps because of—their willingness to challenge the
scope of patent protection, Brazil, South Africa, and Thailand have been
widely hailed as models to follow in the war against AIDS. The World
Health Organization, for example, has touted Brazil as a model, which has
prompted thirty-one other nations to adopt Brazil's guidelines in fighting
AIDS.[101] But much of Brazil's success in fighting the illness is attributable
to its willingness to explore every possible avenue—including challenging
the boundaries of international intellectual property law—to provide access to medicines for its citizens. As a *New York Times* journalist observed,
"[the drug companies'] solution—limited, negotiated price cuts—is slow,
grudging, and piecemeal. Brazil, by defying the pharmaceutical companies
and threatening to break patents, among other actions, has made drugs
available to everyone who needs them. Its experience shows that doing
this requires something radical: an alteration of the basic social contract
the pharmaceutical companies have enjoyed until now."[102]

7

EXPRESSIVE ALTLAWS: COPYRIGHT AND THE
NEW LIBERATION OF INFORMATION

In January 2003, a woman named Bev Harris came across, through Google, a Web site that contained a cache of user manuals, software patches, and the complete source code for the voting machines made by Diebold Election Systems, one of the leading manufacturers of electronic voting systems in the United States.[1] It was an unexpected—and incredible— find. Harris was writing a book about ballot tampering and had found the material on an unprotected Web site. After realizing what the material was, she immediately posted it to her Web site. The sheer volume of the material, not to mention its contents, sparked the interest of the online community, which had long complained about Diebold's refusal to make its source code public. After the material surfaced, the online community began to focus more and more attention on whether Diebold's system was secure, prompting well-founded fears about the company's machines.[2]

Several months later, an unknown person (or persons) went even further. He or she managed to hack into Diebold's servers and collect thousands of internal messages concerning Diebold voting machines.[3] The documents revealed that the voting systems were far from infallible; in fact, they listed numerous problems with the machines' reliability and verification processes, problems that ultimately led California to decertify Diebold's touch-screen voting machines the following year.[4] It turned out that America's votes were far more vulnerable than people had suspected.

In August 2003, a reporter for *Wired News* received a file containing the trove of messages—over thirteen thousand documents in all. Soon afterward, the material began leaking online, and even Harris (who had obtained a copy of the file) joined the fray, posting a few of the memos herself.[5] News began to spread. Terrified of the information becoming even more public, Diebold considered its options and soon turned to copyright law as a tool to limit circulation of the information. Since people were posting the material without Diebold's permission, the company decided to threaten to sue anyone who posted it for copyright infringement. After the material appeared on some Web sites, Diebold sent a series of copyright cease-and-desist letters to Harris, among a few others, and to Harris's Internet service provider (ISP).[6]

Unfortunately for Diebold, a group of student bloggers from Swarthmore College decided to host the e-mail archive on the college servers. Even though officials at Swarthmore, after receiving copyright threats from Diebold, forced the students to disable access to the memos, the students organized a "grassroots cyber-protest," whereby every time a student got disconnected, the files would be posted from another source.[7] Ultimately, students at fifty colleges and universities hosted the memos— in brazen defiance of the cease-and-desist letters that swiftly followed their efforts. An article in the *New York Times Magazine* compared the students to those involved in the famous Pentagon Papers case. "Like aspiring Daniel Ellsbergs," the author wrote, "with their would-be Pentagon Papers, they posted the files on the internet, declaring the act a form of electronic whistle-blowing."[8] The story was picked up by other media outlets, which frequently included hyperlinks to the archive.[9]

As the material continued to circulate, Diebold became extremely concerned about its ailing public image. In October 2003, Diebold sent more letters to several ISPs who hosted Web sites that contained the content, alleging that "the website you are hosting infringes Diebold's copyrights because the Diebold Property was reproduced, placed on public display, and is being distributed from this website without Diebold's consent."[10] The letters further threatened a lawsuit if the material was not taken down pursuant to Diebold's request. But the notices failed to mention something important: Diebold hadn't yet registered a copyright in the material. And to make matters even more complicated, the students argued that they had a fair use right to post the information and make it available to the public.

The conflict between Diebold and the students demonstrated a key flaw in the operation of the law governing copyrighted property in cyberspace. In contacting the ISPs, Diebold was following a special procedure set forth in the Digital Millennium Copyright Act (DMCA), which permits a copyright holder to ask an ISP to take down a particular Web site if the copyright holder has a good-faith belief that the site is infringing.[11] This special provision, known as the "notice and takedown" procedure, had emerged out of the maze of confusion surrounding the reach of copyright protections within the cut-and-paste world of cyberspace. The Internet had ushered in new ways for people to share content freely, but the same technology, combined with the rise of digital media, threatened to make it easy for people to engage in massive amounts of copyright infringement. Copyright owners feared the loss of sales that would result if people posted copyrighted material on their Web sites for the entire world to share, and, at the same time, ISPs feared that they might be held liable for the infringing activities of their subscribers.[12]

As a result, the DMCA, passed by Congress in 1998, contained the notice and takedown provisions, which aimed to protect both copyright owners and ISPs in order to preserve property rights and the continued growth of the Internet. Under the law, copyright owners were responsible for locating incidents of infringement on Web sites and then notifying the ISP who hosted the site to remove the material. In turn, the ISP had to act immediately to take down the infringing material, or face copyright liability.[13]

In most cases of clear-cut infringement, the notice-and-takedown system seemed to be a decent compromise: the copyright owner is rightfully burdened with the responsibility of finding potential infringers, and the ISP provider is burdened with the responsibility of taking down the infringing Web sites. But in harder cases, like the Diebold case, the complexities of freedom of speech, fair use, and other principles highlight the DMCA's failure to ensure that the interests of the public are as protected as those of copyright owners. As one researcher at Harvard Law School's Berkman Center observed, "this swift process might be appropriate for a company whose top-40 song is being traded illegally online, but when it applies to political speech, the process is more problematic."[14] Although the DMCA notice-and-takedown system requires a "good faith" belief in infringement, many sites have been taken down for spurious reasons, and often when the Web site operator disagreed with or criticized a copyright owner. In such situations, the notice-and-takedown system arms a copyright owner with a powerful tool to censor the expression of others and provides unequal recourse for the individuals who are silenced. Since the DMCA provisions require ISPs to take down access to the material immediately, the individual targeted by the procedure frequently lacks an opportunity to respond to the complaint before the Web site is disrupted.[15] The law includes no requirement that subscribers be notified of the subpoena or given the opportunity to challenge the takedown before their identity is disclosed.[16]

Moreover, although it costs almost nothing for a copyright owner to file and serve a DMCA takedown notice, even brief disruptions can be very costly for Web site owners, and it can take the owner a great deal more effort to establish his or her innocence. The DMCA includes a special procedure, called a counter-notification procedure, that enables Web site operators to challenge the takedown if they believe that they have been unfairly targeted.[17] If a counter-notice is filed, the ISP must put the Web site back online within ten to fourteen days, unless the copyright owner has moved to file a case in court. Despite these procedures, many scholars argue that, in practice, the DMCA gives the copyright owner a much greater degree of power than the ordinary Web site owner because the copyright owner can usually procure a DMCA takedown notice with little or no examination of the merits of the dispute.[18] Perhaps because of the sheer number of notices they receive, compounded by their fear of liability for hosting infringing content, few ISPs make an independent assessment of a copyright owner's determination that infringement is occurring. Should an ISP refuse to respond to the DMCA request, it risks losing its immunity under a key "safe harbor" provision of the DMCA. As John Palfrey explained, the DMCA notice-and-takedown procedure is "like getting a temporary restraining order, only without needing to go through a judge."[19]

Despite these flaws, in most cases, the DMCA process operates smoothly and in the interest of copyright owners. Yet the Diebold incident demonstrates the problems caused by the DMCA's failure to provide a mechanism for ensuring that accusations are credible before information is taken down from the Internet. Was the Diebold material copyrighted? And if it was, did the students infringe Diebold's property rights when they posted the material, hoping to circulate it before the election? How should the defense of fair use govern these cases? And what role, if any, should the First Amendment's protection of news gathering play in resolving the dispute? The DMCA makes it difficult to fully address these questions before the disputed material is suppressed. Precisely because it represents such a potent tool for protecting copyrighted material, then, the notice-and-takedown procedure is an equally powerful mechanism for censorship. Even if the students legitimately believed that they were acting within the boundaries of the law, particularly the First Amendment, Diebold could use the DMCA to squelch circulation of the material.

In light of this legal landscape, it made strategic sense for Diebold to do exactly what it did: it attempted to use the DMCA provisions to stop the circulation of the embarrassing information about its voting machines. Diebold reasoned that by alleging infringement and invoking the notice-and-takedown provisions of the DMCA, it could successfully stop the circulation of the documents. So it sent cease-and-desist letters to several Web sites, including those at Swarthmore, warning them that they would be sued for facilitating copyright infringement if they did not immediately disable access to the offending material or remove it from the Internet.[20] "We reserve the right to protect that which we feel is proprietary," Diebold told the *New York Times*.[21] Almost immediately, Swarthmore complied and ordered the students to take down the material pursuant to the DMCA.

The students were understandably furious. They believed that the letters were a "perfect example of how copyright law can be and is abused by corporations like Diebold" to stifle the freedom of expression.[22] Although Swarthmore complied with Diebold's DMCA request to take down access to the material, the school's dean, Robert Gross, was careful to express support for the students.[23] The school's president, Alfred Bloom, concurred, claiming that "the college is deeply proud of its students' resolve to act on behalf of an open and fair democracy."[24] The university recommended that the students respond to Diebold with a counter-notification.[25] "My concern," Dean Gross added, "and I think the concern of the students is to focus attention on electoral fraud. The copyright stuff is a sideshow," he said. "If what the memos suggest is true, this makes hanging chads look like state-of-the-art (election technology)."[26]

Although the students ultimately took the information down from the Swarthmore servers, they decided to go one step beyond the cumbersome counter-notification procedure. After all, by the time they established their rights to post the material under the copyright law, the 2004 elections might well have come and gone. So they opted to defy the DMCA altogether by recruiting students at other schools to post the material on their own servers. Subsequently, every time a student was disconnected for posting the material, the files were given to another student and posted from another location. Eventually, the students launched a nationwide movement—drawing on allies at Harvard, MIT, Carnegie Mellon, Duke, the University of California at Berkeley, and over fifty other campuses to circulate the material by moving the memos from one server to another to ensure access to the public.[27] By staying one step ahead of Diebold and the DMCA notice-and-takedown process, the students were able to keep the information available to the public, despite Diebold's willingness to invoke the DMCA to protect its proprietary hold. Soon, the memos made their way onto peer-to-peer systems. Once there, it became impossible to restrict them from public access, even with the help of the DMCA. "Within days," wrote copyright guru Siva Vaidhyanathan, "one could acquire the memos from peer-to-peer interfaces such as Kazaa, Gnutella, and Freenet. Many other Web sites openly posted the memos and challenged Diebold to try to stamp out every source."[28]

Were the students' activities legal? At the outset, given the substantial murkiness of the DMCA, it was difficult to tell. Diebold's threats obscured the simple fact that the students' behavior fell within a classic gray area between unlawful infringement and lawful fair use. On one blog, Freedom to Tinker, a few lawyers and copyright scholars offered divergent views on whether the students' activities were protected by fair use. One copyright expert, after considering the range of factors—that the use was noncommercial, that the works were unpublished, and that the work was copied in total—concluded in favor of fair use, although he believed that it was by no means a clear-cut issue.[29] A prominent lawyer, Wendy Seltzer, thought that the case was clearer and argued that "fair use and the First Amendment plainly protect our right to use these documents to comment on the mechanisms of our democracy."[30] But another commentator disagreed with this view, arguing that "it's never fair use to use the entire work."[31] And a fourth commentator argued that the real issue was one of unauthorized intrusion into Swarthmore's computers, pointing out that "if they, the students, access the net, via the school's network, in violation of the school's policy, they could be charged with accessing a 'protected computer' in an 'unauthorized manner,' and as a result . . . are likely committing a violation of the CFAA [the Computer Fraud and Abuse Act]." The commentator argued that it was likely that the students acted outside the law, given the likelihood that the various Web sites in question were governed by a terms of service agreement or use policy that did not permit their activities. "Violate it," the commentator observed, "and you are outside the law. I hope people will ponder the implications of this."[32]

In short, at the outset, it was simply not clear who was on the right side of the law: Diebold or the students. At least to the students, the legality of their behavior was a secondary concern. They understood their acts to represent a classic case of civil disobedience, though in an electronic form— they saw their actions as aimed at protecting fair elections, fair use, and free speech.[33] The students thought that the copyright actions constituted a dangerous form of information suppression. Thus, even without a clearcut fair use right to circulate the information, the students felt that they had an obligation to educate the public on the dangers of electronic voting. Nevertheless, the students framed their behavior in legal terms. They contended that the documents were part of an ongoing civic debate and that their activities were therefore protected as a fair use of copyrighted material.[34] They explained: "[We believe] that what we are doing is legal; though we see it as an issue of electronic civil disobedience we believe it is Diebold which is abusing copyright law in an attempt to shut down free speech and the democratic process. . . . We believe the publication of these documents is integral to the function of the democratic process. The memoranda themselves are not marketable products, and in this case we believe the nature of the work, which threatens elections occurring in 37 states, outweighs the need to selectively excerpt portions of the documents. If there is anything the American people have the right to know, it is how their votes are being counted."[35] It became clear over time that the students were faced with a difficult burden: even if they believed that they had a fair use right to circulate the information, the ISPs that hosted them were far more fearful of the legal costs involved, and so the ISPs quietly complied with Diebold's requests.

The Swarthmore students painstakingly chronicled each day's developments in what became a seventeen-day campaign of electronic disobedience, noting not only the media outlets that covered the students' circulation of the information but also the accompanying civic outcry over the voting machines' fallibility. Their diary quoted experts, professors, and citizens who were deeply concerned about the sanctity of their votes.[36] One student from Swarthmore explained on the site: "Diebold can't win! Each takedown request is simply met with more mirrors. We are willing and able to continue this campaign until the 2004 presidential elections. We will not allow Diebold's faulty voting machines to replace democracy."[37] The participants, however, were careful to argue that they believed that copyright law was being used to suppress information that rightfully belonged in public hands. "It's not like people are reading these memos in order to steal Diebold's election system," one student pointed out. "[The company] is trying to use this law, and specifically the mandatory take-down section, to conceal flaws that directly affect the validity of election results. This is a threat to our democracy," he concluded.[38]

A graduate student in computer science at MIT, C. Scott Ananian, downloaded the files from a Web site and posted links to the copies through MIT's Internet connection. "As a patriotic American," Ananian explained, "I felt that people needed to know and that I had a duty to tell them about [the issues surrounding Diebold's electronic voting systems]. People need to see the primary documents to convince themselves that this stuff was real."[39] After Diebold sent MIT two cease-and-desist messages, MIT informed Ananian that he had forty-eight hours to remove the content. Ananian complied with the university's request.[40] Others did the same. One student from Indiana University who posted the material and received a letter told the *New York Times,* "I'm starting to worry about the ramifications for my entire family if I end up in some sort of legal action."[41]

The Indiana student's fears were well grounded. Given the lack of clarity over the reach of the fair use defense and the DMCA, even copyright experts were unsure which side would win. "The DMCA issues do muddy the water," expert John Palfrey observed. "I don't think this is a slam dunk on either side," he concluded.[42] Although the conflict centered on the reach of copyright law in the context of a strong public interest in access to the information, many copyright lawyers were concerned about the initial appropriation of the private information.[43] One lawyer from the intellectual property firm Darby & Darby explained, "There is no copyright misuse when a company uses its rights under copyright to stop unauthorized reproduction of its writings." The lawyer continued, "It is no defense to say 'the subject of the writings is an important one.' . . . This is tantamount to arguing the end justifies the means. If Diebold has misrepresented its products, the law provides remedies. Thieves, however, don't get a free pass."[44]

For a time, Diebold continued to send cease-and-desist letters to the Web sites that hosted the material. Soon, nearly every major news outlet was covering the story, informing the public of the risks of unverified electronic voting. Ballot security became part of the political conversation. One presidential hopeful, Dennis Kucinich, even posted a link to the archive, criticizing Diebold for its alleged abuse of the DMCA to bar access to information, and asked Congress to investigate.[45] In an accompanying statement, Kucinich wrote: "Diebold has been using coercive legal claims to intimidate internet service providers and even universities to shut down websites with links to its memos and remove the memo content. . . . By abusing the Digital Millennium Copyright Act, Diebold has intimidated numerous internet service providers to comply with its requests. The damage is two-fold: (1) limiting the public's information about the security of its voting machines, and (2) expanding corporate control over our most free medium of expression, the Internet."[46]

Finally, on November 24, 2003, facing widespread public criticism from copyright and free-speech advocates, Diebold relented, claiming that it would retract the copyright notices and promising that it would not file suit against ISPs or other individuals who posted or linked to the archive.[47] "We've simply chosen not to pursue copyright infringement in this matter," a Diebold spokesman explained.[48] Nevertheless, the students chose to initiate litigation themselves in order to obtain a ruling in their favor that would effectively prevent Diebold from threatening any further litigation relating to the publication, linking, or hosting of the archive. "We have sued Diebold with the intention of making them stop their misuse of intellectual property law to terrorize students across the nation who care about the state of the democratic process in our country," stated one of the Swarthmore students, Nelson Pavlosky.[49]

Rather than waiting to be sued as defendants, the students chose to act as plaintiffs to use the DMCA to protect their activities. They sought a declaratory judgment—a legal finding from a judge—establishing that the students had a fair use right to post and link to the internal information, as well as damages and attorneys' fees against Diebold for its misuse of copyright law. The students thus attempted to force the court to make a profound legal shift in perspective: rather than focusing on their own conduct, the students hoped to focus attention on the legality of Diebold's acts instead. They relied on the doctrine of "copyright misuse" in making their legal claim—a doctrine that essentially makes it illegal for a copyright owner to extend the boundaries of his or her entitlement in a manner that violates the public-policy values that copyright is supposed to protect.[50]

In what marked a watershed victory, the students prevailed.[51] In reaching its decision in favor of the students, the trial court employed a seldom-used section of the DMCA that makes anyone who materially misrepresents the infringing character of the material liable for damages and attorneys' fees,[52] and required Diebold to pay $125,000 in damages and fees to the students. The court chided Diebold for its strategic use of the takedown provisions under the DMCA. It observed that at least part of the archive would have been protected by fair use, noting that each of the relevant factors of a fair use determination weighed in favor of the students, rather than Diebold: "The purpose, character, nature of the use, and the effect of the use upon the potential market for or value of the copyrighted work all indicate that at least part of the email archive is not protected by copyright law. The email archive was posted or hyperlinked to for the purpose of informing the public about the problems associated with Diebold's electronic voting machines. It is hard to imagine a subject the discussion of which could be more in the public interest. If Diebold's machines in fact do tabulate voters' preferences incorrectly, the very legitimacy of elections would be suspect." Given the complete absence of evidence that the students' posting had any pecuniary effect on the original market for the documents, the court concluded that the students' use of the material was a fair one. The court emphasized that the students engaged in a transformative use of the documents, concluding, "[The plaintiffs] used the email archive to support criticism that is in the public interest, not to develop electronic voting technology." Perhaps most importantly, the court also found that Diebold had materially misrepresented the extent of its proprietary protection over the documents, asserting that "no reasonable copyright owner could have believed" that its documents were protected by copyright, concluding that Diebold "specifically intended" that its cease-and-desist letters would prevent publication. Indeed, the court noted, Diebold was attempting to use the DMCA as a sword to suppress publication of material that could prove embarrassing, rather than as a shield to protect intellectual property that it actually owned.[53]

The court's decision marked several important changes in the judicial treatment of the DMCA's notice-and-takedown provision, which had long been criticized for its potential to censor valuable content.[54] Prior to the case, the notice-and-takedown provision largely "default[ed] to an assumption that infringement has occurred," a presumption that might be appropriate for some forms of established illegal behavior (like uploading protected MP3s), but that can often seem far less justified in other contexts in which infringement is alleged, most obviously political speech.[55] In such situations, as in *Diebold*, the DMCA offered a private copyright owner a speedy way to short-circuit the circulation of embarrassing information without legislative or judicial oversight; the result, as the *Diebold* court concluded, was an almost wholesale delegation of power to the copyright owner to decide what does and does not constitute infringement.

In most cases, there is little consideration within the DMCA process of the possibility of fair use protections, which are murky and difficult to evaluate. However, the students in the Diebold case, in making fair use the centerpiece of their defense, ensured that these considerations would become an important part of crafting a forward-thinking legitimate defense before an ISP. Even more important, the outcome of the case pointed towards the possibility of limiting the power of purported copyright owners to use intellectual property law as a tool to silence criticism. No longer, it seemed, could a copyright owner prevail simply by threatening an online speaker with a lawsuit. Instead, the *Diebold* case suggested that misrepresentation of the scope of a copyright constituted "misuse" of copyright altogether and ran the risk of substantial liability. In short, the outcome of the case sent an important signal that the notice-and-takedown provisions were no longer the blank check that copyright owners might have hoped for. Instead, it signaled an important compromise—as in many other areas of copyright law—between freedom of speech and proprietary boundaries.

Finally, the *Diebold* case provides an example of how challenging the boundaries of intellectual property can serve democratic goals of social justice, inclusion, and dialogue. As Siva Vaidhyanathan pointed out, "by using methods both within the law (via the federal courts) and beyond the law (by facilitating anarchistic distribution of the memos regardless of threats from Diebold and cowardice by the Swarthmore administration), [the students] set an example for activists and citizens' groups . . . to follow."[56] Not only did the accompanying legal response lead to a fair use right to post and circulate the information, but the court also invigorated an important rule of prohibitory restraint through its implicit invocation of the doctrine of copyright misuse, a doctrine that has the potential to impose significant limits on the copyright owner's entitlements regarding exclusion and control.

The students' actions therefore demonstrate how actions taken outside the intellectual property system can foster the reevaluation or clarification of property entitlements. Not only did the students' initial acts of resistance force Diebold to relent, but the success of their litigation highlighted the occasional need for property rights to give way to other competing values, like democratic discourse and access to vital information. As the Diebold case illustrates, challenging property entitlements can engender valuable forms of formal and informal legal change.

The *Diebold* case therefore highlights the potentially productive value of the expressive altlaw.[57] Like many other altlaws, the students were motivated by a form of necessity—apart from challenging asserted boundaries of proprietary ownership, there was no other way to ensure that others had access to the material. At the same time, however, the students' actions were also expressive in that they were principally designed both to share the information and to demonstrate (through litigation) the need for copyright entitlements to shift in response to other competing interests. And in turn, the law shifted to validate their claim and to limit the reach of the property right in Diebold's information. The case vindicated the students, but it also demonstrated how the law can operate as a tool to limit copyright owners' attempts to silence activities that fall within fair use. As part of the settlement, Diebold was required to send out a series of retractions of its cease-and-desist letters. One student, Derek Slater, whose Web site was targeted, was thrilled about the news of the retraction. "I think I'll frame it," he announced.[58]

PART

RESPONDING TO PROPERTY OUTLAWS

8

TWO PERSPECTIVES ON PROPERTY OUTLAWS

In part 2, we described several cases in which property disobedience yielded important shifts within existing legal regimes governing property and intellectual property. In this part and the next, we explore the ways in which the law responds to property disobedience, both for better and for worse. Along the way, we point to several doctrines that seem to recognize the value of leaving some space for property disobedience and suggest some ways in which the law (especially the law of intellectual property) might be changed in order to encourage productive disobedience while continuing robustly to protect rights of private ownership.

Inasmuch as property disobedience plays an integral part in forcing the evolution of property law, the property outlaw also faces a substantial risk of punishment or liability. Given the important position that outlaws have occupied in the evolution of property law, however, we believe that it is essential for the law to retain a certain flexibility in its response to them. Although much of our focus in this discussion is on criminal enforcement of property law, the same general observations apply to noncriminal enforcement through sanctions such as damages and fines.

For the purposes of our analysis, we will accept the common characterization of the dominant theories of criminal punishment as either broadly deterrent or retributive. By the former, we mean theories that view the purpose of punishment as creating disincentives that self-interested potential criminals will take into account in deciding whether the possible rewards of a criminal act outweigh the risk of punishment. By the latter, we refer to theories that identify the purpose of punishment as rooted in moral theories about culpability and just deserts. Although we decidedly do not intend to take sides between these two approaches, our description of the appropriate legal response to property outlaws must vary depending on which theory one prefers. Our argument is premised on the general notion that certain categories of property outlaws are less culpable (or, in consequentialist, deterrent terms, create less social harm—or perhaps even create more social benefits) than ordinary criminals. Accordingly, we analyze a variety of ways in which adherents of both deterrent and retributive approaches can (and, to a certain extent, already do) take into account the productive aspects of disobedience in order to preserve the inherent dynamism that it introduces within property law.[1]

Property Outlaws in Deterrent and Retributive Perspectives

In the classic view, the ultimate goal of deterrent punishment ought to be something very close to zero incidence of the proscribed behavior.[2] Some contemporary theorists have suggested a similar goal, at least as an (admittedly impossibly expensive) ideal.[3] Most recent discussions, however, have abandoned the goal of zero disobedience in favor of punishment that seeks to achieve an "optimal" level of disobedience by forcing criminals to internalize the social costs of their behavior, including both the harm to victims and the costs of law enforcement. These approaches treat the question of punishment as "a generalization of the economist's analysis of external harm or diseconomies."[4] Typically, the process of calculating the optimal level of punishment is described by deterrent theorists as one involving some variation on a mathematical calculation linking, among other things, the likelihood that a criminal will be caught with an aggregation of the harm to victims and the enforcement costs generated by the criminality.[5]

Our argument is that these calculations, whether framed in terms of general or specific deterrence, fail to consider or recognize the productive informational and redistributive potential of some kinds of legal transgression. By overlooking this potentially useful function and failing to recognize that some elements of property disobedience may be more socially productive than others, deterrent models of punishment are likely to call for levels of punishment that overdeter or preclude certain forms of productive transgression. Further, the general tendency of criminal law to overdeter property violations is particularly acute when the technology of law enforcement suddenly improves. Under such circumstances, levels of deterrence that may have been appropriate when the activity in question was relatively difficult to detect are especially likely to prove excessive.

What is the value of some property disobedience that deterrent theorists have overlooked? Two categories are particularly significant. First, there may in certain situations be value in the outlaw's directly redistributive conduct. We refer to this broad category of utility gains as "redistributive value." As scholars have observed, the law of tangible property contains several doctrines that permit forced transfers under certain circumscribed conditions.[6] Second, in cases of persistent, widespread disobedience, citizen behavior communicates vital information to property owners and to the state, indicating that some element of a property law or of the owner's use of the property may be out of date, unjust, or illegitimate in some respect. We refer to this signaling function provided by outlaw conduct as its "informational value." The information generated by outlaw conduct can, under the right circumstances, persuade property owners or the state to reevaluate their commitments to the status quo.

In contrast to the forward-looking, consequentialist approach associated with deterrence theory, the retributive theory centers not on the consequences of outlaw conduct but rather on the punishment the offender deserves in light of the moral character of the conduct. As Michael S. Moore has put it, "*retributivism* is the view that punishment is justified by the moral culpability of those who receive it. A retributivist punishes because, and only because, the offender deserves it."[7] From a broadly retributive point of view, the argument that certain categories of property outlaws should be tolerated (or subject to reduced sanctions) by the state relies on two intuitions: first, as a general matter, those who nonviolently break property laws are less morally culpable than other types of lawbreakers; and second, the violation of outdated laws or of laws that perpetuate unjust distributions of property is less blameworthy than other criminal acts and may even at times be justified. The first intuition is already embodied, albeit incompletely, in the criminal law, which treats crimes against persons as much more serious than similar crimes against property. The second intuition, which is similarly appealing, has also been incorporated into existing law, though not as robustly.

The foregoing discussion suggests that retributive theorists would be far more interested in the (re)distributive justice of property-outlaw behavior than in its informational value. After all, the notion of informational value resonates more strongly with the consequentialist focus of deterrence theorists. Nevertheless, assuming a degree of punitive indeterminacy within retributive systems of punishment, the informational value generated by property outlaws can be relevant within retributive theories as well.

The Types of Outlaws Revisited

Acquisitive Outlaws

ACQUISITIVE OUTLAWS IN DETERRENT PERSPECTIVE Through the forward-looking prism of deterrence, the law is rightfully viewed as reluctant to encourage disorder by loosening the punitive sanctions associated with property lawbreaking. Economists generally regard encroachments on property rights as socially wasteful rent seeking. Indeed, this analysis forms the principal basis for the most common economic arguments against theft.[8] Nevertheless, the consequentialist case for involuntary transfers of property can be quite strong when there is reason to believe that the outlaw places a higher value on the property in question than the true owner and there is some obstacle to a consensual transfer between the parties. People who have nothing (or very little) will have limited means to express in market offers the value they place on an item of property.[9] Consequently, involuntary transfers may be one of the few options available to them. The difficulty lies in identifying situations in which the outlaw truly does value the property more than the owner and in which the long-run effects of permitting occasional violations of the default rule against involuntary dispossession will not swamp the benefits created by permitting the transaction.[10]

The doctrine of adverse possession, which permits long-term trespass to mature into formal title, provides a useful illustration of this tension at work. The adverse possessor's long-term use (and improvement) of the property, combined with the risk of civil and criminal sanctions, will in many cases constitute strong prima facie evidence that the lawbreaker places high value on the property.[11] When these factors are coupled, as adverse possession requires, with a lackadaisical response by the true owner, the law achieves a high degree of confidence that the possessor values the property more than its absentee owner does. The relative ease with which property owners can protect their rights and the heavy burdens placed on adverse possessors diminish the ancillary costs of creating such a legal mechanism for forced transfers.

But situations in which the rigorous requirements for adverse possession are met are not the only circumstances under which the law might be justified in inferring that the lawbreaker places a higher value on property than its true owner does and in which the benefit of recognizing a forced transfer would not be outweighed by the long-term effects of recognizing the lawbreaker's claim. Traditional adverse-possession law gains confidence from the failure of the true owner to step forward and enforce his or her property rights, which indicates that the owner places abnormally low value on the property. Comparable confidence may arise when there is good reason to think that the nonowning claimant values the property at an abnormally *high* level in the absence of any countervailing evidence that the true owner places similarly exceptional value on the property. This might occur, for example, when the distribution of property rights is extremely skewed, the true owner is very wealthy, the acquisitive outlaw is very poor, or other conditions, like survival or a broader conception of necessity, weigh in favor of a legal reevaluation of entitlements. On a dangerously cold night, the homeless man almost certainly values the sheltered entrance to a large shopping center more highly than even the most attentive owners value their right to exclude him. He simply cannot communicate his preference in an intelligible way within a system of consensual market transactions. Under these and similar circumstances, consequentialist considerations would seem, as a prima facie matter, to call for the law to at least temporarily accommodate the demands of the nonowner.

Apart from the direct redistributive value that results from certain involuntary transfers, pervasive and persistent acquisitive outlaw conduct can generate important and valuable information about the existence of misallocations of property rights. Concentrations of disobedience clustered around discrete legal entitlements might suggest that transaction costs or wealth effects are standing in the way of what would otherwise be a beneficial transfer of rights. In England, for example, it was common in the twentieth century for outdoors enthusiasts to trespass on private land as they "rambled" over the countryside. Such acquisitive outlaw conduct went on for decades, sometimes accompanied by expressive forms of disobedience, until it caught the attention of the Labour Party, which ultimately responded by eliminating landowners' rights to exclude ramblers from "open" rural lands that did not implicate concerns for privacy.[12] Particularly when their conduct is pervasive and protracted, acquisitive outlaws generate an informational value above and beyond any redistributive value their behavior may have. This informational value, however, has been largely disregarded in economic discussions of nonconsensual transfers.

Of course, in the case of acquisitive outlaws, the quality of the information generated is undermined by the self-interested nature of the outlaw's behavior. In the context of market transactions, an offer to give something up in order to consummate the purchase gives us fairly reliable information about the value the acquiring party places on a shift in legal rights, though this information is distorted by wealth effects.[13] In the case of a forced transfer, however, we cannot tell from the outlaw's conduct the extent to which he or she values a shift in entitlements, whether for the limited purpose of the specific transaction in question or for systemic legal change more broadly. The truth of two (at least) plausible assumptions, however, would reinforce the informational value of persistent, widespread disobedience. First, in a well-functioning society, it is likely that most citizens possess an intrinsic willingness to obey the law, a willingness that is particularly pronounced when the law faithfully reflects broadly shared values.[14] And this seems true irrespective of the private gains some citizens might derive from breaking the law, particularly when they perceive that the law is fair and is widely obeyed by their fellow citizens.[15] Although empirical evidence in support of this view of the effect of criminal deterrence is unsettled, our position is at least a plausible one and has been embraced by a number of leading scholars.[16] This assumption is not meant to deny the reality that some people may actually resemble the Holmesian "bad man." For such people, cold, probabilistic considerations of deterrence will be paramount. Barring a widespread breakdown in the social order, however, most people will opt for legal mechanisms of acquiring property, and clusters of lawlessness will convey important information. Second, as behavioral economists have found, most people are less eager to pursue someone else's property than they are to keep something they already possess.

The combination of these two factors suggests that, as an initial matter, the behavioral balance is tipped in favor of departing from existing allocations of property only through legal transactions. That bias in turn suggests that when large numbers of people persistently engage in illegal actions aimed at shifting property entitlements away from the status quo, they are likely to be acting in response to fairly powerful incentives or objections. Widespread failure to resort to the market within a particular subgroup, or an intentional and coordinated strategy to shun the market, will therefore often suggest some sort of market failure or widely perceived injustice.[17]

None of this discussion is meant to suggest that we are unmindful of the potential costs involved. As rule utilitarians have frequently (and plausibly) pointed out, associated with any government decision to permit violations of general laws against forced transfers is the risk of creating negative spillover effects that could easily outweigh any short-term gains achieved by a specific forced redistribution. The long-term negative side effects of permitting the activities of individual acquisitive outlaws could take several forms. First, permitting outlaws to either temporarily or permanently retain the property they seize might well encourage property owners to resort to violence in order to protect their property or might discourage them from making productive investments in their property out of fear of losing it. Second, tolerating forced acquisitions in one case might erode the general deterrent effect of the criminal law and encourage further acquisitive behavior in broadly analogous situations by opportunists with less compelling claims than the original lawbreakers. And third, permitting lawbreakers to profit from their actions could more generally undermine respect for the rule of law.[18]

Of particular concern is the possibility that, over the long run, the general deterrent effects of permitting certain forced transfers will generate harmful feedbacks that actually magnify the harm caused by the illegal act, repercussions that would minimize the possibility that ratifying the forced transfer could be beneficial for society as a whole. For example, numerous adherents to the "broken windows" theory of criminal behavior have repeatedly hypothesized about the crime-amplifying effects of visible disorder.[19] Permitting some forced transfers might conceivably contribute to such a feedback process, especially if the forced transfers were concentrated around neighborhoods already suffering from the effects of pervasive disorder.

Although these effects raise serious concerns and should not be treated lightly, none of them rules out in advance the possibility that if the benefit of a forced transfer is great enough for a large enough number of people, legalizing certain categories of forced transfers, temporarily or permanently, can be a productive solution that ultimately reinforces, rather than undermines, the rule of law. As Frank Michelman has observed, the nature and extent of owners' responses to "forced sharing" raise difficult empirical questions that cannot be determined a priori through abstract reasoning.[20] In other words, in cases of extreme want, permitting forced transfers could be beneficial, even over the long run.

Further, if the pressure for the particular type of forced transfer within a community is broad enough, legalizing the transfer may *increase* order and respect for the rule of law and for property rights by bringing the official law into greater conformity with people's sense of justice and fairness.[21] For example, among squatting communities in the nineteenth-century United States, the perception that land policy was patently unfair and unworthy of obedience threatened to undermine squatters' respect for the rule of law more broadly.[22] Bringing the law of land distribution into conformity with the widely held views of the local community—by ratifying squatters' (illegal) appropriations—converted a group of outlaws into a group with something at stake in protecting the (modified) property system.

A similar intuition appears to underlie the arguments made by Hernando de Soto with respect to the benefits of granting title to squatters in Lima, Peru. In Peru, where the mass of people are cut off from property ownership by their own poverty, residents have frequently resorted to concerted land invasions to occupy underutilized land, both public and private.[23] As de Soto observes, "people are capable of violating a system which does not accept them, not so that they can live in anarchy but so that they can build a different system which respects a minimum of essential rights."[24] De Soto notes that 69 percent of the houses built in Lima in 1985 were constructed on unlawfully occupied land. Under the circumstances de Soto describes of widespread rejection of the existing distributive order, ratifying the conduct of property outlaws—or accommodating them by creating a formalized process by which they can accomplish the goal of ownership—can ultimately become an order-enhancing, not an order-destroying, strategy.

Other observers of squatter communities throughout the developing world have commented on their impressive, albeit largely informal, orderliness. Robert Neuwirth ultimately concurs with de Soto and others who have argued that—for better or for worse depending on one's orientation—once squatters' claims are recognized, squatters typically become fierce defenders of their property rights and, by extension, supporters of the legal order from which they were formerly excluded.[25] The simultaneous radicalism and conservatism of squatters explains why they have so frequently been attacked by commentators on both the left and the right: they are suspect to the right because their squatting begins in an act of defiance of the established legal order; and they are suspect to the left because when they succeed, they reinforce the very systems of private ownership they initially transgressed.[26]

For analogous reasons, how others respond to a system of forced sharing will depend on the precise means by which that sharing is accomplished. Not all disobedience, even of the acquisitive variety, need contribute to a sense of widespread disorder that would undermine broader crime-control efforts. An act of illegal appropriation may actually contribute to visible *order*. For example, squatters in the American West created elaborate (and ordered) systems of informal law to protect their investments should their legality some day be recognized.[27] Similarly, de Soto has observed that organized squatters in Peru often keep meticulous land records indicating who "owns" which parcel and take great pains to defend their informal property rights against owners and "ordinary criminals."[28] A great deal of urban squatting in the United States in the 1970s and 1980s was highly organized and likewise may have worked to displace the preexisting disorder generated by extensive urban abandonment.[29] Urban squatters were fixing broken windows, not breaking them. It is perhaps for this reason that neighborhood residents were typically supportive of urban squatting efforts, notwithstanding their illegality.

ACQUISITIVE OUTLAWS IN RETRIBUTIVE PERSPECTIVE   It is commonplace within theories of civil disobedience to distinguish between conscientious disobedients who violate laws with the self-conscious purpose of drawing attention to the injustice of the laws they oppose and mere criminals motivated by greed or selfishness. Ronald Dworkin's theory of civil disobedience, for example, actively privileges conscientious lawbreakers (who overlap substantially with our own category of expressive lawbreakers) over other types of criminals.[30] Indeed, for Dworkin, the principal difference between the most justified and least justified forms of civil disobedience turns on the degree of intensity with which the disobedient citizen views the violated law as unjust. Accordingly, under his view of civil disobedience, many of the people we have called acquisitive lawbreakers would not fare particularly well. Their subjective motivation, although often a mystery, frequently appears to be little more than a self-interested desire to acquire property rights currently in the hands of others.

The central message sent by the acquisitive outlaw's actions is that another person owns something that the outlaw wants (or needs) but that he or she will not (or cannot) purchase in a voluntary transaction. In most cases, this desire for the property of another will be unworthy and unjustified, and society correctly responds to the lawbreaker's behavior by punishing the transgression. But, as we have shown, at times external conditions might call into question, or at least lead us to soften, our reflexive tendency to penalize the lawbreaker.

In contrast with Dworkin, we believe that the justification of an act of acquisitive disobedience can turn on the objective content of the law and the facts on which the law itself operates, not just on the subjective attitude of the outlaw. In reaching this view, we draw on a long, though recently neglected, tradition within Western property thought.

Early Christian thinkers, for example, viewed the failure of the rich to share with the poor as tantamount to theft.[31] John Chrysostom typified this point of view when he wrote that "not to share our own wealth with the poor is theft from the poor and deprivation of their means of life; we do not possess our own wealth, but theirs."[32] In the thirteenth century,

Thomas Aquinas built on this tradition when he argued that a poor person who takes what he needs from the "superabundance" of another is simply taking that to which he is already morally entitled, and consequently, does not commit the crime of theft.[33] Indeed, in Aquinas's time, canon lawyers believed that the destitute were permitted to complain to ecclesiastical authorities when local elites failed to comply with their duty to share their resources with the poor. A priest or bishop could then compel the wealthy to give alms, using the denial of absolution and the threat of excommunication, if necessary, to achieve his goals.[34]

On the American frontier, squatters frequently invoked the doctrine of necessity, often expressed in terms that echoed medieval natural law ideas, in order to justify their own trespass on public and private lands. Writing about squatter conceptions of ownership on the nineteenth-century frontier, Donald Pisani observed that the American Revolution popularized the notion that "God had given the Earth to mankind in common and that human beings had the same right to land as they had to air and water." In addition, Pisani noted, settlers believed that "human beings had a right to life and self-preservation—and hence to subsistence." So common were these sentiments among squatters that one military officer charged with the task of removing squatters from mission land in California in 1847 complained that "if there was one more word of the *Law of Necessity* . . . I should be compelled to send [the squatters] forthwith to [Mexico] in irons."[35]

More recently, Jeremy Waldron has endorsed a redistributive principle that "nobody should be permitted ever to use force to prevent another man from satisfying his very basic needs in circumstances where there seems to be no other way of satisfying them."[36] Within modern criminal law, analogous intuitions appear to underlie the justificatory doctrine of necessity, although in practice (as we discuss further in the next chapter), the doctrine has been so hemmed in by qualifications and exceptions that it has become virtually inoperative in circumstances of economic need.

It is important to note that, unlike its role within the dominant theories concerning civil disobedience, the subjective attitude of the acquisitive outlaw with respect to the justice of the violated law is not the most relevant factor in this analysis. Calling the lawbreaker's action an act of self-ishness, even if the allegation is true, does not undermine its justification under our inquiry. Instead, what matters is whether, as a question of objective distributive justice, the lawbreaker took what he or she badly *needed* from the superabundance of another in such a way that those actions avoided an even greater evil. Someone in dire need is certainly not justified in taking from someone else in dire need. The outlaw's subjective view regarding the objective injustice of the existing property distribution, however, is not the critical factor.[37]

Even assuming the justice of acquisitive actions under the most extreme circumstances of need, the more interesting question is whether there is an argument that the category of justified acquisitive conduct extends beyond the situation of the person in immediate need of sustenance for physical survival. We limit ourselves to the observation that there are plausible theories of distributive justice that would be amenable to permitting some additional room for self-help beyond the extreme case of, say, imminent starvation. In large part, the question turns on the breadth of one's definition of "necessity." Many people would admit the validity of some acquisitive actions to fulfill basic human needs but then argue for an extremely narrow understanding of "need" as encompassing only those items necessary to sustain physical survival.

Notwithstanding substantial economic inequality and poverty, in an affluent society like ours, the number of people who might need to violate property laws in order to stave off imminent physical harm attributable to poverty is likely to be very small, though not zero.[38] In a highly unequal society in the developing world, the numbers will be much larger, as de Soto's work illustrates. Worldwide, roughly a billion people live on land that is not their own, many of them in conditions of extreme deprivation. Some observers estimate that by 2030, one in four people on the planet will be squatting. As one commentator has put it, "the overwhelming majority of the world's one billion squatters are simply people who came to the city, needed a place to live that they and their families could afford, and, not being able to find it on the private market, built it for themselves on land that wasn't theirs."[39]

Many theorists have argued for a broader understanding of necessity beyond these situations of dire need in both the developing and developed world. Thinkers as diverse as Aristotle, Adam Smith, and, more recently, Amartya Sen and Elizabeth Anderson have, for example, agreed that the category of human need extends well beyond the basket of goods necessary to stave off starvation and exposure.[40] In particular, they have focused on the intuition that because human beings are social animals, their legitimate "needs" include the property necessary to facilitate a minimally acceptable degree of participation in the social and political life of their respective communities. Given the differences in material circumstances of various communities and, accordingly, the different material preconditions for effective participation, this understanding of necessity is likely to yield different concrete definitions of need for differently situated societies.[41]

As Adam Smith put it in his *Wealth of Nations,* the category of "necessaries" includes "whatever the custom of the country renders it indecent for creditable people, even of the lowest order, to be without"—for example, leather shoes, a commodity that might be viewed as a luxury or perhaps as an eccentricity in other cultures, but that was a minimum requirement for even the most basic level of social respectability in Smith's England.[42] Building on Smith's culturally relative definition of needs, Amartya Sen has proposed a definition of poverty that considers the material commodities necessary to permit a person to survive physically and to participate, at least at some minimal level, in the social life of the community.[43]

If we employ this metric while shifting our attention away from subsistence economies, the commodities necessary to participate minimally in the life of a community are likely to expand.[44] Presumably, in some communities or at some time in human history, a loin cloth, some tools or weapons, and a makeshift shelter would have been sufficient to be a member of the community in good standing. A comparable list for life in the twenty-first-century United States would include substantial quantities of clothing, a fairly sophisticated shelter with indoor plumbing and various utilities (electricity, gas, telephone service), a series of functional household appliances, and an effective means of transportation.[45]

As a community becomes more affluent, the list of commodities needed to participate in community life tends to expand. This is why items that were once regarded as luxuries, such as indoor plumbing, are now considered minimal requirements of habitability and why, notwithstanding indoor plumbing's onetime status as a luxury item, we are justified in continuing to refer to housing that lacks indoor plumbing (and even to much housing that has it) as unacceptably "poor." Seen in this light, arguments that the poor are materially well off in comparison with the poor of the last century often come off as incurably obtuse.

To a limited extent, existing law recognizes the importance of this expanding list. For example, landlord-tenant law permits tenants to engage in self-help by, for example, refusing to pay rent or deducting the cost of certain essential repairs from the rent when the landlord fails to maintain the property adequately.[46] And the circumstances that would justify such a refusal to pay rent encompass features of residential property, such as running water, that would have been viewed as housing luxuries a century ago.[47] Unfortunately, the legal protection of an individual's right to receive most of these services is inadequately protected by existing law.

Extending Sen's context-specific definition of "need" to the question of self-help, one could plausibly argue that the propertyless person is entitled to take from the property of others not just what is necessary to sustain physical existence but also at least some of those commodities needed to permit a minimal participation in the life of the community. This assertion sounds fairly radical when stated in the abstract. Nevertheless, existing property doctrines like the implied warranty of habitability, adverse possession, and necessity suggest that self-help redistribution is already accepted, in a circumscribed way, by current property laws. As we discuss at greater length below, we are not calling for the creation of new legal categories so much as the expansion of existing tools. The necessity doctrine, for example, need not encompass every element of the expanded list of needs. After all, on most accounts, the entitlement protected by the doctrine does not guarantee the right to avoid any need at all, but only "dire" or some similarly qualified need. Still, a broader understanding of human need might justify expanding the prerequisites for an assertion of necessity beyond a showing of imminent physical harm.

Expressive Outlaws

EXPRESSIVE OUTLAWS IN DETERRENT PERSPECTIVE Expressive outlaws present deterrent theorists with a different calculus, in large part because of the relative modesty of their demands. They do not seek to take possession of someone else's property for themselves. Indeed, because expressive outlaws are not attempting to acquire property for themselves, they have fewer incentives—aside from a desire to express their legal preferences—to engage in the lawbreaking activity to begin with. As Eric Kades has argued, their willingness to risk injury or jail in order to express their dissent therefore suggests that they place an exceptionally high value on changing the legal status quo. Moreover, the visibility they bring to what may have been a sublimated legal disagreement (for example, the myth of black acquiescence in the private segregation of the Jim Crow South) means that their activities generate information for those in political power. And, unlike in the case of acquisitive outlaw conduct, this information is not tainted by the same degree of material self-interest.[48] Finally, because expressive outlaws are typically organized, their activities may not contribute to the same extent as decentralized acquisitive outlaw behavior to an increase in visible disorder that could undermine respect for the rule of law among the general population. The lunch-counter sit-in protesters, for example, were nothing if not orderly, as even some of their opponents conceded.

But a rigorous examination of the expressive outlaw requires recognition of a paradoxical caveat: to legitimize, *ex ante,* the lawbreaker's activity would radically undermine the expressive message itself.[49] That is, part of the message is intrinsically tied to its status as disobedience; to legitimize the disobedience would therefore dilute, and even counteract, the message's vitality.[50] Accordingly, although we advocate a reevaluation, after the fact, of the proper level of punishment of expressive outlaws, we remain cognizant of the expressive value that is generated by the lawbreaker's willingness, before the fact, to accept punishment, and we thus are reluctant to advocate a prospective change in rules.

Given the intrinsic link between the illegality of their conduct and the quality of the information that the conduct provides, it is not clear that generally applicable and substantive legal accommodation before the fact is a desirable response to expressive outlaws, even from the point of view of the outlaws themselves. It is not surprising, for example, that many of the lunch-counter sit-in protesters specifically wanted to be jailed and in some cases even objected when judges proposed suspending their sentences.[51] The converse was also true, and opponents of civil rights were sometimes eager to avoid enforcing the law against protesters in order to deny them the platform created by acts of civil disobedience. As Kades correctly puts it, "if it is the illegal nature of civil disobedience that grabs the attention of the rulers, then eliminating all sanctions will render the tactic less effective."[52] However, as Kades further points out, this logic does not preclude substantially lightening the punishment meted out to expressive outlaws.[53] Expressive lawbreakers do appear to generate less social harm than the typical criminal. Any consequentialist accommodation of expressive outlaws would, however, seek to minimize harm to property owners while preserving the expressive value of the disobedience itself.

EXPRESSIVE OUTLAWS IN RETRIBUTIVE PERSPECTIVE The retributive justification for expressive violation of criminal laws is, to a certain extent, less controversial than the case for acquisitive outlaws. As Dworkin puts it, "Americans accept that civil disobedience has a legitimate if informal place in the political culture of their community."[54] Much of the standard rationale for tolerating classic manifestations of civil disobedience stems from a widespread recognition of the importance of conscience to individual autonomy. Dworkin, for example, argues that lawbreaking is most easily justified when it is expressive of the view that one is being compelled by the law to perform what one conscientiously believes to be a deeply immoral or unjust act.[55]

Daniel Markovits goes further than Dworkin, arguing that intentional lawbreaking can be acceptable even in the absence of a strongly held belief in the deep injustice of the existing law. Indeed, he argues that disobedience is "an unavoidable, integral part of a well-functioning democratic process" when it is employed to expose and overcome "democratic deficits" caused by inertia built into the democratic political process. Consistent with his majoritarian theory of legal obligation, Markovits limits the scope of permitted "democratic disobedience" to situations in which the act of legal defiance expresses a view that has "significant support among the citizenry" but that has been held in check by the inertia of the democratic process. Disobedience that lacks such majoritarian support cannot persist in the face of a clear expression of majority support for the legal status quo.[56]

Although we welcome Markovits's broader view of the acceptable scope of expressive disobedience, we would go a bit further. In our view, expressive disobedience represents an important part of the political process even in the absence of the democratic deficits that arise when the law fails to reflect already-existing majority sentiment. Instead, we view such law-breaking as having as a legitimate goal the *creation* of majority sentiment where none existed before.

As Robert Cover understood, allowing groups to live out their alternative legal conceptions uniquely fosters the normative diversity that is essential to life in a free society.[57] Though not all such expressive disobedience need ultimately be embraced by the official lawmakers, its social value provides a reason to create space for such expression, at least to a certain extent. By allowing people to live out an alternative vision of legal possibility, lawbreaking can help overcome what might (to paraphrase Hannah Arendt) be called imaginative deficits, deficits that may well prevent majorities from embracing the previously unexplored shapes that the law might take.[58] As we have already argued, the ability of lawbreaking to demonstrate the range of imaginative legal possibilities beyond the parameters of existing democratic debate is particularly (though not exclusively) strong for those who intentionally violate property laws (as opposed to other sorts of laws).

Even beyond property lawbreaking's imaginative power, however, the formal ratification of concerted illegality can play an important role in protecting minorities against majoritarian oppression. When a minority group demonstrates the intensity of its preference for legal change through an embrace of illegality in the face of a policy supported by only the most apathetic of majorities, considerations of fairness arguably favor legal change, notwithstanding the persistent absence of majority support for affirmatively implementing such change. Under these circumstances, a fair solution might be to put the strength of majority sentiment to the test (that is, to gauge its ability to overcome the inertial forces Markovits describes) by providing the opportunity for legislative override of the requested legal accommodation. Such a move would reverse the direction of the inertial forces to determine whether such mildly favorable majority sentiment can summon up the energy to reassert itself in favor of the old rule.[59]

It is important to note that a significant part of the reduced culpability associated with expressive disobedience, at least as compared with revolutionary action, stems from the civil disobedient's implicit affirmation of the democratic process through his or her voluntary submission to criminal punishment for the unlawful acts. In other words, expressive outlaw conduct affirms the authority of the community's democratically enacted laws even as it forcefully challenges one particular product of that system. It seems clear that expressive outlaws are less blameworthy than other sorts of criminals, but what is not clear is that the proper response to their reduced culpability is a complete elimination of criminal liability, as opposed to, for example, reduced punishment or targeted relief offered after the fact. We discuss several possible responses to the conduct of expressive outlaws in the next chapter.

9

RESPONDING TO PROPERTY OUTLAWS

Our principal purpose in this book has been to highlight the importance of certain categories of intentional property disobedience to the evolution of property law. In particular, we wanted to bring to the forefront two neglected values generated by some intentional property disobedience—what we have called its redistributive value and its informational value. Given the power of these two values, we argue for a reconfiguration of sanctions in certain contexts. This does not mean that sanctions are always (or even usually) inappropriate; indeed, as we argued in the context of our discussion of expressive outlaws, the expressive outlaw's willingness to face the imposition of legal penalties is part and parcel of the outlaw's expressive force.

We are concerned, however, that, in its approach toward enforcing property norms, the law may aim to preclude too much. As we have argued, the law must take into account the socially productive nature of some property disobedience, not just its social costs. In fact, total deterrence does not appear to be the goal of most contemporary theorists. Moreover, at least in practice, the degree and likelihood of punishment for most property-law violations have left sufficient play in the joints of the system to permit some kinds of intentional disobedience to lead to significant legal change.

As we discuss in chapter 11, however, the dynamically evolving technologies and strategies of law enforcement constantly threaten to eliminate the needed flexibility within the enforcement of property laws. In crafting their responses to property outlaws, decision makers must therefore pay careful attention to these shifts in the technology or strategy of law enforcement that dramatically increase the risks of property disobedience. When enforcement becomes cheap, easy, and pervasive through the advent of new technology, preexisting legal responses can easily become excessive—particularly in cases where the law previously engaged in only sporadic enforcement. If too effective, harsh sanctions can inadvertently stamp out the informational benefits of some property disobedience. In short, dramatic improvements in the ability to detect and punish property disobedience have the ability to shift the potential outlaw's calculus in significant ways, not all of which are socially beneficial.

This focus on the possibility that improvements in the technology of property enforcement can suppress productive disobedience is particularly crucial in the context of intellectual property, where the technology (and policy) of property enforcement is undergoing revolutionary change. But our point is a general one that, as our discussion of adverse possession below illustrates, applies with equal force in the context of tangible property. Of course, there are reasons to doubt that the deterrent force of some punishments, such as those accompanying most trespass statutes, could possibly be excessive, because the crimes are misdemeanors accompanied in practice (at least in this country) by relatively light punishments.[1]

In some cases, however, even nonviolent trespassing protesters have been made to suffer harsh penalties through creative prosecution. For example, in the United Kingdom, nonviolent trespassers advocating the "right to roam" were, in one famous case, sentenced to over a year in prison through the creative use of criminal statutes. More routinely, even misdemeanor criminal trespass can carry prison sentences of up to a year.[2] In addition, in some instances, particularly those involving expressive behavior, injunctions and contempt sanctions have dramatically increased the penalties for even minor property crimes. Added to the actual sentences imposed, the ancillary effects of criminal convictions of *any* sort, such as reputational and professional harm, can magnify the force of even minor criminal sanctions.

Outside the specific context of trespass, punishment for minor property crimes can, through the application of "three strikes" laws and similar laws targeting repeat offenders, lead to the imposition of harsh sentences that might cause even someone in the most dire and uncontroversial situation of necessity to think twice before violating the property rights of others. In California, for example, under a "three strikes" regime, petty larceny can be punished as a felony if the defendant has a prior conviction for the crime, and any felony (including such elevated "petty theft" convictions) can count as a third strike. The possible effect of this practice was shown in the U.S. Supreme Court case *Lockyer v. Andrade:* the defendant, who had a history of committing property and drug crimes, was sentenced to twenty-five years to life in prison after being caught attempting to steal videotapes valued at roughly $150.[3]

When confronted with a pattern of pervasive and protracted property disobedience, legislators and prosecutors are often tempted to respond by increasing penalties in an effort to increase the deterrent effect of the law. That increased repression often takes the form of enhanced sentences, but it can also occur through increased certainty of law enforcement, as prescribed by the social-influence theories of criminal behavior.[4] Although the strategies of heightened penalties and heightened enforcement are not inherently inconsistent, they are often presented as the only valid alternatives. A third possibility, typically overlooked, is to ratify widespread property disobedience through targeted legal accommodation.

We suspect that most legislators unthinkingly favor the option of increased repression, primarily in the form of longer sentences, over the possibility of legal reform.[5] This is certainly the correct response under many circumstances. Some norms are sufficiently important and entrenched that their violation should not be tolerated. Moreover, the avarice of some people means that a certain level of property crime will persist, no matter how just society's wealth distribution. Much of the conduct that contributes to such background levels of crime is typically unjustified and is unlikely to convey much useful information. Nevertheless, our analysis counsels against the common knee-jerk tendency toward ever higher penalties and instead encourages lawmakers to consider the possibility that spikes in or concentrations of property disobedience can provide an opportunity to reevaluate society's commitment to property law's status quo. Extremely high penalties, combined with the unpredictability of the criminal-justice system, can make the cost of engaging even in justified outlaw conduct too high for most people.[6] Although they may prevent crime, high penalties can stifle the informational value generated by property disobedience—information that is essential to maintaining property's evolutionary dynamism.

The social-influence approach of increased law enforcement, which advocates an engagement with both the "price" of crime and its social meaning, presents more of a puzzle for our analysis. Proponents of this school of thought often favor a higher-certainty—lower-penalty strategy of criminal punishment.[7] Our analysis lines up, at least to an extent, with the prescriptions of the social-influence theory, but we are also cognizant of the potential chilling effect on justified disobedience of frequent, albeit low-level, punishment endorsed by this strategy. A proper concern with the importance of permitting some leeway for productive and justified disobedience suggests the need to retain a degree of flexibility within strategies aimed at aggressively eliminating disorder—in some cases even counseling in favor of tolerating intentional underenforcement.

Although we believe that property outlaws are sometimes justified in their conduct and can offer society valuable information about inefficiencies or injustices in the property system, the unlawful nature of their behavior *is* cause for concern. In part, this concern stems from the likely uneven and potentially unfair effects of outlaw behavior on property owners and third parties. If property reform is left to the individual actions of outlaws, it is unlikely that the losses imposed on owners will be fairly distributed. Because outlaws typically operate in their own neighborhoods, the result might be actions that perversely make the situation of the poor as a whole even worse.

In part, however, our concern also stems from the dangers that criminal behavior poses to the well-being of outlaws themselves. By engaging in illegal behavior, even if justified, property outlaws take substantial risks. In light of the potential that property owners and their sympathizers will engage in violent self-help, outlaws risk their physical safety. In addition, they risk being burdened by substantial fines, imprisonment, or social stigma. Although their actions may be useful in highlighting areas of needed legal reform, it would be wrong to conclude that the existence of property outlaws is a matter of indifference.

A concern with the unfair potential burdens both on property owners and on outlaws themselves suggests that lawmakers should favor the enhancement of alternative means for potential outlaws to express opposition to the legal status quo. With these qualifications in mind, in this chapter we discuss several possible legal responses to property outlaws. In the next part, we turn our attention to the law of intellectual property. In the context of traditional tangible property law, we divide our discussion of possible legal responses to outlaw behavior into two categories; each corresponds to one of the two principal values we view as being created by property outlaws. Viewing outlaws' redistributive and informational value through the bifurcated lens of outlaw actions and possible alternatives to such actions yields four possible strategies. In response to outlaws' redistributive value, the state may either (1) selectively ratify certain forced transfers or (2) increase systems of government-sponsored redistribution. In response to outlaws' informational value, the state may either (1) incorporate the information generated by outlaw behavior into the political process through deliberative feedback mechanisms or (2) increase subsidies of legal substitutes for expressive disobedience.

Increased governmental redistribution will tend to reduce the need for reliance on forced transfers and on expensive and unreliable procedural mechanisms for weighing the justifications for such transfers after the fact.[8] Similarly, increased subsidization of speech that is subversive of the status quo reduces the pressure to engage in illegal expressive conduct to draw attention to groups' complaints. Conversely, however, in the absence of the state's willingness to create and adequately fund viable alternatives, we can expect continued or increased reliance on disobedience.[9] It is important to note, however, that these two types of strategies are not mutually exclusive.

Responding to Property Outlaws' Redistributive Value

Ratifying Certain Forced Transfers

PRIVATE ACQUIESCENCE One obvious possibility when confronted with an acquisitive outlaw is for the owner to simply make an assessment of the outlaw's need for the property the outlaw has appropriated. In *Habits of the Heart,* Robert Bellah and his coauthors relate a story about John Winthrop, the first governor of the Massachusetts Bay Colony. "When it was reported to him during an especially long winter that a poor man in his neighborhood was stealing wood from his woodpile," they write, "Winthrop called the man into his presence and told him that because of the severity of the winter and his need, he had permission to supply himself from Winthrop's woodpile for the rest of the cold season. Thus, [Winthrop] said to his friends, did he effectively cure the man from stealing."[10] The same response is open to each owner: to recognize the justice of another's claim on one's own surplus and to act accordingly. This is not "charity," strictly speaking, but rather a private assessment of the justice of the outlaw's claim to one's property. It is only after owners decide against acquiescence in the unauthorized behavior that the sorts of formal legal mechanisms we describe in the remainder of this chapter come into play.

As we explore in more depth in our discussion in chapter 12 of private acquiescence in the context of intellectual property, the nonrivalrous nature of information makes such private accommodation a much more palatable course of action for owners of intellectual property than it is for owners of tangible property; in the context of tangible property, the decision to acquiesce may deprive owners of their own enjoyment of the property in question. Of course, even with tangible property, acquiescence need not entail any disruption in the owner's use and enjoyment of his or her own property. This is particularly true in the case of land, where the same parcel may support multiple nonconflicting uses. And we suspect, although the data would be extremely difficult to gather, that private acquiescence in intentional trespass is a very common response when the trespass has a minimal impact on the use to which the owner has decided to use the land.

ADVERSE POSSESSION The doctrine of adverse possession permits a trespasser who makes sufficiently open and notorious use of someone else's land for a specified period of time to obtain title ownership.[11] In most states, the law permits even the knowing trespasser (or so-called bad-faith adverse possessor) to take advantage of this doctrine. Although not a criminal law doctrine, adverse possession ultimately converts someone who would otherwise qualify as a criminal trespasser into an owner.

Lee Fennell has called bad-faith adverse possession a case of "efficient trespass," but "efficient theft" would be a better term.[12] The result of adverse possession is not merely permission to continue trespassing on another's property without being able to exclude the true owner, as one would expect from a theory of efficient trespass. Nor is it merely an option to purchase the property at fair market value in a forced sale. Instead, the result of successful adverse possession is an outright involuntary and uncompensated transfer of ownership from the original owner to the unlawful possessor.

Under certain circumstances, such a forced transfer can be justified in consequentialist terms. And, as Fennell has persuasively argued, the broad contours of adverse-possession law seem to be well crafted to isolate a category of situations in which we can have a great deal of confidence that such transfers are efficient. But the doctrine can also be justified in nonconsequentialist terms. The intentional adverse possessor, or squatter, has typically been someone without much property but with a great deal of time and a willingness to invest substantial labor in improving the unoccupied property of another. In addition, the intentional adverse possessor seeks to put the property in question (real estate) to valuable use, either for shelter or the pursuit of a livelihood. Finally, the property must be sufficiently unimportant to its true owner that the owner permits an interloper to intrude on the property and occupy it for a lengthy period of time, typically seven to ten years.

One could justify the legal ratification of intentional adverse possession by applying something like the nonconsequentialist principle we have previously discussed in relation to the retributive response to acquisitive outlaws: it is not wrong to appropriate someone else's surplus property in order to provide for one's own need when viable legal alternatives are not available. The application of this nonconsequentialist principle would seem to track fairly closely the acquisitive outlaw behavior most strongly justified by consequentialist approaches. This principle, of course, generates substantial epistemological problems when it comes to determining whether its conditions are actually satisfied. Adverse possession gets around these problems by adopting onerous conditions that ensure its application will be radically underinclusive.

It is true that the adverse-possession doctrine does not on its face pay much attention to the "need" of the adverse possessor, but when the doctrine is applied to the knowing adverse possessor, that need will very likely be manifest. With the exception of boundary disputes, it seems unlikely that many of the property rich will have either the time or the inclination to intentionally adversely possess someone else's land. And the status of the property in question as "surplus" property of the true owner is also likely to be satisfied when the owner cannot be troubled to assert his or her property rights within the prescribed period of time.

In the past, the doctrine of adverse possession sometimes served an important redistributive function and constituted a significant threat to absentee ownership.[13] Its significance in recent years, however, has declined to such an extent that it is now plausibly described as merely a mechanism for clearing title errors and resolving inconsequential border disputes.[14] This diminished role for adverse possession is the natural result of the increased affluence our developed economy coupled with reductions in the cost of property surveillance that make it cheaper for property owners to oust potential adverse possessors, both of which diminish the incentives for potential adverse possessors to seek out property to possess in the first place.

All things being equal, improvements in the technology for enforcing property rights make the category of adverse possession even more radically underinclusive than it would otherwise be. Owners need not expend much energy monitoring their property, and prospective squatters are confronted with a minuscule likelihood of successfully obtaining title. This observation suggests that as the technology of property monitoring improved, property law should have responded by easing the requirements for adverse possession. Because the behavioral requirements of adverse possession continue to serve the purpose of putting reasonably attentive owners on notice that their property is occupied by another, the most straightforward way to maintain the balance struck in the past by adverse-possession law in the face of technological advances in property surveillance would be simply to reduce the period of time for which the adverse possessor must possess the property. We have seen such a reduction in New York, where the period was originally twenty years but was shortened over the course of the twentieth century, first to fifteen years, and then to ten. And in the United States, adverse-possession statutes are generally shorter in the younger, western states. But even shorter periods than those that presently prevail might make sense. Although seven to ten years may have been a fair period of time to require of an adverse possessor in the nineteenth-century West, when a trip from the East Coast to the West Coast and back could take months, a shorter period would seem to be more than sufficient to protect the interests of even moderately vigilant property owners in this era of six-hour transcontinental flights and instantaneous, ubiquitous telecommunication. The case for such a reduction in the time period required for adverse possession seems particularly strong in the context of urban properties, where it is virtually impossible for even the most careless owner not to notice an adverse possessor's use of his or her land.

A trend in the United States in recent years has been to do away with so-called "bad-faith" adverse possession, that is, adverse possession in which the possessor knows that the property belongs to another. At the level of formal doctrine, this trend represents a dramatic change in direction. The traditional test for adverse possession in the United States has typically ignored the state of mind of the adverse possessor, or when the test has taken it into account, either has simply required the adverse possessor to act as if the property was his or her own or has required the adverse possessor to know that it belonged to another. Richard Helmholz has argued that, notwithstanding the formal doctrine, courts have, at least in recent years, favored good-faith adverse possessors over those who knowingly occupy the property of another. If Helmholz is correct, then the recent trend toward the formalization of the requirement of good faith is more properly understood as bringing doctrine into conformity with practice than as a dramatic legal shift.

Whether we describe the trend as a legal revolution in adverse-possession law or a long-needed updating of the law to bring it into line with actual practice, the question remains whether the requirement of good faith (both in doctrine and in practice) is a wise one. Understood as a mechanism for redistribution, as we have proposed, adverse possession likely has less of a place in a wealthy, modern capitalist society in which nearly everyone has the basic necessities of life. Accordingly, it is perhaps understandable that modern adverse-possession law in the United States is narrowing the scope of permissible nonconsensual transfers of property. On the other hand, in the current economic crisis, the explosion of home foreclosures has resulted in enormous numbers of absentee-owned, unoccupied dwellings. According to the U.S. Census Bureau, 15 percent of housing units in the United States were vacant at the end of 2008.[15] These vacant houses posed a threat to neighborhood property values, as foreclosing banks failed to maintain the empty properties.[16] At the same time, homelessness among families suffering from the economic downturn is a growing problem. Given this combination of pervasive need and widespread underutilization of existing housing units, there seems to be a continuing place for a redistributive conception of adverse possession, even in the United States.

In any event, there can be little doubt that extremely skewed landownership patterns in the developing world constitute a serious barrier to development, particularly where landownership provides access to a livelihood. With one billion (intentional) squatters worldwide, bad-faith adverse possession remains one promising means of providing security of tenure and legal formalization for an enormous number of people. In other words, even if the prohibition of intentional adverse possession makes sense in the United States, there are substantial reasons for developing countries to resist emulating that trend, at least for the time being.

NECESSITY The doctrine of necessity permits nonowners to trespass on, and under certain circumstances even to appropriate, the property of others in order to avoid a grave harm.[17] In the criminal context, the basic insight of the doctrine, which has been recognized by nearly every state and federal court in the country, is that a person should not be punished for being forced by circumstance to choose between two evils, the lesser of which involves breaking the law.[18] Although it varies significantly by jurisdiction, the criminal defense of necessity has traditionally been understood to justify the defendant's otherwise unlawful appropriation of the property of another when (1) the defendant's illegal conduct was committed to avoid a significant evil; (2) the defendant reasonably believed that his or her actions were necessary to avoid this evil; (3) the defendant had no alternative legal means of preventing this harm; and (4) the evil sought to be avoided is greater than the harm expected to result from the defendant's criminal conduct.[19]

A related doctrine applies within the noncriminal law of property, privileging access to private property when necessary to protect those in dire need from death or serious bodily harm. Such property users are not obligated to compensate property owners unless they damage or consume the property in question. (So, for example, a stranded hiker would not have to pay for mere access to a vacant hotel in order to seek shelter from a snowstorm, but the hiker would have to pay for any damage caused by the break in.) Moreover, the law protects the right of access of the person in need, even permitting that person to engage in reasonable self-help in order to overcome attempts by property owners to interfere with access in times of dire need.[20]

The doctrine can be fairly easily justified in consequentialist terms. But it can also be explained in moral terms that are similar to the redistributive principle we have been discussing. Like adverse possession, however, the doctrine of necessity creates substantial epistemological problems, to which the law has responded by couching the doctrine in qualifications that end up making it profoundly underinclusive.[21]

In its traditional formulation, the necessity doctrine falls squarely within the circumstances that approximate those in which we have argued that acquisitive outlaw behavior would be justified: situations in which someone in need nonviolently takes what he or she needs from the surplus of another. The conduct of many squatters, both those of the nineteenth-century American West and those in many parts of the developing world today, as well as those in the modern urban context, would appear to fall within the boundaries of this description. In addition, many of the behaviors of homeless people that have been criminalized by local governments in recent years fit comfortably within a plausible understanding of necessity.[22]

Most courts, however, have interpreted the necessity defense in an artificially narrow way that would restrict it to extremely unusual circumstances, such as natural disasters. Most significant for our purposes, several courts have held that, as a categorical matter, the doctrine is not available when the evil the defendant seeks to avoid is caused by economic forces alone.[23] We reject these narrow reconstructions of the defense and would require courts to treat dire economic necessity in precisely the same way that they treat necessity caused by natural disasters. In a predominantly market-based economy that relies almost exclusively on consensual transactions to get property from one person to another, economic necessity can be as dire an evil as catastrophic flooding.[24] Moreover, as in the case of natural disasters, third parties who assist those in situations of dire necessity should also be entitled to take advantage of the defense.[25]

In one Texas case, a woman was charged with welfare fraud after she unlawfully obtained work to supplement her welfare income in order to provide food for her children. Her lawyer proffered the testimony of several experts that the defendant's children were suffering from malnutrition prior to her attempt to supplement her income and that the state welfare benefits available to her were insufficient to provide minimally adequate nutrition for herself and her children. The trial court refused even to allow the defendant to present the evidence to the jury, and the defendant was convicted.[26]

In *Southwark v. Williams,* a 1971 case involving urban squatters in London, the court endorsed an equally narrow interpretation of the necessity doctrine. Homeless families had been living on the streets of London and had, with the assistance of an urban-squatting advocacy group, nonviolently occupied an abandoned home owned by the Borough of Southwark. When the borough brought suit to oust them from possession, the defendants pled the defense of necessity. The court categorically rejected the defense's applicability, arguing in sweeping terms that necessity could never be used outside the context of imminent threats to physical safety caused by environmental calamities and the like: "When a man, who is starving, enters a house and takes food in order to keep himself alive[, our] English law does not admit the defense of necessity. It holds him guilty of larceny." The court's justification rested entirely on the long-term side effects of a broad necessity defense on public order and the security of property. "If homelessness were once admitted as a defense to trespass," the court implausibly argued, "no one's house could be safe."[27]

The court's worries for the security of home ownership were needlessly alarmist in the context of a case about homeless urban families occupying abandoned and derelict housing. There is no reason that the necessity doctrine cannot be tailored to steer its beneficiaries toward underutilized, abandoned, or other obviously neglected property. Nevertheless, the court's concern with the long-term consequences flowing from a broad definition of necessity is a reasonable one.

Necessity would actually be applied only after the fact by a jury (or judge) whose decision would not bind future courts or juries.[28] Moreover, in a society in which most people perceive the system of social welfare to be adequate to provide for the needs of the poor, few fact finders would be willing to conclude that acquisitive conduct was justified in any but the most obviously justified circumstances. Although permitting a greater number of defendants to argue the necessity defense to juries would marginally raise the cost of law enforcement and might yield a slightly lower conviction rate for property crimes, it is unlikely that these effects would encourage many people to undertake additional criminal actions.

The impact of broadened consideration of necessity by juries could be diminished even further if the defense were styled as an excuse or mitigation, rather than as a justification. Characterizing arguments beyond the traditionally narrow limits of the necessity doctrine—as excuses or as factors to consider in mitigation of the prescribed punishment, rather than as outright justifications—would further permit judges and juries to consider the role that economic need played in the defendant's decision to violate the law outside the confines of the traditional necessity defense and without confining their options to the binary choice of conviction or exoneration.

Obviously, the jury is a less-than-perfect mechanism for operationalizing and assessing outlaws' informational and redistributive value. Juries are small and are usually not representative of the electorate as a whole. Nevertheless, they are the only direct point of involvement by citizens within the criminal process. Juries have therefore almost always played crucial roles in bottom-up lawmaking.[29]

To be clear, we have no illusions that the jury process constitutes an ideal mechanism for disseminating information to the broader political community. The feedback between the jury and the democratic process, for example, cannot work when the jury system is itself fatally flawed or reflects unbridgeable cleavages within the polity. When a segment of the population is excluded from the jury, as was the case in the Jim Crow South, juries simply cannot function as a stand-in for the conscience of the community or as a means of filtering information back into the political process. Similarly, when a segment of the community is excluded from the political process, or when a political community is so segmented by class or race that there is an utter lack of basic respect for certain members of the community, the jury mechanism for feeding information back into the political process will be impaired. But as long as the jury system operates in a relatively nondiscriminatory manner and the society is not already irreparably cleared by racial, gender, or class divisions, broadening the use of the necessity defense would provide destitute defendants with a meaningful opportunity to explain the motivations for their conduct and provide jurors with important insights into the challenges or hardships faced by the poorest members of society—insights that they can then disseminate to the larger political community.

Robert Ellickson has reasonably questioned the educative value of brief encounters with the poor, such as the typical fleeting interaction with panhandlers on the street.[30] But in the context of a protracted interaction, as in a criminal trial, it is plausible to think that exposure to the hardships faced by the poorest citizens could help educate the jury, as well as any members of the public or press who might be attending the trial, about the nature of economic injustice, and thereby feed useful information back into the democratic political process.[31] Additionally, a large number of acquittals under the necessity defense would provide a powerful signal to the relevant authorities that the public perceived the jurisdiction's provisions for the poor to be inadequate.

Increasing Government-Sponsored Redistribution

Of perhaps greater concern than the long-run effects on law and order is the cumulative effect of justified acquisitive outlaw conduct on certain property owners. It is impossible to predict with any certainty the extent to which the costs imposed on property owners by concentrated outlaw conduct would lead to further deterioration of economic activity in areas of concentrated poverty. If the consequences were extensive, however, they would further harm those living in economically depressed communities. Whether these long-term costs exceeded the benefits of the forced transfers would depend on the degree of need satisfied by the transactions. Of course, for nonconsequentialists, those costs would be irrelevant to the inquiry whether the acquisitive outlaw was justified in taking the property to satisfy his or her needs. Nevertheless, even a nonconsequentialist can favor an effort to provide for the justified needs of the poor through the most efficient means possible.

Compensation or other risk-spreading mechanisms for property owners affected by justified self-help might work to cabin negative side effects. In his recent book on global constitutional property, Greg Alexander discusses *Modderklip East Squatters v. Modderklip Boerdery (Pty) Ltd.*, a South African Constitutional Court case considering how to treat forty thousand squatters who had illegally occupied property owned by a Johannesburg farmer. The court refused to compel the squatters to leave the land they had taken but, acknowledging the unfairness of the burden they had imposed on the landowner, commanded the government to compensate the landowner for his losses.[32] The judgment recognized the legitimacy of each party's claims: the squatters' claim to land on which to live and the landowners' claim not to be forced to bear the entire cost of honoring the squatters' legitimate claims. In effect, the court concluded that both parties' rights had been violated by *the state's* failure to adequately address the country's maldistribution of land, and the court crafted a remedy that mimicked as closely as possible the benefits of a centralized solution to the problem. As the South African property scholar Andre van der Walt puts it, this remedy treats the state's "failure to protect one right (access to housing) as the direct cause of failure to protect the other right (property). . . . If the one right was protected properly, the other one could have been protected as well."[33] In other words, the *Modderklip* decision perfectly illustrates the interdependence between owner and nonowner that lies at the heart of the phenomenon we are describing.

The costs associated with self-help suggest that it would usually be far cheaper for society to provide for the needs of the poor in a more organized and proactive fashion. A comprehensive system of government-sponsored redistribution and social insurance is an obvious substitute for the sorts of self-help redistribution envisioned by doctrines like adverse possession and necessity, and would generate far fewer spillover effects. Louis Kaplow and Steven Shavell argue, for example,[34] that legal rules are generally a less efficient redistributive mechanism than the tax system, and Robert Ellickson has commented that "if redistribution is to be carried out, families, charities, and welfare agencies know far more than judges about who is deserving of aid."[35] But it is important to note that, although a system of voluntary or mandatory redistribution may be more efficient than distributive-minded changes in property law, it does not follow that self-help is inferior to a highly unequal status quo and therefore not justified when adequate redistribution is not forthcoming.

As a society expands its formalized systems of redistribution, we should expect that its members will rely less and less on simply taking what they need and express less tolerance for those who do. Nevertheless, the status quo biases within the property system resist the expansion of redistributive systems, and, as Markovits argues, the political process itself generates its own inefficiencies that prevent redistributive programs from being kept up to date. Accordingly, it seems likely that even in societies that make substantial efforts to provide adequate social safety nets, movements of outlaws will crop up from time to time to prod the process along.[36]

The potential for the natural interplay between these two strategies of redistribution is illustrated by the homeless. The services currently available to the homeless are viewed by many as inadequate to provide for even their most basic needs.[37] In addition, because of their uniquely challenging circumstances, the homeless find it very difficult to take advantage of those social services that are provided by the state and by private actors.[38] Accordingly, they are frequently forced to resort to informal (and, increasingly, illegal) mechanisms of providing for their needs, such as illegal begging and trespass.

Surveys of public opinion indicate that citizens generally believe that the resources available to the homeless are inadequate and should be expanded. Members of the public also appear to believe that the criminal law should not penalize the homeless for taking actions necessary for survival.[39] Making the necessity defense available to the homeless who nonviolently break laws against trespass, theft, or panhandling might well result in a substantial number of acquittals. If, however, the services were improved to the point that they were widely perceived to be adequate, jurors would become less sympathetic toward those homeless people who continued to prefer illegal means to satisfy their needs. A broadening of the necessity defense, therefore, need not be a harbinger of chaos or the collapse of private ownership, as the *Williams* court feared.[40] Instead, it seems capable, through the jury process, of calibrating itself to the circumstances.

Responding to Property Outlaws' Informational Value

Ratifying forced transfers in order to accommodate certain categories of outlaws is likely to have some effect on the value of the information communicated by disobedience. Deterrence theories of punishment (and common sense) suggest that making the perceived punishment for crime less certain or less severe will itself increase *to some extent* the likelihood that people will be willing to break the law.[41] Moreover, excusing, *ex ante,* certain categories of disobedience is likely to generate strategic behavior on the part of lawbreakers that may well blur the boundaries distinguishing justified from unjustified behavior. The trick is to avoid completely foreclosing certain types of productive disobedience without encouraging broader criminal behavior to such a degree that the informational value of productive disobedience is itself destroyed. The task, therefore, is to preserve the expressive and communicative value of the disobedience in such a way that the law (1) reduces spillover effects and (2) avoids diluting the message, but (3) still provides an adequate level of deterrence against other less productive forms of disobedience. The law can accomplish this by selectively awarding a combination of case-specific immunities and particularized sentence reductions, all of which can help preserve any informational value without necessarily blurring the boundaries between productive and unproductive disobedience.

However, it is very difficult to specify in advance the content of the category of justified property disobedience with any precision. It is far easier to assess the justification of such actions on a case-by-case basis after the fact. Accordingly, most of the legal responses that we advocate in this part focus on *ex post* evaluations, often discretionary and nonprecedential in nature, that permit government decision makers to take into account the full complexity of the circumstances in determining how, or whether, to punish a particular act of disobedience.

The use of *ex post* mechanisms that operate on a case-by-case basis has two benefits. First, these are the sorts of mechanisms best suited to the moral complexity of outlaw conduct. Second, because deterrence operates through the *expected* sanctions of potential outlaws, the case-by-case, nonprecedential operation of the reforms we suggest limits their potential long-term effects for those contemplating future disobedience. The general deterrent-decreasing effect of building an *ex ante* exception into laws of theft and trespass is likely to be more substantial than that of granting after-the-fact case-by-case relief from criminal sanctions for individuals whose conduct happens to satisfy the requirements of, say, necessity.[42] This would remain true unless (1) *ex post* relief were predictably granted in an appreciable number of cases and (2) the substantial likelihood that they would be able successfully to take advantage of such *ex post* relief were communicated to other potential lawbreakers. The decision whether to rely on prospective rules or standards that are subject to clarification after the fact is frequently presented as an all-or-nothing choice, but the use of discretionary, *ex post* remedies can be coupled with the prospective reassertion of rule-like prohibitions and therefore can help to preserve the informational value of protracted outlaw conduct.

These mechanisms are not without their shortcomings, however. Giving discretion to public officials presents the danger of abuse and partiality in its exercise. Moreover, case-by-case adjudicative methods of relief have difficulty taking into account relevant consequences that flow from the aggregation of decisions in individual cases. On the other hand, much of the discretion we advocate already exists, but it is probably not being exercised along the lines we are suggesting. Consequently, our proposals would not do much to make the existing state of affairs worse. And, as we have argued, the *ex post* strategies we are recommending would help minimize long-term costs. Moreover, even where the legislature is better situated to take into account the implications of an emerging pattern of disobedience, the results of case-by-case adjudication can help draw the legislature's attention to the problem in the first place. For example, in the Netherlands, a judicial decision in favor of urban squatters generated a firestorm of controversy that led to the enactment of a law prohibiting property owners from keeping their property vacant or unused for long periods of time.[43] In other words, the sorts of mechanisms we advocate do not operate in isolation from the legislative process but are in constant dialogue with it.

Engaging Property Outlaws

EXPRESSIVE NECESSITY Although we favor the broad availability of the necessity defense for acquisitive outlaws, our analysis suggests that the necessity defense is somewhat less justifiable in the context of expressive outlaw conduct. And in fact, federal courts have been particularly reluctant to allow civil disobedients to avoid punishment by arguing necessity.[44] Most instances of expressive property disobedience, however, involve what is known as "indirect" civil disobedience, in which the law that is expressively broken, such as the law against criminal trespass, is not the law that the protesters are trying to change. This is the case, for example, with protesters who trespass on military bases in order to express their condemnation of nuclear deterrence. But intentional disobedience by those we are calling property outlaws aims at protesting the very property law being broken. That was the case, for example, with the 1960s civil rights protesters and the urban squatters of the 1970s and 1980s.

Application of the doctrine of necessity is more appropriate in situations involving direct civil disobedience. This argument depends on the greater informational value provided by direct civil disobedience. When someone violates a property law to protest some other sort of law, the only information conveyed is the intensity and seriousness of the protestor's moral opposition to the law in question. In contrast, when someone violates the very law to which he or she is opposed, the outlaw conveys both his or her intensity and seriousness and, in addition, provides a visible example of the alternative state of affairs the outlaw hopes to bring about.[45] Moreover, although there are a variety of ways to express seriousness and intensity of belief without violating the law, the only way for some nonowners to produce a concrete example of the property regime they seek is by violating the very law holding that reality back. This combination of the informational advantage of direct civil disobedience and the more effective means of expression it provides may justify widening the range of cases in which defendants may plead necessity.

It might be that the legal status quo is supported by reasons more weighty than sheer inertia or a lack of imagination on the part of the dominant majority. If that is the case, allowing the defendant to assert necessity will not do much harm. It is unlikely that a jury would find the expressive outlaw's conduct justified under most circumstances. But if a great number of people come to see the existing state of affairs in a different light as a result of the disobedience itself, they may come to view those who first showed us the way as heroes rather than criminals.

Courts have already recognized a role for something very similar to "expressive necessity" in a number of cases involving the right to engage in political and religious speech on private property. Interestingly, a number of these cases have involved property outlaws who were willing to risk conviction for criminal trespass in order to assert a right to access audiences located on private lands. In *Marsh v. Alabama,* for example, the defendant, a Jehovah's Witness, entered Chickasaw, Alabama, a "company town" near Mobile, Alabama, owned by the Gulf Shipbuilding Corporation, and began distributing religious materials. Representatives of the corporation told the defendant to leave the town, but she refused. She was arrested and charged with criminal trespass. The U.S. Supreme Court reversed the conviction, concluding that, even though Gulf Shipbuilding owned the land, the town operated for all practical purposes like a municipality and was therefore subject to the same constitutional norms that apply to public property. "Ownership," the Court said, "does not always mean absolute dominion. The more an owner, for his advantage, opens up his property for use by the public in general, the more do his rights become circumscribed by the statutory and constitutional rights of those who use it."[46] In *Amalgamated Food Employees Union, Local 590 v. Logan Valley Plaza, Inc.,* the Supreme Court expanded *Marsh* to cover the right to engage in speech in a privately owned shopping center.[47] Although the Court later backtracked from its *Logan Valley* decision in *Lloyd Corp. v. Tanner,* it declined in that case to overrule it, preferring instead to narrowly construe the implications of the earlier case. But even that narrow construction was consistent with the notion of expressive necessity. The Court in *Lloyd Corp.* read *Logan Valley* as recognizing a First Amendment right to engage in speech in a private shopping center when that speech relates directly to the shopping center's operations. In such situations, the Court suggested, "no other reasonable opportunities for the pickets to convey their message to their intended audience were available," and the absence of viable substitute locations—that is, the expressive necessity of speaking at that particular location—entitles speakers to disregard owners' commands to leave.[48]

The Supreme Court ultimately overturned *Logan Valley* in *Hudgens v. NLRB,*[49] expressly rejecting its prior position, but it has continued to leave space for states to interpret their own constitutional protections of speech on private property more broadly than the federal constitutional rights.[50] Several state courts, but perhaps most expansively the New Jersey Supreme Court, have continued to provide substantial constitutional protection to political and religious speech on private property under legal theories remarkably similar to the kind of expressive necessity we are advocating.

For example, in the 1994 case *New Jersey Coalition Against War in the Middle East v. J.M.B. Realty Corp.*, the New Jersey Supreme Court held that under New Jersey's constitution, people handing out leaflets in opposition to the Gulf War could not be excluded from a large regional shopping mall. The court's reasoning depended in significant part on the necessity of reaching audiences where they were, even if that meant, under certain circumstances, recognizing a constitutional right to speak on private property. "We look back and we look ahead in an effort to determine what a constitutional provision means," the New Jersey court said. "If free speech is to mean anything in the future, it must be exercised at these centers. Our constitutional right encompasses more than leafletting and associated speech on sidewalks located in empty downtown business districts. It means communicating with the people in the new commercial and social centers; if the people have left for the shopping centers, our constitutional right includes the right to go there too, to follow them, and to talk to them. We do not believe that those who adopted a constitutional provision granting a right of free speech wanted it to diminish in importance as society changed, to be dependent on the unrelated accidents of economic transformation, or to be silenced because of a new way of doing business."[51]

DISCRETIONARY RELIEF   In addition to the doctrine of necessity, there are other *ex post*, discretionary, and nonprecedential tools at the disposal of the criminal law. Prosecutorial discretion and sentencing are both areas where legal decision makers could, in cases of clear necessity, exercise their authority in ways that would recognize the legitimacy of the defendant's actions while only minimally undermining the strength of criminal norms. Prosecutorial discretion differs from sentencing, however, in its binary nature, which causes it to operate more like a jury's decision to acquit. Accordingly, it should perhaps be reserved for situations in which the merits of the defendant's actions are the clearest.

A related, though less risky, strategy is for judges or the executive to treat subsequent legal reform or social consensus ratifying the property outlaw's conduct as grounds for vacating a conviction and sentence. This is the approach the U.S. Supreme Court took in cases involving civil rights protesters. In a number of cases, the Court vacated the convictions of participants in the lunch-counter sit-ins in light of the subsequent enactment of state and federal statutes prohibiting restaurant owners from excluding on the basis of race.[52] As the deeply divided Court said in *Hamm v. City of Rock Hill,* when the legislature has substituted a "right for a crime," there is a strong basis for vacating convictions, even for conduct that occurred before the legal change.[53]

The majority opinion in *Hamm* does not fully capture the power of the legislative transformation at work in that case. The statutes that shifted the legal landscape were no fortuitous coincidence; they were enacted in direct response to the very disobedience for which the defendants before the Court stood convicted. When outlaws and legislatures engage in such fruitful dialogue, judges (or executives) are on particularly strong ground in granting relief from criminal liability. Forgiveness of disobedience that the community has come to embrace only marginally reduces the deterrent effect of criminal sanctions for most criminals. In addition, it encourages those who are contemplating the possibility of setting out on an outlaw strategy for legal change to carefully assess the likelihood that they are on the wrong side of history.

Finally, unlike a broader exemption of expressive disobedience from criminal liability, this approach would not itself undermine the expressive power even of the conduct to which it applied. There is substantial truth to the notion that the moral courage of civil disobedience depends on the willingness of the outlaw to risk (or even welcome) criminal punishment in order to express the depth of his or her dissent. But selective *ex post* decisions to exempt certain outlaws from criminal punishment would preserve the moral power of the disobedience at the moment it occurred (since the outlaw would have no assurance at the time of the disobedience that such actions would fall within the scope of the exemption) while also signaling that, at times, such behavior is indeed a legitimate form of political expression.

Subsidizing Alternatives to Outlaw Behavior

Outlaw strategies are particularly appealing to those who cannot challenge the existing legal regime, whether by amplifying their voice with monetary donations to political actors or through mass media, or by pursuing civil litigation. In the case of expressive outlaws, the public subsidization of criminal defense counsel means that criminal litigation may well constitute a more practicable mechanism for pursuing legal change than the civil litigation that is the focus of many discussions of evolution within private law.

It stands to reason that some of the pressure to engage in outlaw behavior would be reduced by affirmatively creating legal alternatives to expand the voice of the "property poor." Two obvious mechanisms present themselves. First, the state could (as it has in the past) subsidize civil litigation on behalf of the poor. Expanding legal aid for the pursuit of civil complaints might well provide a viable alternative outlet for a significant amount of discontent that would otherwise be directed toward outlaw strategies for legal change. Second, expanded state subsidies for access to the political process or to means of mass communication would help amplify voices that might otherwise go unheeded, perhaps encouraging legal change that would otherwise await the pressure provided by property outlaws.

RESPONDING TO INTELLECTUAL PROPERTY ALTLAWS

10

THE INFORMATIONAL VALUE OF
INTELLECTUAL PROPERTY DISOBEDIENCE

In January 2006, Larry Downes, at the time the associate dean of the U.C. Berkeley School of Information Management and Systems, proclaimed in an influential column that, even though the U.S. Supreme Court had recently ruled in favor of the recording industry in an important case involving peer-to-peer file sharing, "copyright is effectively dead." "Any law that is ignored by nearly every young adult in the country," he observed, "is no law at all."[1] His argument was, in part, supported by a study that found that 72 percent of Americans between eighteen and twenty-nine years old "do not care whether the music they download onto their computers is copyrighted or not."[2] Downes's general observation posited the existence of a massive copyright revolution in the United States, fueled by disobedience to a system of laws that young adults viewed as outdated or even unjust.[3] Moreover, far from discouraging file sharing, copyright owners' efforts to enforce their statutory rights against private parties only seemed to pour fuel on the fire, further discrediting the legitimacy of their property rights in the eyes of some users.

At the time, Downes's observations generated a fair amount of discussion regarding the extent and significance of copyright disobedience and its potential to alter the direction and scope of enforcement.[4] Downes foresaw a continued trend of disregard for the law, characterized by a yawning divide between what intellectual property laws formally authorize and what consumers actually do. Downes predicted that intellectual property laws could undergo a "dramatic reversal," largely because of consumer backlash as well as the rise of an information society that celebrates the free circulation of information.

Three years after Downes's observation, many of his predictions seem, in retrospect, deeply insightful. We have watched tens of thousands of citizens—college students, grandmothers, preteens—become targets of lawsuits by the recording industry. But at the same time, we have also watched countless music distributors—iTunes and others—learn how to accommodate the expectations of consumers regarding sharing music files and other forms of content with one another. And we have watched some musicians themselves embrace the seemingly "lawless" world of downloading music, culminating in Radiohead's famous decision in 2007 to release its new album to fans with the request that they pay as much as they wanted instead of a set price. A *Times of London* survey found that a third of album downloaders had paid nothing but that the average price paid for the album (which retailed in the United Kingdom for ten pounds) was approximately four pounds.[5] Just a few months later, however, physical copies of the album, sold at a fixed price, debuted at the top of both the U.S. and U.K. music charts.[6] Far from being the death of copyright, the disobedience on which Downes was commenting was becoming a key ingredient in creative marketing schemes and was perhaps stimulating important changes in the law of intellectual property.

The argument Downes introduced—and the debate that ensued—is valuable because it captures several themes that are relevant to our discussion of the interaction between property regulation and disobedience. The first of these themes highlights the importance of cultural acceptance. The more confusing, the more outdated, and the more unfair copyright law seemed, Downes argued, the less inclined people would be to follow its restrictions. Downes thus foretold the persistence of several different kinds of disobedience—and we continue to see examples of acquisitive disobedience (illegal downloading and uploading of content, and the like) and expressive disobedience (evidence of some consumer backlash and distrust of intellectual property law). Most importantly, his comments suggest that persistent disobedience may (should?) result in a grand reversal within intellectual property law, whereby, instead of reflexively increasing the repression, the law eventually gives way and creates a new synthesis, ratifying and legitimating consumers' previously unlawful conduct.

In recent years, we have seen some signs of accommodation on the part of private and public entities. In the private sector, corporations have learned a variety of ways to respond to disobedience, sometimes gleaning new insights about consumer preferences and sometimes recognizing that some unauthorized uses (like remixes) can actually benefit, rather than hurt, a copyright owner. The responses of many copyright holders—suing infringers, initiating DMCA takedown notices, and the like—has also engendered a fierce degree of criticism from those who believe that information, like other public goods, should be more accessible.[7] Contemporary debates in intellectual property—the enclosure of the commons, sharing copyrighted music, and pharmaceutical patents and human rights—benefit from a more nuanced picture of the property altlaw.[8] Inasmuch as they center on deep philosophical principles of distributive justice and democracy, the fact that the debates are occurring unwittingly honors the role of the altlaw (or outlaw) in legal evolution.

Despite the broad range of available responses to disobedience, policymakers and scholars alike often seem to overlook the possibility that expressive and acquisitive disobedience is instrumental in provoking productive legal transitions that themselves foster innovation or equity. All too often, intellectual property owners appear to adopt what we have already referred to as a "classic" view of deterrence—whereby the ultimate goal of intellectual property law enforcement ought to be zero (or near zero) incidence of property transgression.[9] In the case of copyright law, this goal may be pursued through vigorous legal enforcement, using such mechanisms as the DMCA notice-and-takedown procedures, as well as digital rights management (DRM) and other technological "lock out" systems that preclude unauthorized uses. But copyright law, as any intellectual property historian will acknowledge, has always been a leaky regime, permeated with exceptions and incomplete means of control and surveillance over unauthorized copying. The role of the altlaw suggests that this leakiness may not be a problem, but may actually be beneficial.

The difficult task is to conceptually isolate the productive elements of disobedience and to try to determine how to preserve the former while combating the latter. Of course, it may not be easy to tell the difference between the two. Our discussion in the next few chapters, therefore, suggests several tools, many of them of a procedural variety, that intellectual property law can use to separate the productive from the unproductive sorts of piracy, free riding, and disobedience. Applying the same model we developed in the context of tangible property, we propose a series of reforms aimed at restoring the necessary space for some tolerance of free riding and disobedience in order to preserve their expressive and redistributive value.

The Informational Value of Disobedience

As in the tangible property context, there is a tendency, even among those who discuss the importance of intellectual property disobedience, to privilege expressive disobedience over more self-interested, acquisitive varieties of disobedience. This tendency is understandable. Much of the time, acquisitive altlaw behavior is unjustified and produces more harm than good. Sometimes, however, acquisitive altlaw behavior can be justified or can generate a variety of benefits for society. That is, some sorts of unauthorized acquisitive uses play a crucial role in facilitating needed shifts in the architecture of intellectual property law. Cases of particularly widespread free riding offer valuable information concerning the degree to which entitlements may be outdated or the result of some kind of political or market failure that might, on its own merits, justify legal reform or redistribution. The virtue of intellectual property lies in the law's capacity, if properly calibrated, to mediate between the owner and the altlaw, sometimes favoring the altlaw over the owner, rather than deferring automatically to owners' determinations of what constitutes legal and illegal conduct.

As we pointed out earlier, property disobedience can play a powerful role in correcting for democratic and imaginative deficits in law and policy.[10] Some will reject this notion, arguing that our democratic system already adequately protects dissent by providing formal institutional mechanisms for enacting reform through the political process. The example of the civil rights sit-ins, however, draws attention to the potential for blindspots within the democratic process, which in turn demonstrate the occasional need for unlawful dissent. In the words of Elliott Zashin, during the civil rights era, "many citizens felt they could no longer operate within the limits of existing democratic institutions and could only achieve their social and political goals by openly breaking the law."[11]

Largely as a result of the civil rights movement, civil disobedience is to-day accorded a privileged place in our political culture, and new generations of activists often return to its powerful symbolism in debates over current issues. However, as we have already noted, many contemporary political theorists, such as John Rawls, have characterized disobedience aimed at re-forming economic institutions and policies as being inherently less justified than disobedience targeting political institutions—"unless tax laws, for ex-ample, are clearly designed to attack or to abridge a basic human equal lib-erty, they should not normally be protested by civil disobedience," Rawls writes, because of the taint of self-interest.[12] Instead, Rawls offers examples of minorities being denied the right to vote, to hold property, and to travel, and the mistreatment of certain religious groups as clear examples of viola-tions of civil liberties that might justify the symbolic and expressive power of disobedience.[13] Rawls's observations suggest that two foundational characteristics operate against a justification of civil disobedience in the eco-nomic context—the self-interested character of the disobedience and the availability of the political process.

As we suggested in prior chapters, these qualities—the self-interested nature of some disobedience and the availability of legislative options—are not disqualifying and may, in certain narrow circumstances, actually weigh in favor of the validity of particular transgressions. Indeed, the value of civil disobedience may be heightened when disobedients see the politi-cal system as failing to represent their concerns. This is particularly true with respect to intellectual property protections, where legislators have long been criticized for succumbing to pressure by intellectual property owners to expand intellectual property rights at the expense of consumers, whose diffuse interests often seem to be inadequately represented in the legislative process.

Perhaps most significantly, however, the condemnation of self-interested disobedience fails to recognize that some kinds of self-interested disobedi-ence have played integral roles in clarifying unsettled areas of law and facili-tating the creation of innovative legal privileges. Indeed, altlaw behavior can be all the more valuable *because* intellectual property laws are so unsettled; regardless of the motivations, each incident of altlaw behavior provides an opportunity for the sort of clarification and fine-tuning that intellectual property protections require to operate successfully. Moreover, as we noted in part 3, people by and large obey laws they believe to be legitimate, apart from the risk or severity of threatened punishment. When those laws are perceived to be illegitimate, however, the deterrent calculus becomes more salient. For this reason, even in the absence of net redistributive value, acquisitive outlaw behavior can generate useful informational value.

In addition to providing useful information about consumers' attitudes toward intellectual property norms, acquisitive altlaw behavior can generate important information for intellectual property owners about consumer preferences. Particularly in cases of protracted and pervasive acquisitive free riding, these transgressions may demonstrate the need for a responsive legal shift to update an ossified regime of entitlements or to address the presence of high transaction costs that preclude efficient transfers. Of course, in the case of the acquisitive free rider, the quality of this information is diluted by the self-serving nature of the transgression. As we noted in chapter 8, in the context of market transactions, an offer to give something up in order to consummate the purchase provides information about the value the acquiring party places on a shift in legal rights. We cannot tell from the acquisitive altlaw's conduct, *ex ante,* the extent to which he or she values a change in property rights. But notwithstanding these reasons to discount the value of *isolated* instances of acquisitive free riding, widespread free riding frequently signals some sort of obstacle to a market transaction—market inefficiencies, transaction costs, or the lack of an appropriate avenue for the distribution of the protected content.

Consider how this insight might be applied to the phenomenon of illegal file sharing. A great number of file sharers are just people expressing a preference to obtain for free something that might otherwise cost them money. The desire of consumers to obtain goods for lower prices is not useful information to intellectual property owners. We already know that most people would prefer to get their entertainment for free. But consumers' widespread engagement in file sharing also conveys useful information to copyright owners about consumers' strong preferences to purchase music online, on a song-by-song basis, and to be able to freely transfer songs between digital devices. Inquiring into the reasons for infringing behavior can be an important source of innovative marketing ideas for copyright owners.

Setting the penalties for copyright violation too high can deter these violations to such an extent that their informational content goes largely undetected. A broad and festering rejection of the legitimacy of copyright restrictions, kept under wraps by virtue of the severity of the penalty for violating copyrights, will create an undesirable and potentially unstable situation for intellectual property owners. High sanctions (or a high certainty of getting caught) may lead to relatively low levels of violation for a time, lulling owners into a false sense of security. But adherence to intellectual property norms under such circumstances will depend on owners' ability to maintain the same degree of enforcement. Indeed, the high sanctions may themselves undermine the perceived legitimacy of intellectual property norms, since consumers may judge the sanctions to be unfairly severe compared with the actual harm caused by such violations and may deem the sanctions themselves to be a sign that copyright owners have captured an unfair advantage in the legislative process.

Thus, a sudden change in the technology of lawbreaking coupled with an underlying broad-based rejection of the legitimacy of copyright law can result in epidemic levels of disobedience. Reliable information about the degree to which consumers have internalized intellectual property norms is thus invaluable to copyright owners, who can take action to increase consumers' internalization of existing norms or perhaps can work to alter copyright norms to accommodate consumers' sense of legitimacy and fairness. The result will be less pressure on the technology and surveillance of copyright enforcement, which will reduce the need for owners to engage in a costly arms race with potential infringers.

Against Overdeterrence

To preserve some room for these sorts of informational value, the law should be especially careful not to overdeter infringement *ex ante* through an overreliance on laws whose penalties are so severe that they foreclose all types of transgressions. Over the past few years, we have witnessed the rise of increasingly draconian strategies of enforcement through a combination of harsh civil and criminal penalties. In the intellectual property arena, supracompensatory damages are the norm rather than the exception. Under the Copyright Act, for example, a single act of willful infringement is punishable by fines of up to $150,000.[14] A teenager illegally copying songs within a peer-to-peer network can theoretically incur millions of dollars of statutory damages in a single sitting. Even when violations are not deemed willful, courts have broad discretion to award damages of up to $30,000 per infringing act.[15] The Copyright Act even imposes criminal penalties for certain willful violations for personal gain.[16] In addition, the fair use defense—intellectual property consumers' principal defense against allegations of infringement —is notoriously vague and unpredictable, frequently leaving consumers to guess as to the scope of their rights with respect to copyrighted material.[17]

Although such supracompensatory sanctions may have made some sense in an era when enforcement was difficult or when the prohibitive cost of the technology for copying copyrighted material meant that few people were susceptible to prosecution for copyright infringement, technological shifts in recent years have radically altered the landscape of both infringement, surveillance, and enforcement, raising the risk of overdeterrence. The risk of overdeterrence is particularly strong in the area of copyright, on which we focus most of our attention, primarily because of the ease of obtaining a copyright under the current regime. But recent developments in patent law, specifically reinterpretations of existing law that have lowered the bar for patentability, make the discussion of overdeterrence relevant to other intellectual property contexts as well.

This shift toward greater assertions of private control has been facilitated by recent changes in both the law of intellectual property and, more importantly, enforcement technology. Over roughly the past two decades, new developments in technology not only have facilitated infringing behavior but have also made it much cheaper and easier for intellectual property owners to locate and punish infringers. Digital technology and the Internet have made it easier to copy information and have therefore radically reduced the cost and increased the quality of copies.[18] Indeed, the ubiquity of digital technology has made infringement an almost effortless feature of everyday life.[19] Moreover, as Madhavi Sunder has observed, our popular culture makes (arguably) infringing activities a normal, almost indispensable, part of social expression and participation.[20]

At the same time, however, digital technology has enhanced owner control. The rise of the Internet's global information network has made infringing activity much easier for copyright owners to track down. Accordingly, even as the digital revolution has reduced the physical cost of infringement, it has simultaneously reduced the costs of searching for and finding infringing uses. As John Tehranian has put it, the same technology that has facilitated increased file sharing has "brought individual piracy into the light of day and made enforcement a viable option for copyright holders."[21] The result has been an explosion of intellectual property litigation (and threats of litigation) against previously anonymous private citizens. Professor Tehranian describes his experience representing "a middle-aged, terminally ill Mexican immigrant on welfare" who had been sued by the Recording Industry Association of America for the alleged file-sharing activities of his son (and ended up using funds from his welfare check to pay for the settlement).[22]

Increasing the visibility of infringing activities is just one of the ways that technology has extended the reach of intellectual property law into our everyday lives. The digital revolution has also given rise to digital rights management (DRM), which refers to restrictions on the copying and use of digital material that are encoded directly in the material itself. DRM makes it possible for Apple to prevent iTunes customers from using the music they purchase on any device other than an Apple iPod. Of course, no DRM scheme is foolproof, and for virtually every form of DRM in existence, tech-savvy users have devised electronic means of breaking through the limitations intellectual property owners impose.

In addition to these technological changes that have increased the reach of intellectual property law, the law itself has shifted in ways that reinforce the rights of intellectual property owners. The DMCA does this by prohibiting the circumvention of "copy-protection measures" (that is, DRM) as well as prohibiting the trafficking in tools used for circumventing DRM.[23] In addition to substantial civil penalties, the DMCA provides for criminal penalties for those who "willfully" violate its provisions for financial gain. The DMCA thus supplements traditional copyright protection by legally enforcing private owners' technological efforts to prevent infringement. As Dan Burk has observed, this sort of intermingling of legal and technological deterrence can dramatically decrease the flexibility enjoyed by consumers. Where legal regulation constitutes the barrier to a preferred use, Burk observes, "users may breach it at their discretion, avoiding penalty until they are apprehended and legal process is complete." In contrast, technological barriers are easier to enforce. "Unless users are technologically sophisticated," Burk observes, "unauthorized uses are simply impossible."[24]

When coupled with the DMCA's anticircumvention provisions, DRM also prevents users from engaging in activities that might be clearly protected by fair use. By blocking all forms of unauthorized activity, however, or alternatively, by increasing the costs of the disobedience through unreasonably high criminal and civil penalties, these measures also have the undesirable effect of foreclosing judicial or legislative intervention. As a result, these measures prevent fair use defenses from keeping up with the changing needs of technology, thereby contributing to the undesirable ossification of intellectual property law. In other words, by foreclosing unauthorized uses, the law becomes frozen in time, wholly beholden to a private content owner's determination of what constitutes allowable and unallowable use, and unable to shift to accommodate future uses that might in fact be legally protected. It may be more productive for the law to aim to preserve some of the signaling value of some unauthorized uses, precisely in order to facilitate periodic adjustments, either through legislative, judicial, or private acquiescence, as we discuss further below.

Against Delegation

Improved surveillance, legal protection for intellectual property owners' copy-protection measures, and vague legal standards defining the rights of intellectual property consumers have combined to create an environment in which risk-averse intellectual property consumers are eager to avoid activities that might lead to even the accusation of intellectual property infringement. This atmosphere of consumer fear lends itself to scattershot assertions of intellectual property rights, even when those assertions are completely unfounded. Observers have recently noted an epidemic of exaggerated assertions of copyright, what copyright scholar Jason Mazzone has dubbed "copyfraud."[25] These overly broad assertions of copyright extend in two dimensions: (1) claims of copyright over works that are already in the public domain; and (2) assertions of rights that exceed the actual scope of what is granted to copyright owners by the law—for example, characterizing as infringement certain activities that are actually lawful or fair uses. As Professor Mazzone puts it, "Copyright notices appear on modern reprints of William Shakespeare's plays, even though the new publisher had nothing to do with their creation, and Shakespeare's writings are squarely in the public domain."[26]

The problem goes beyond copyright. Similar problems have arisen in the context of patent and trademark as well. Confronted with an array of draconian penalties and an intellectual property regime in which the rights of users are only vaguely defined, consumers frequently find it easier to take the path of least resistance, acquiescing in intellectual property owners' self-serving interpretations of their rights and paying licensing fees to engage in uses to which they are already entitled.[27]

For their part, as intellectual property owners exert more and more control over the boundaries of their rights, they face powerful incentives to expand the definition of disobedience itself by hurling the epithet of "pirate" or "outlaw" at those who stand in their way, even when their opponents are acting within the boundaries of traditional legal rights of access. But there is a hidden cost to this effort. As the (asserted and perceived) domain of ownership grows, previously innocent acts become tarred as piracy, and the domain of piracy (and the community of pirates) likewise expands proportionally in response.

These trends, of course, center in part on the rhetorical power of the term "piracy," which was originally meant to refer to the distribution for profit of counterfeit copies of software, music, and motion pictures, but today extends to a much wider variety of unauthorized activities. There is a vicious circularity regarding disobedience in copyright. As the definition of disobedience expands, the law seems to necessitate (and implicitly justify) a greater delegation to the owner to control and to deter its incidence. This redefinition expands the definition of piracy, justifying further expansions of owners' legal protections, which further expands the notions of piracy, and so on.

Consider a recent example. During oral argument for the landmark case *Metro-Goldwyn-Mayer Studios Inc. v. Grokster, Ltd.*, the attorney for the recording industry, Donald Verrilli, offered the following observation regarding the much-accepted practice of consumers "ripping" the songs on a CD to a computer: "The record companies, my clients, have said, for some time now, and it's been on their website for some time now, that it's perfectly lawful to take a CD that you've purchased, upload it onto your computer, put it onto your iPod."[28] At the time, Verrilli was referring to the fair use defense of "space shifting," which allows consumers to take material that they have purchased and move it to other media for the purposes of accessibility or mobility.[29] Yet just a few months later, the recording industry's tune sharply changed. As part of its rule-making submissions for the DMCA, the industry decided to reverse its position and argue instead that such forms of space shifting constituted an "authorized use" rather than a fair one: "Nor does the fact that permission to make a copy in particular circumstances is often or even routinely granted, necessarily establish that the copying is a fair use when the copyright owner withholds that authorization. In this regard, the statement attributed to counsel for copyright owners in the *MGM v. Grokster* case is simply a statement about authorization, not about fair use."[30]

This terse statement radically changes—and reverses—the architecture of copyright law. Rather than copyright law defining what constitutes allowable use through the concept of "fair use," the recording industry attempts to define the boundaries through the more limited notion of "authorized use." Not only does this rhetorical shift alter what constitutes disobedience, but it also places the power to make such determinations squarely within the hands of the copyright owner rather than a judge or the legislature.

The trend toward broadening the definition of piracy is also roughly coextensive with the increasing efforts to moralize intellectual property protection, an effort in some tension with intellectual property's broadly instrumental justification. As Lawrence Liang has masterfully explained, the figure of the pirate looms over contemporary intellectual property discourse, where scholars tend to characterize the pirate "as the ultimate embodiment of evil."[31] Julie Cohen too has noted this tendency, observing that the entertainment and publishing industries have recently embarked on a set of initiatives to "invest unauthorized private copying with moral significance."[32] "Scholars working on understanding the phenomenon are accused of romanticizing illegality, and a sympathetic look at piracy is equated to a support for anarchy and lawlessness," Liang explains.[33]

Industry norms also play an integral role in crafting definitions of disobedience. Within the realm of intellectual property, there is a wide range of social norms and customary practices that govern use and permission. These norms frequently shift and change in relation to the challenges faced by both owners and consumers, in contrast to tangible property, which carries with it long-standing customary definitions.[34] As Jennifer Rothman's important work in custom reveals, for example, there is an entrenched industry practice in certain contexts to procure licenses for all uses of another's intellectual property, even when there are strong fair use or First Amendment defenses at stake.[35] For example, in the areas of film, television, and even written works, a "clearance culture" prevails, as Patricia Aufderheide and Peter Jaszi have shown, that often encourages risk-averse publishers and authors to abandon projects, even when there are substantial fair use defenses.[36] In film and television production, clearances are routinely demanded (and procured) for any use of copyrighted and trademarked works, as well as for images of public figures—so much so that fair use defenses, however credible, often recede to the background.[37] These industry practices in turn shape the law because courts often consider the failure to conform to industry practices in assessing the credibility of a fair use defense. The "clearance culture" contributes, just like the other forms of private ordering we have examined, to an expansion of the definition of disobedience and a narrowing of potential defenses.[38]

Maintaining the Spectrum

There are powerful and overlapping reasons why the law should be uncomfortable with this state of affairs. As we have already discussed, markets do not always permit property to find its way into the hands of those who most need it. And although the effort to tar all types of infringement with the label of immorality might be a powerful means of combating counterfeiting, it also carries with it the inaccurate suggestion that disobedience of an owner's wishes is always wrong. In this book, we have described intellectual property disobedience, in a deliberately broad fashion in the hope of bringing out the substantial gray areas in the law. In fact, as we have suggested, what might look like illegal disobedience, at first, can wind up comprising an unauthorized activity that is lawfully protected and even, at some points, desirable for innovation or expression.

In addition, excessive assertions of ownership can end up being self-defeating insofar as they undermine the public's identification with property norms and increase the public's tendency to identify with opponents of those norms.[39] Although the sorts of disobedience we study usually involve some form of free riding, not all free riding implicates the theory of productive disobedience that we offer in this book. Some sorts of free riding are performed with an intentional disregard of a property owner's entitlements; others are less intentional. Free riding periodically forces the law to reconsider (or even just consider in the first place) its allocation and definition of entitlements. The law must therefore aim to strike a balance between protecting the stability of intellectual property norms—otherwise, those norms would lose a great deal of their value—and tolerating a marginal degree of disobedience in order to keep this dynamic system in motion.

In her influential book *Digital Copyright,* Jessica Litman discusses the potentially counterproductive nature of intellectual property owners' expanding demands for legal protection: "The less workable a law is, the more problematic it is to enforce. The harder it is to explain the law to the people it is supposed to restrict, the harder it will be to explain to the prosecutors, judges, and juries charged with applying it. The more burdensome the law makes it to obey its prescriptions, and the more draconian the penalties for failing, the more distasteful it will be to enforce it. The more people the law seeks to constrain, the more futile it can be to enforce it only sporadically. Finally, the less the law's choices strike the people it affects as legitimate, the less they will feel as if breaking that law is doing anything wrong. If a law is bad enough, in other words, large numbers of people will fail to comply with it, whether they should or not."[40]

Rather than aiming for complete deterrence in an effort to stamp out infringing activities, the law should instead seek a level of deterrence that accepts periodic disruptions as both necessary and healthy. In the context of the acquisitive or expressive altlaw, the law can respond in one of two ways: either by condemning the behavior through the imposition of civil and criminal liability, or by legalizing the behavior through fair use provisions, levies, or other forms of compulsory licenses. The possibility that these latter solutions might be desirable in the end suggests that a degree of disobedience, *ex ante,* may be essential to the health of the intellectual property system as a whole. As we further discuss in the next two chapters, there are a variety of ways in which the law can be shaped to preserve some of the informational and redistributive elements that certain forms of disobedience offer.

11

RESPONDING TO ACQUISITIVE ALTLAWS

In part 3 we outlined a variety of different approaches that the law might take in responding to property disobedience in the context of tangible property. How we described those responses depended on whether we approached the question from a utilitarian or nonconsequentialist perspective. In the intellectual property context, our analysis would similarly differ. For a variety of reasons, however, this distinction looms less large in the intellectual property context, where utilitarian considerations often predominate. Nevertheless, when it becomes relevant, we will distinguish between these two broad approaches, identifying situations in which favoring one or the other lens could make a difference to our legal prescriptions.

When property disobedience overcomes a market failure and transfers property entitlements to those who value it more highly, it generates redistributive value. And when property disobedience produces information that is valuable to economic and political actors, it generates informational value. Even some self-interested acquisitive free riding can serve as a valuable tool for producing both of these sorts of value.

As with tangible property, maintaining the dynamism needed to preserve the system as a whole depends on preserving a space for the expressive function played by altlaws (and outlaws) in drawing attention to these market failures that may require judicial or legislative intervention. With respect to the preservation of redistributive value, we focus on specific ways that the law can retain its flexibility in protecting property rights so that it accommodates other competing values, such as efficiency, distributive justice, and innovation. In addition to the considerations we have outlined in the tangible property context, we introduce considerations that focus largely on the purpose and differences between *consumption* and *innovation* in intellectual property. When an altlaw takes or uses intellectual property without authorization for the purposes of consumption, the conduct bears a significant resemblance to the acquisitive outlaws we discussed in the real property context. In discussing the law's response to the acquisitive altlaw, therefore, we focus on a variety of ways that the law might (or, in some cases, already does) occasionally make room for disobedience in order to foster consumption (particularly by those who could not otherwise afford access). However, at least part of the tale of disobedience in the intellectual property context centers on innovation as well—the use of intellectual property to create new goods in the marketplace—and we argue that this consideration may weigh even more heavily in favor of protecting the conduct in some cases.

Distinguishing between Consumption and Innovation

In an important 1965 article in the *Columbia Law Review,* Adolph Berle called for a new approach to property in the modern era.[1] He argued that the industrial age had ushered in a new form of property ownership—one that substantially altered our previously individualistic notion of property, derived in part from our agricultural background. Although Berle focused primarily on the growing dominance of corporations in modern economic life, he also focused his readers' attention on a helpful distinction with deep roots in Western property thought. He distinguished between two broad categories of property: property for consumption and property for production. Berle's distinction between the productive and consumptive uses of property, or at least one like it, goes back as far as Aristotle.[2] And the basic distinction between property for consumption and property for exchange has played an important role in the thinking of theorists as diverse as Adam Smith, Karl Polanyi, and Karl Marx.[3]

The distinction between consumptive and productive uses of property is particularly important to keep in mind as we contemplate the growth of intangible forms of information, like intellectual property and telecommunications networks. As we suggested in chapter 2, technological innovation does not occur in a vacuum—it requires both the ability and the freedom to build on others' inventions. These follow-on innovations, whether they take place in the context of copyright or patent law—require us to reframe how we regulate, or respond to, disobedience, particularly when it is tied to valuable forms of innovation. For this reason, we believe the law should be mindful of the distinction between free riding for the purposes of innovation and free riding for other purposes, such as consumption, and should avoid conflating the two.

Consider, for example, a recently proposed French law that would, on a "three strikes, you're out" basis, require the government to cut off a person's access to the Internet—for as long as a year—if that person is accused by the recording industry of sharing files.[4] The law enables the recording industry to make unilateral determinations about what constitutes legal behavior, leaving the decision up to the party least likely to reach a balanced and thoughtful outcome. Such a proposal also tends to conflate unauthorized uses that are consumptive from those that might involve innovation, like remixes, commentaries, or "mashups." Our proposals below are aimed not just at deconstructing the phenomenon of disobedience altogether, but also at highlighting some of the ways the law as currently structured might overdeter transgression.

Fair Use as Market Failure

Fair use is perhaps the most obvious mechanism by which intellectual property law accommodates and incorporates the redistributive value of altlaws and outlaws, both acquisitive and expressive.[5] The privilege of fair use works as an active limitation; it empowers other future creators to use and build on existing works without the consent of owners. As the Supreme Court noted in *Campbell v. Acuff-Rose Music, Inc.*, "some opportunity for fair use of copyrighted materials has been thought necessary to fulfill copyright's very purpose."[6] Section 107 of the Copyright Act provides that "the fair use of a copyrighted work, including such use by reproduction in copies or phonorecords or by any other means specified by that section, for purposes such as criticism, comment, news reporting, teaching (including multiple copies for classroom use), scholarship, or research, is not an infringement of copyright."[7] In determining whether a potentially infringing activity constitutes a "fair use," the statute instructs courts to consider, nonexclusively, four factors: "(1) the purpose and character of the use, including whether such use is of a commercial nature or is for non-profit educational purposes; (2) the nature of the copyrighted work; (3) the amount and substantiality of the portion used in relation to the copyrighted work as a whole; and (4) the effect of the use upon the potential market for or value of the copyrighted work."[8]

The fair use defense as a whole can be viewed as a legal recognition of the validity of certain forced exchanges of intellectual property rights when market failures stand in the way of consensual transactions. In most situations, a consensual, mutually beneficial transaction is preferable to a "court's distant judgment."[9] Yet there are situations in which the possibilities of consensual bargaining break down for one reason or another. For example, market failure might occur in the case of noncommercial use that yields benefits to society that go uncompensated. In such circumstances, as Wendy Gordon points out, fair use is especially appropriate, particularly if the price the defendant would offer would understate the real social value of the use.[10]

Conceived of in this way, fair use (like adverse possession in the context of land) appears to be a prime example of the law's incorporating a mechanism for identifying and ratifying productive acquisitive altlaw conduct—for the purpose of either consumption or innovation. Although it is possible for Congress to authorize regulatory solutions to widespread problems of market failure, as it has on several occasions, such solutions are prone to be either too sweeping or too limited. For this reason, Wendy Gordon argues that a case-by-case, judicially administered doctrine like fair use might be the best legal tool. She explains that the fair use doctrine serves as an "equitable rule of reason" and is justified when "(1) defendant could not appropriately purchase the desired use through the market; (2) transferring control over the use to defendant would serve the public interest; and (3) the copyright owner's incentives would not be substantially impaired by allowing the user to proceed." For the second prong, Gordon advocates considering the narrow question whether "transferring the use to the defendant gives rise to a net social benefit." In order to preserve the incentive-based system that is at the heart of copyright, however, Gordon also advocates taking into account the extent of the losses that are likely to follow in the marketplace as a whole and focusing, in part, on whether the use affects the incentives of other similarly situated plaintiffs.[11]

Implicit in the market-failure analysis of fair use is the baseline notion that the user's right to copy, at times, ought to be purchased from the copyright owner, as well as the recognition that, at other times, some barrier to bargaining might stand in the way of such a productive redistribution of intellectual property rights. Gordon outlines several uses for which fair use analysis is justified because of market failures:

- The use of a work that is out of print or otherwise unavailable;
- The spontaneous, individual, and often unsystematic use of copyrighted material by a teacher who circulates materials for class;
- Uses characterized by high transaction costs and low per-transaction anticipated profits, such as individualized "home use" of new technologies, for which the costs of enforcement are likely to outweigh anticipated benefits for the copyright owner;
- The use of public goods that confer external social benefits beyond a market transaction;
- Noncommercial uses;
- Uses for which there are nonmonetizable values, like contribution to a public debate;
- Uses that conflict with a copyright owner's anti-dissemination motives, such as criticism or parody (for which a copyright owner is unlikely to license the use of the work).[12]

Each of the situations Gordon identifies draws on protecting consumptive uses of copyrighted works. In each, however, the user's inability to license the work—either because of antidissemination motives or the presence of transaction costs—still weighs in favor of allowing fair use to justify the appropriation of the work. The fact that each of these uses is consumptive does not foreclose the possibility of protection; what matters more is the public's interest in accessing the information.

The same principle applies even more strongly when addressing the role of "disruptive" innovations in the marketplace. Here, we would argue that the law's calculus, just as it considers the private interest in protecting the copyright owner, must also consider the public interests at stake in protecting certain kinds of unauthorized activity for the purposes of follow-on innovation. In 1984, the Supreme Court honored the acquisitive innovator in its landmark *Sony* decision, in which Justice Stevens, writing for the Court, noted that "the sale of copying equipment, like the sale of other articles of commerce, does not constitute contributory infringement if the product is widely used for legitimate, unobjectionable purposes."[13] To be legitimate, he concluded, the technology "need merely be capable of substantial non-infringing uses."[14] The *Sony* Court's protection of other devices with "substantial non-infringing uses" enabled other manufacturers to develop similarly innovative products without the entertainment industry's permission. Maintaining these decentralized entitlements for innovation owes much to the acquisitive altlaw, who challenges boundaries and facilitates the reconsideration of existing boundaries in cases of market failure.[15] On Gordon's view, the fair use defense, in effect, evaluates after the fact the legitimacy of the barriers to which the acquisitive infringer points as the reason for not seeking a license from the intellectual property owner, and judges the infringer's self-help appropriation to be either justified (or excused) or unjustified (or unexcused). The fair use defense, then, at least in the abstract, is a good example of the law's mixture of condemnation and accommodation of infringing conduct. It is therefore the sort of doctrine we favor.

The fair use principle can extend to other contexts as well, particularly in the context of acquisitive innovation. In such circumstances, avoiding overdeterrence of disobedience in order to preserve innovation may be even more important. Consider this example. In the early 1990s, despite the widespread popularity of decompilation[16] to promote innovation and interoperability in the software market, copyright owners decided to mount a vigorous campaign of litigation against reverse engineering (a trend that continues even today within private contractual agreements).[17] As Michael Carrier, Julie Cohen, and Mark Lemley have argued, the software market is a "network effects" market, where users benefit from expanding the number of other users in a system,[18] and where competitors soon realize the benefits of promoting greater compatibility (or interoperability) between products.[19] At the same time, however, the market for commercial software products recognizes the need for and the value of promoting interoperability, which is why protecting reverse engineering in these fields has been so important.[20]

In a dramatic *Sony*-like display of judicial intervention on behalf of software innovation, the Ninth Circuit held in *Sega Enterprises Ltd. v. Accolade, Inc.*, that reverse engineering of software constituted a fair use.[21] Accolade, a developer and manufacturer of computer entertainment software, attempted to develop compatible video games by reverse engineering the software for Sega's Genesis game console.[22] Sega promptly sued Accolade for copyright infringement. The court noted that "when technological change has rendered an aspect or application of the Copyright Act ambiguous," the Copyright Act must be construed in light of its basic purpose: "to stimulate artistic creativity for the general public good."[23] Because there was no other means of accessing this unprotected information, the court found that the unauthorized copying of the software was necessary to determine the functional aspects of the console. Had it chosen to protect Sega against such activities, the court warned, it would have permitted a copyright owner to gain an unlawful monopoly over the functional aspects of the product, an extension expressly outside the scope of copyright protection.[24]

Was Accolade free riding off of Sega's creative work by copying the software in order to reverse engineer it? Yes. Was this illegal? No. The court noted that empowering such types of interoperability advanced the public benefit by increasing the number of independently designed video game programs. "It is precisely this growth in creative expression, based on the dissemination of other creative works and the unprotected ideas contained in those works, that the Copyright Act was intended to promote."[25] The significance of the *Sega* case lies not just in its exploration of the Copyright Act but in its complex understanding of the limitations of intellectual property rights in the face of countervailing forces like necessity and innovation. Where an original inventor has the ability to block another innovative exchange, courts must assess the desirability of a voluntary bargain with a strong eye toward social welfare.

There are, however, substantial problems with the way that the fair use defense operates in practice that mitigate its effectiveness in performing this balancing role. The most obvious and frequently discussed defect of the defense is its vagueness. Courts have been, for the most part, unable to derive any clear rules of application from the broad statutory language. As Gideon Parchomovsky and Kevin Goldman observe, "the repeated application of the fair use doctrine has resulted in it growing increasingly unpredictable." Moreover, Parchomovsky and Goldman continue, "academics, for their part, have been unable to rescue fair use from its murkiness. Despite numerous attempts to distill a coherent conception, none of these formulations has been adopted by the courts, and scholars generally agree that it is now virtually impossible to predict the outcome of fair use cases."[26]

As numerous commentators have noted, the vagueness of the fair use defense has had a distorting impact on copyright practices, as risk-averse users attempt to avoid potential liability by being overly cautious in their fair use of copyrighted materials. Moreover, the lack of clarity emboldens intellectual property owners to define their own legal rights expansively. The fair use defense would benefit from reforms aimed at better distinguishing among intellectual property altlaws. Proposed reforms discussed in the academic literature have tended to revolve around establishing clear rules that would enhance predictability in the fair use area.[27] Our own proposals are, first, to reduce the stakes for potential "fair users" by reducing sanctions for intellectual property infringement to a more compensatory level and, second, to balance the allocation of risk regarding the vagueness of what constitutes fair use by raising the costs to intellectual property owners of guessing wrong as in the *Diebold* case, thereby generating incentives for intellectual property owners, *ex ante,* to be more modest in defining their own rights. We return to the topic of fair use and to our proposed solutions to its vagueness problem in the next chapter in connection with our discussion of expressive altlaws.

Rethinking Necessity

Reniger v. Fogossa, an early case on necessity, involved a shipmaster who threw valuable cargo overboard as a storm approached. Discussing the shipmaster's dilemma, the court observed that "for in every law there are some things which when they happen a man may break the words of the law, and yet not break the law itself. . . . And therefore the words of the law of nature, of the law of this realm, and of other realms, and of the law of God also will yield and give way to some acts and things done through the words of the same laws, and that is, where the words of them are broken to avoid greater inconveniences, or through necessity, or by compulsion, or involuntary ignorance."[28]

We have already discussed, and defended, in chapter 8 the plausibility of a moral principle that people are entitled to take for themselves the things they need in order both to survive and to achieve some minimally acceptable degree of participation in society. This principle applies just as strongly in the context of intellectual property as it does with regard to tangible property. Within current law, the doctrine of necessity is exceedingly narrow, to the point of practical irrelevance. But a more capacious definition of "necessity" would permit decision makers at various steps in the law-enforcement process to consider the permissibility of the altlaw's (or outlaw's) actions along distributive lines. Public-health emergencies—for example, a widespread epidemic or biological attack—represent particularly clear examples of material necessity justifying encroachment on the robust property rights guaranteed by patent law.[29] And as we have discussed, both the altlaw and outlaw have often played a key role in encouraging the law to recognize situations in which such emergencies justify setting aside existing property entitlements.

As a rule of thumb, instances in which the nonconsequentialist version of the redistributive principle applies are also likely to be situations in which utilitarian considerations would favor forced transfers from the intellectual property owner to the party in need. Indeed, the utilitarian case for forced transfers in situations of necessity may be even stronger in the intellectual property context than in the context of tangible property because of the nonrivalrous nature of information. Because the party in need presumably cannot afford to purchase the intellectual property on the open market (at least on the terms demanded by the intellectual property owner), permitting that party to appropriate the intellectual property for his or her own use does not deprive the intellectual property owner of anything tangible. Consequently, in the intellectual property domain, we favor—even more than we do in the context of tangible property—a broader conception of "need" that recognizes the right to a minimal level of expressive social involvement.

Of course, the law must explore the particulars of each acquisition to determine whether the acquisition is actually morally correct, or if morally incorrect, to be tolerated for pragmatic reasons. This last distinction roughly corresponds to the difference between an "justification" and an "excuse" for lawbreaking in criminal law.[30] In cases where lawbreaking is justified, we would not want the lawbreaker to be subject to the property owner's veto power.[31] On the other hand, the law may choose to "excuse" some behavior when something occurs "that we do not want to have emulated—a behavior, a lack of permission, or lack of compensation—but which we allow without imposing liability because of the particular facts of that case."[32] Cases of appropriation in the presence of high transaction costs are one example. If we could lower transaction costs in some way, then we would want to honor the desirable goal of allowing the parties to strike a bargain between themselves. But without a mechanism for lowering those costs, we may choose to accept the unilateral appropriation. According to Professor Gordon: "'Excuse' connotes 'if only'—if only some discrete fact were different, we could apply the law as written. In instances of 'market malfunction,' we are in the world of 'if only': we would prefer the market to govern if only the market could function well, but when it fails to do so (because of, e.g., transaction costs), a court may excuse a participant from adhering to the usual market rules."[33] The law might then "excuse" the defendant's decision without holding it up as exemplary. At times, by imposing a "price" on the use, a court can cure a market failure in a way that still preserves some of the incentive structure underlying copyright and patent law. Applying this logic, Gordon advocates determining the proper response to an unauthorized, acquisitive use by considering whether the defendant's behavior is desirable, whether the defendant sought permission first, and whether failing to compensate the intellectual property holder for the use is justified.[34]

The case of HIV drugs, which we discussed at length in chapter 6, provides the clearest example of necessity's redistributive principle in action. The owners of the patents for several antiretroviral drugs essential to the survival of those infected with HIV refused to provide their drugs at low cost to patients in extremely poor countries, where HIV infections were quickly becoming national emergencies. The actions of these governments and the generic-drug manufacturers, which led the drug developers to reconsider their stance and begin offering the HIV drugs at lower prices to customers in the developing world, were almost certainly justified under the redistributive principle on which we have been relying.

Another example where a necessity defense, properly understood, would almost certainly be appropriate involves the drug Iplex, a promising treatment for amyotrophic lateral sclerosis (also known as Lou Gehrig's disease). Iplex is no longer available on the market because of a successful patent-infringement suit brought by the manufacturer of a similar drug for treating short stature; however, the stature medication is not as effective as Iplex for treating Lou Gehrig's disease, a fatal condition with no known cure and few effective treatments.[35] The unlicensed manufacture of Iplex (whether by Insmed—the drug's developer—by or some third party) to provide to patients with Lou Gehrig's disease would easily fall within the scope of the redistributive principle.

Both the HIV-drug story and the Iplex case clearly illustrate the redistributive principle in action—dire need permits the direct appropriation of the intellectual property of another. But they are important for another reason as well: they both illustrate the importance of third parties to the operation of the redistributive principle in the intellectual property context. People with HIV and Lou Gehrig's disease are in no position to make use of the patented information related to the manufacture of the drugs they needed to survive. Only with the help of generic-drug manufacturers willing to violate drug patents in order to supply them with those drugs would they be able to exercise their right to appropriate the patented information they need. The specialized nature of a great deal of intellectual property means that in most cases, those who would benefit from the appropriation require the assistance of others in accomplishing the appropriation to which they are entitled.

Discussions of intellectual property infringement often focus on the negative impact that infringing conduct has on the *ex ante* incentives of potential intellectual property creators. Too much infringement, the argument goes, and incentives will drop, resulting in inadequate investment in the creation of new intellectual property. Law professor Richard Epstein, a long-standing advocate of property rights, published a scathing editorial in the *Financial Times* that criticized the "short-sighted" nature of both Thailand and Brazil's decisions to threaten compulsory licensing, predicting that the decisions to weaken patent protection would harm consumers in the long run by "crippl[ing] incentives to invest in new drugs."[36] Another analyst reached the same conclusion, asking, "If a company stands no chance of recouping even a portion of that investment, where is its incentive to tackle the many diseases that ravage the developing world? Further, if it is acceptable for generic drug producers to make a substantial profit on the distribution of large amounts of drugs—none of which they invented—why are the companies that created the medicines not justified in turning a profit?"[37] Epstein called on both private industry and governments to pay "commercially reasonable price[s]," arguing that "no nation should be able to circumvent the voluntary market solely because it doesn't get the best deal possible." "In the end," Epstein wrote, "the AIDS imbroglio replays a familiar morality tale: disregarding property rights in the name of human rights reduces human welfare around the globe. Even strong claims for distributional equity always come at the price of technological innovation."[38]

Under Epstein's approach, the calculus for determining the proper sanctions for intellectual property infringement looks a great deal like the calculus utilitarians employ in setting the optimal level for criminal punishment for tangible property crimes. But although permitting certain sorts of infringing conduct might reduce the *ex ante* incentives for the production of new intellectual property, several considerations suggest that the interaction between such conduct and intellectual property production is, at best, extremely complicated.

For starters, although increased protection of intellectual property rights plausibly yields increased incentives to engage in production, and decreased protection arguably decreases those incentives, it is far from obvious what the magnitude of the impact of any given increase or decrease in intellectual property protection will be. The question is surely an empirical one, and yet it is virtually impossible to test. Music sales have been declining for nearly a decade. And at least some of that decline is almost certainly attributable to increased music piracy. Yet despite the continued protestations of each generation of parents that today's music is not as good as the music they listened to as teenagers, there is no indication that the quantity or quality of music being produced in recent years has begun to decline. The point here is not to deny that incentives matter, but simply to question whether the fact that incentives matter (as they surely do) necessarily means that any decrease in the value of those incentives, however marginal, will translate into a noticeable decrease in the quantity or quality of new production.

The Iplex example illustrates this point. Since the drug's use for Lou Gehrig's disease is not a market for the drug on which it has been found to infringe (that drug was for short stature and was not effective at treating Lou Gehrig's disease), its production for patients suffering from Lou Gehrig's disease would do nothing to diminish the expected or actual pay-off for the owner of the infringed patent. Any impact its production (or the production of any drug under similar circumstances) had on patent incentives would be highly indirect and almost certainly *de minimis*.

Relatedly, as numerous commentators have already pointed out, protecting intellectual property rights is not without its costs, even in terms of sheer productive output. New production depends on access to a robust public domain on which to build and borrow. As Rebecca Eisenberg and Michael Heller have argued, too much intellectual property protection can yield a tragedy of the "anticommons" that may ultimately inhibit the creation of new works.[39] In other words, beyond a certain point, additional intellectual property protection can prove counterproductive. If we are operating on the wrong side of the boundary between productive and counterproductive intellectual property protection, the space created by tolerating a degree of altlaw or outlaw conduct may well enhance (rather than inhibit) intellectual property production.

In addition, ensuring a robust supply of intellectual property is just one half of the utilitarian equation. Utility can be enhanced by providing more intellectual property for consumers to enjoy, but it can also be increased by ensuring that a broader range of consumers actually have the ability to make use of the intellectual property that has already been created. If altlaw conduct makes intellectual property more broadly available than it would be in the absence of that conduct, determining whether the enhanced utility generated by this broader accessibility is outweighed by any decreases in future intellectual property production due to reduced incentives becomes a complicated empirical question. Maximizing incentives to produce by single-mindedly defending property rights will tend to overdeter infringing conduct if it fails to account for the utility gains that can result from increased consumption enabled by infringement.

Finally, the unpredictable nature of emergencies makes it unlikely that the failure of intellectual property owners to fully exploit them for profit would have much of an impact on incentives to innovate. Generally speaking, the less foreseeable an emergency, the stronger the (utilitarian) case for setting aside or temporarily suspending (or weakening) intellectual property rights. On this score, the HIV epidemic is a tricky case. The public-health emergency it represents has been something of a slow-motion disaster, unraveling over a long enough period of time that pharmaceutical companies have been able to engage in extensive research-and-development efforts in its wake. One might plausibly argue that weakening the protection of HIV drugs undermines incentives for companies to continue developing new tools for responding to the crisis. On the other hand, the scale of the destruction the virus has unleashed, particularly in the hardest-hit parts of the developing world, has sometimes come as a surprise. As a result, profits from those regions might represent something of an unexpected windfall for drug producers such that depriving them of that windfall arguably would not have much of an impact on *ex ante* incentives. If we step back for a moment, the HIV case seems ideally suited for a compromise solution in which drug companies are, for the most part, permitted to reap the rewards of protection, with the limited use of compulsory licensing or the production of generic substitutes (perhaps with some form of limited compensation to drug makers) as a tool to alleviate the burdens on the poorest and most heavily burdened communities.

The real risk to intellectual property incentives (and likely the reason pharmaceutical companies do not already make drugs available to low-income consumers at discounted prices) is that some of the drugs produced under the auspices of a necessity defense will find their way into the broader market, substituting themselves in gray markets for products that might have been sold to consumers willing and able to pay higher prices. The risk of such diversion, though real, can be mitigated by regulatory action, although such regulation will not be free. It is fair to say that in most cases, permitting intellectual property infringement on the ground of economic necessity will impose some costs on intellectual property owners. Determining the magnitude of the impact of such a decrease in intellectual property incentives on investment in the development of lifesaving drugs is a difficult task, but the potentially harmful long-run consequences of applying the redistributive principle can be softened in a variety of ways. The most obvious would be to follow the lead of the South African *Modderklip* case, which we discussed in chapter 9, and require justified infringers or governments to compensate intellectual property owners for the losses due to the diversion of copied drugs into gray markets. The requirement to compensate should be structured, however, to reward infringers who minimize such diversion. If a system of differential pricing that provides some protection against gray-market arbitrage could be established, one group of consumers could be made better off without causing undue harm to the incentives to produce new drugs.[40]

Compulsory Licensing

As we noted at the outset of this chapter, property can be used for consumption or for production. Intellectual property is used for production when it plays a role in the construction and invention of follow-on innovations. In intellectual property law, free riding is often a necessary part of innovation, particularly in industries that seek to develop a more efficient means for disseminating content.[41] The innovator (frequently an altlaw, but sometimes an outlaw) may engage in free riding because the law is unclear or because he or she is optimistic about the path the law is likely to take in the future.[42]

Overdeterrence of actions that challenge existing entitlements in intellectual property can cut off this potential avenue of legal change. The specter of DRM and the concomitant protections within the DMCA have shifted the paradigm to what Fred von Lohmann has called a "permission first, innovate later" state of affairs, in which the law delegates determinations of legality to the copyright owner, even when the interpretation of the law is far more complicated.[43]

In copyright law, as Timothy Wu has explained, there is always the possibility that a more efficient means for dissemination of content will be invented, forcing courts to confront the law's lack of clarity.[44] In such cases of legal uncertainty, the acquisitive innovator seeks to use some part of an original invention or protected work for the purposes of facilitating downstream innovation.[45] At times, the law has accommodated the innovator's activity, either through judicial or legislative ratification. Whether the law ultimately adopts the innovator's position or not, however, is less important than the opportunity the innovator affords decision makers to consider the need for legal change.

Although there are countless examples of acquisitive innovation in intellectual property (indeed, much of copyright law is premised on addressing the issue of follow-on innovation), the most powerful examples stem from a set of legislative developments during the twentieth century, which highlight the emergence of what Joe Liu has referred to as a regime of "regulatory copyright." This regime is characterized by greater legal intervention into the structure and operation of particular markets, as illustrated by a greater reliance on Congress, rather than the courts, in fashioning industry-specific responses to issues of liability.[46] Copyright law's evolution, at many of these points, has been punctuated by the emergence of legislative and judicial decisions establishing the boundaries of authorized and unauthorized activity that later paved the way for compulsory licensing and other liability rules as a solution that redefined (and ultimately protected) unauthorized uses.

The most important element of the regulatory copyright structure involves the repeated resort to compulsory licensing, which emerged largely as a result of—and as a solution to—disobedience. Consider the early history of the recording industry, which developed in the late 1890s and early 1900s. By 1899, almost three million records had been sold—without any royalties being paid to the copyright owners.[47] During this period, the player piano, which used a perforated piano roll to mechanically reproduce a song's melody, was introduced into the market. In time, thousands of rolls, which reproduced a wide variety of songs, were produced, and all failed to pay royalties to music's composers. By 1902, at least a million piano rolls were on the market.[48] The law had few precedents to guide its determination whether the mechanical reproduction of a song, without permission, constituted a "copy" for the purposes of copyright infringement.

For Tim Wu, this case at the turn of the century marked not only the birth of the recording industry but also the birth of a new model of copyright law that has pervaded our current debates about the relationship between intellectual property protection and innovation, a model that Wu has dubbed "copyright's communications policy." Wu uses this label to refer to copyright's tendency to serve as a key mediating tool between the copyright owner, challengers, and innovators. As Wu explains, today's pirate may be tomorrow's incumbent. Wu quotes the famous American composer John Philip Sousa, who complained before Congress about the piano roll and the phonograph: "I see my compositions . . . stolen bodily by the phonograph trust and piano-player combination, and ground out daily from thousands of cylinders, disks, and rolls, without paying me or any of us one single, solitary penny."[49] As Wu explains, in these debates, the composers repeatedly used the rhetoric of piracy, characterizing the recording industry as "irresponsible pirates whose reckless copying of music threatened to destroy American creativity."[50]

Frustrated beyond imagination, the composers sought help from both the courts and Congress to alleviate their perceived losses of royalties, and finally, in 1908, their case was heard by the Supreme Court in *White-Smith Music Publishing Co. v. Apollo Co.*[51] They hoped for an unambiguous affirmation of their understanding of the nature and scope of their property rights in their music, but to everyone's surprise, the composers lost. The Court ruled in favor of the recording industry in a judgment that defended innovation from an overbroad interpretation of copyright law. In its opinion, the Supreme Court drew an interesting distinction between sheet music, which was protected under copyright law, and the new technology of the piano roll, which was considered a completely distinct mechanism and, according to the court, fully outside of the purview of copyright law as it then existed.[52] Given Congress's failure to extend copyright law to govern this new innovation, and given the Court's perceived differences between a piece of sheet music and a piano roll, the Court declined to find for the composers and sided with the piano-roll manufacturers instead, striking a victory for the "pirates" in the dispute.

In the end, despite the outcome of the case, the parties decided to settle the dispute once and for all by asking Congress to institute the first statutory compulsory-licensing scheme: Congress would extend copyright protection in compositions to mechanical recordings, and the recording industry would receive complete and full access to all copyrighted recordings in exchange for a set royalty fee. According to Wu, the case set a precedent whereby the courts would decide technologically sensitive copyright cases in favor of a challenger industry, a "pirate," in order to force Congress's hand."[53] Then, in turn, instead of reflexively favoring the copyright owner and forcing piano-roll manufacturers to bargain for licenses on the open market, Congress set the terms of the license, devised specific penalties for failure to comply, and established a system of industry-specific reporting procedures.[54]

In many cases of acquisitive free riding, courts and Congress have readily chosen to scale back copyright entitlements and enact a series of measured refinements through industry-specific regulation. According to Jane Ginsburg, when new technology develops a mode of dissemination that does not supplant known markets and copyright owners attempt to prevent such dissemination, Congress has historically intervened to "split the difference" between the copyright owners and innovators by providing for compensation but not exclusive control over the new means of dissemination.[55] However, if the new mode threatens to replace or compete with traditional markets and copyright owners might seek to exploit these new markets, then Congress will instead provide for exclusive rights, enabling the copyright owners to refuse to license and to charge market prices.[56] We do not mean to suggest that free riding is always acceptable; instead, Ginsburg's observations suggest that free riding can—and should—provide an opportunity to reevaluate existing entitlements or, perhaps, to shift from property-rule to liability-rule protection through the exploration of some form of compulsory-licensing solution.[57]

In the context of peer-to-peer transmissions, a number of prominent scholars have argued that compulsory licensing may be a more desirable solution to the current regime of industry lawsuits. Neil Netanel and William Fisher, for example, have both argued strongly in favor of imposing a noncommercial-use levy on the sale of any consumer product or service whose value is substantially enhanced by peer-to-peer file sharing.[58] Their proposals call for a fixed rate that would be built into the sale of the product or service, with the proceeds distributed to interested copyright holders. In many ways, this proposed solution echoes the frequent resort to levies and compulsory licenses throughout copyright's history.

The levy solution also underlines what copyright law should be designed to achieve: a balance between private owners and consumers, facilitated by government intervention. It also, importantly, follows the approach taken by a number of other jurisdictions, including Germany and Britain, in addressing the issue of at-home private copying. Britain's decision to adopt at-home safe harbors for private copying were apparently influenced by the futility of enforcing copyright law in the home. As a British court explained:

> From the point of view of society the present position is lamentable. Millions of breaches of the law must be committed by home copiers every year. Some home copiers may break the law in ignorance, despite extensive publicity and warning notices on records, tapes and films. Some home copiers may break the law because they estimate that the chances of detection are non-existent. Some home copiers may consider that the entertainment and recording industry already exhibit all the characteristics of undesirable monopoly—lavish expenses, extravagant earnings and exorbitant profits—and that the blank tape is the only restraint on further increases in the prices of records. Whatever the reason for home copying the beat of Sergeant Pepper and the soaring sounds of the Miserere from unlawful copies are more powerful than law-abiding instincts or twinges of conscience.[59]

The court concluded, "A law which is treated with such contempt should be amended or repealed."[60] Given the difficulty of finding infringers, and related considerations, Parliament chose to enact a limited safe harbor for at-home copying, along with a complicated system of levies to compensate artists.

The story we have just told begins with copyright law, but it almost certainly extends beyond into the areas of telecommunications, trademark, and even patent law.[61] Of course, levies are imperfect solutions to a massively complicated problem, particularly where piracy is concerned. People often criticize compulsory licenses and levies as inflexible, unwieldy, and prone to ossification.[62] Nevertheless, they do represent an opportunity for Congress to weigh the various interests in play—those of consumers, innovators, and others. For example, after a variety of decisions narrowed the scope of the experimental-use exception for patent researchers, a number of commentators voiced interest in exploring a compulsory license for universities and nonprofit research, further underscoring the need for a more malleable view of patent law's exclusivity.[63]

Abandonment

In the context of tangible property, when an owner is no longer interested in making use of his or her property, the owner can "abandon" it by throwing it away or leaving it in a place where someone who might want it is likely to pick it up and keep it. Once abandoned, tangible property is subject to lawful appropriation by its first (subsequent) possessor. The question whether property is "abandoned" turns largely on the intent of the owner when he or she parts company with the property or, in the absence of any clear evidence of such intent, on our best inference of the owner's intent given the circumstances.[64] Property thrown in the garbage, for example, will be deemed to have been abandoned by its owner absent some compelling evidence to the contrary.[65] Of course, not all abandonment is so obvious. Typically, mere nonuse of property does not support a claim of abandonment. On the other hand, in certain contexts, nonuse over a sufficiently long period of time may give rise to an inference of intent by the true owner to abandon the property.[66] And even if an appropriator guesses wrong, the most he or she can expect to lose is possession of the claimed item of property.

As a general matter, land cannot be abandoned.[67] But the doctrine of adverse possession, which we have already discussed at length, may constitute an example of such owner neglect "maturing" into abandonment, at least when there is a party willing to assume the responsibility of ownership. As we saw in part 3, that doctrine permits a nonowner to establish good title to a parcel of land by using it openly and notoriously for a specified period of time.

The doctrine of abandonment plays an important role in the law of property. By protecting subsequent appropriators of unused and apparently unwanted property, it helps bring that property back into circulation. The doctrine therefore reduces both waste and need. Indeed, entire subcultures have sprung up in the United States around the use and appropriation of abandoned property. In the 1970s, urban squatters occupied and rehabilitated abandoned buildings in decaying downtown neighborhoods. But the virtuous circle of abandonment and reuse encompasses more than just land. The United States produces nearly five pounds of solid waste per person per day. This is a literal treasure trove of material goods whose owners no longer want them. The "freegans" are a growing subculture of people who, for a variety of reasons—often having to do with environmental and social-justice commitments—choose to live off discarded food and clothing. A *New York Times* profile of freegans gave the following account of a "dumpster dive" near a New York University dorm:

> Ms. Brewster and her mother, who had come from New Jersey, loaded two area rugs into their cart. Her mother, who declined to give her name, seemed to be on a search for laundry detergent, and was overjoyed to discover a couple of half-empty bottles of Trader Joe's organic brand. (Free and organic is a double bonus.) Nearby, a woman munched on a found bag of Nature's Promise veggie fries.
>
> As people stuffed their backpacks, Ms. Kalish, who organized the event (Mr. Weissman arrived later), demonstrated the cooperative spirit of freeganism, asking the divers to pass items down to people on the sidewalk and announcing her finds for anyone in need of, say, a Hoover Shop-Vac. . . . She rooted around in the trash bin and found several half-eaten jars of peanut butter. "It's a never-ending supply," she said.[68]

If we were to apply to intellectual property the same legal standards that we apply to tangible property, that is, the standard of subjective intent to relinquish ownership rights as evinced by owners' behavior towards the property (and by other objective indicia of an intent to abandon), a large percentage of intellectual property would legally be deemed "abandoned." Of course, the problem would be determining what owners' intentions actually were, since it is much more difficult to express the intent to abandon in the context of intangible property. Owners cannot just throw their copyright into the garbage can.[69] But, with the exception of trademark law, which has a robust doctrine of abandonment, intellectual property law makes it extremely risky for nonowners to infer from an owner's long-standing neglect of intellectual property that the owner has "abandoned" it.

The problem is particularly acute for copyright, with its long-term of protection and its supracompensatory statutory damages. The owner of a copyright can allow a written work to fall out of use for decades, but "finders" still run the risk of being sued for infringement should they attempt to sell copies of the copyrighted work (even if they do not seek to profit from doing so). For tangible property (except land), when an owner engages in actions that signal an intent to abandon, a third party who appropriates that property will find himself legally protected against subsequent claims by the original owner. The absence of such a doctrine in the cases of both land and copyright lays the foundation for a form of redistributive value from unlawful conduct that is not as necessary for other forms of tangible property. In the case of land, at least some of that redistributive value is liberated through intentional trespass, which, over time, matures into ownership through adverse possession. In the context of factually abandoned intellectual property, that redistributive value is partially liberated through infringing conduct. But copyright offers no corresponding legal mechanism by which that act of infringement can become legal.

The absence of safe harbor like abandonment, combined with the length of copyright protection, is an enormous body of ostensibly "owned" material as to which rights holders (whose identity can be extremely difficult to ascertain and who may not even be aware that they own the rights to a work) may have no interest in enforcing their rights but for which there is no protection for subsequent appropriators. This lack of a safe harbor, coupled with copyright's routine use of supracompensatory damages, makes appropriators extremely reluctant to engage (at least in public) in any potentially infringing uses of these "orphan works" (as they are known)—for example, by bringing an orphan work back into print. They cannot be sure that, once they have engaged in the infringing (but seemingly harmless) use, a rights holder will not come out of the woodwork to claim crippling copyright damages or injunctive relief.

The problems this poses are perfectly illustrated by the controversy over Google Books. Google has proposed scanning, indexing, and making available over the Internet roughly twelve million out-of-print (but in millions of cases still copyrighted) books, in the process rendering the books both text searchable and far more accessible to the general public. The service would allow users to search through the "library" for particular words or phrases. They could download entire books that are in the public domain. For copyrighted books, the search results would be displayed in snippets of text, with the option to purchase the entire work. As of this date, Google has scanned over seven million books into its digital library. Publishing companies originally opposed the plan as the equivalent of a massive theft of copyrighted property, even though the vast majority of the books will never be printed again.[70]

In 2005, five publishers and the Authors' Guild, which represents several thousand writers, sued Google, alleging that the scheme amounted to copyright infringement. Google initially took the position that its copying was protected fair use because it would enhance public access to out-of-print books. In late 2008, Google and the plaintiffs (using the mechanism of the class-action lawsuit to strike a deal on behalf of all authors and publishers) agreed to a proposed settlement, which is, as of the time of this writing, still subject to final approval by the trial court. The agreement creates the Book Rights Registry, which acts on behalf of copyright holders. Google will have the nonexclusive right to use the content contained within the digital library to provide its search service, a library that will contain virtually *every* book ever published in the United States before 2009 (unless rights holders who do not want their books included opt out in time). Google would be allowed to display up to 20 percent of the copyrighted books in the library as part of its free search service and could offer its users the *full* copyrighted book for a fee (or as part of a subscription service). A percentage of the revenue Google derived from the search service would go into a pool (administered by the registry) to compensate qualifying rights holders who register to receive payments.[71]

Although it superficially resembles the sorts of compulsory licensing schemes we support in order to overcome the kinds of market failures represented by the existence of orphan works, the proposed settlement is, in many ways, the worst of all possible worlds. By licensing the content of the digital library, Google ratifies the content owners' most expansive proprietary claims. In effect, it abandons its claim that it has fair use rights to make digital copies of existing books in order to make them text searchable and to make orphan works available to the public. Moreover, even though the license Google enjoys under the settlement is nonexclusive, the access the license provides to orphan works is wholly a creature of the class-action opt-out device, which automatically extends the settlement to orphan works unless a rights holder opts out in time (something that is very unlikely for a true orphan work). Consequently, no one will be able to offer a competing service containing the orphan works without (1) creating its own digital copies; (2) being sued by authors and publishers; and (3) if sued, striking a similarly favorable deal as the Google settlement or prevailing in a fair use defense. Google in effect ends up with a monopoly on the orphan works its library will make available. The original lawsuit against Google, and the potentially monopolistic proposed settlement that threatens to emerge from it, are direct consequences of the absence of a doctrine like abandonment in copyright to provide a clear safe harbor to downstream appropriators of unused and apparently unwanted intellectual property.

The 110th Congress considered a bill that attempted to remedy the absence of an abandonment mechanism in copyright law. The Shawn Bentley Orphan Works Act of 2008, which did not pass, would have provided something of a safe haven for users of copyrighted work who conduct a diligent search but are unable to locate the work's owner in order to negotiate a license.[72] Under the proposed law, users of such an orphan work would not be exposed to the full force of copyright's supracompensatory damages structure but would instead be required to pay only what the bill calls "reasonable compensation" for the use of the copyrighted work, a term defined to mean the fair market value of a license for the copyrighted work had the user been able to negotiate one. Crucially, the value of the license would be determined as of the moment before the infringement began, thereby permitting the infringing user to capture any increase in market value in the underlying work that is attributable to the infringer's own efforts to revive interest in the orphan work.

Lawrence Lessig criticized the bill, both for its unfairness to copyright owners (particularly those abroad) and for its failure to define its safe haven with sufficient clarity. In an op-ed in the *New York Times*, he wrote:

> Precisely what must be done by either the "infringer" or the copyright owner seeking to avoid infringement is not specified upfront. The bill instead would have us rely on a class of copyright experts who would advise or be employed by libraries. . . . The bill makes no distinction between old and new works, or between foreign and domestic works. All work, whether old or new, whether created in America or Ukraine, is governed by the same slippery stan-

dard. The proposed change is unfair because since 1978, the law has told creators that there was nothing they needed to do to protect their copyright. Many have relied on that promise. Likewise, the change is unfair to foreign copyright holders, who have little notice of arcane changes in Copyright Office procedures, and who will now find their copyrights vulnerable to willful infringement by Americans.[73]

We share Lessig's concern with the bill's failure to provide a clear definition of "diligent search." The bill would also mitigate the danger of unfairness to copyright owners were it to focus on older copyrighted works. Moreover, we agree with Lessig's proposal to return to a model of a shorter period of initial protection, followed by an additional period (or periods) of protection only when copyright owners are willing to take some affirmative step to renew their copyrights. But, whatever the bill's flaws, we are sympathetic to Congress's effort to find some solution to the problem of "abandoned" copyrighted works. And we are less concerned than Lessig with the potential unfairness such a solution might present to existing copyright holders. As long as the mechanisms for protecting their work are sufficiently clear, copyright holders interested in protecting the value of their existing rights should be expected to keep abreast of legal developments in the same way that owners of real property, even those residing abroad, have to monitor changes in environmental and land-use regulations that might affect the value of their property. In any event, we cite the bill primarily in order to draw attention to the intuition (clearly at work behind the bill) that unauthorized conduct is sometimes essential to achieving intellectual property law's goal of facilitating both productive and consumptive uses of information, an intuition that is at the heart of our argument about the importance of leaving some room within property systems for infringing conduct.

12

RESPONDING TO EXPRESSIVE ALTLAWS

In 2003, a little-known disc jockey by the name of Brian Burton, also known as Danger Mouse, came up with a unique idea: mixing the Beatles' *White Album* with the contemporary vocal sounds of the recently released *Black Album* by the artist Jay-Z.[1] After methodically sampling and combining the beats, rhythms, and lyrics from the two works, Burton produced an innovative combination of the two albums, which he then titled, quite aptly, *The Grey Album*.[2] Danger Mouse knew that the album would never be commercially released, because of the unlicensed use, but he believed that it was still worth the effort.[3] ("It's illegal, I know that and it may get me in trouble, but if I had thought about that I would have never made what I thought turned out to be one of the best things I ever did," he later mused.)[4]

Danger Mouse then released his work to thunderous appreciation across cyberspace. *Rolling Stone* magazine described *The Grey Album* as "the ultimate remix album" and "ingenious"; the *Boston Globe* called it "the most creatively captivating" album of the year.[5] It was mentioned in the *New Yorker*'s "Talk of the Town" as well.[6] Danger Mouse's resulting hybrid was part of an emerging, mostly illicit, subset of songs known as "mashups," which refers to a variation of sample-based creation that has been circulating in clubs or on the Internet since about 2000—artists essentially mix two or more songs to create a completely different sound from both original works.[7] Although they certainly constitute an important arena of appropriation art, mashups also demonstrate a classic reversal of the roles between producers, creators, and consumers.[8] Far from passively accepting the traditional distinction between audience and performer, the mashup movement demonstrates "amateur" participation in the world of the creation of cultural products.[9] Paul Morley describes the "bootleg mix" or mashup as follows: "Anonymous raiders of the twentieth century, or "bastards," armed with a decent hard drive, a lust for life, a love of music that borders on the diseased, and a warped sense of humor mash up tracks taken off the Internet, twist genres across themselves, and rewrite musical history in a way musicians would never think of. Access on the Internet to a capella vocals and instrumental backing tracks means that homebodies, who are all in the mind, can ignore legalities and logic and all manner of niceties and splice together any music that takes their fancy."[10] As the journalist Sam Howard-Spink writes, "There is no brick wall between musician and listener; they are part of the same whole."[11]

The Grey Album immediately faced threats from the recording industry for its unlicensed use of the copyrighted songs.[12] EMI Records' cease-and-desist letter, which was sent to Danger Mouse, and to many of the sites distributing his work, demanded that the participants stop distributing the album and that they identify the names and addresses of all third parties involved in the distribution, reproduction, or public performance of the album.[13] The recording industry equated the work with simple piracy at a time when musical sampling was being widely attacked in the courts for its use of copyrighted works without permission.[14] The fact that the material was used without authorization was the key problem, not the use of the material itself. "We authorize sampling and remixes all the time," a spokeswoman for EMI explained. "But he didn't ask for our permission. That's illegal."[15]

Yet the underground character of the music—and the silencing mechanisms of copyright law—only seemed to enhance *The Grey Album*'s desirability. A movement began in cyberspace to "liberate" the music from copyright's control. The organization Downhill Battle, whose activities we discussed in the introduction, organized a "day of digital civil disobedience," Grey Tuesday, to draw attention to the legal suppression of the album. Downhill Battle described Grey Tuesday as "an act of civil disobedience against a copyright regime that routinely suppresses musical innovation."[16] Underlying its criticisms was a passionate philosophical critique of the copyright system, which the participants argued had strayed far from its utilitarian justifications. In response to EMI's cease-and-desist letter, Downhill Battle argued that the group enjoyed "a fair use right to post this music under current copyright law and the public has a fair use right to hear it," claiming that its posting constituted a political act with no commercial interest. Downhill Battle continued: "For people to make an informed decision about whether the major record labels and existing copyright law serve the interests of musicians and the public, they need to be able to hear the music that is being suppressed."[17] Downhill Battle called the cease and desist letters "a clear, simple, downloadable example of how the major record labels stifle creativity . . . and it's the perfect way to explain to non-experts why the copyright system needs to be reformed."[18]

On Grey Tuesday, February 24, 2004, over 170 participating Web sites and blogs offered Danger Mouse's album for download in clear defiance of EMI's legal threats; over 400 sites went "grey" in support of the album. The event was a massive success: the album was downloaded approximately 100,000 times that day, enough to qualify for gold-record status within the industry.[19] The point of Grey Tuesday was not to reargue the merits of excluding works of appropriation from copyright; it was to provide a symbolic and educative opportunity to highlight the way copyright law managed to deny consumers access to innovative artistic goods. Like sit-in participants, the Grey Tuesday protesters were motivated by a desire to express their disagreement with a particular legal situation and to call for reform.

In the previous chapter, we distinguished concerns about consumptive disobedience from those involving questions of innovation, suggesting that the law should consider the difference between disobedience for consumption and disobedience for downstream product development. Among expressive altlaws, we similarly distinguish between the "commentator" and the "creator."

The expressive *commentator,* like the students in the *Diebold* case, seeks to use a protected work for discussion, commentary, or reporting, but faces the risk of censorship because of the copyright owner's control over the information. In such circumstances, a voluntary bargain cannot be struck between the parties themselves (usually because of the nature of the information or commentary in question), but the circulation of the information creates public benefits. In these situations, the case for legal intervention to protect access to the work is strongest.

In contrast, the expressive *creator* seeks to use a piece of work to advance his or her own artistic projects. Whereas the commentator might be a journalist or blogger using the copyrighted material solely for communicative purposes, the creator is more interested in using material to generate new creative works. Although these new works are arguably expressive in some sense, they are less easily disentangled from the artist's self-interest, since artists often earn income by selling them. Accordingly, the activity of the expressive creator straddles a middle position of sorts between expressive and acquisitive altlaw behavior. Though we treat these altlaw creators under the rubric of expressive disobedience, we acknowledge the ambiguity of their conduct and recommend slightly different responses to their activity within copyright law.

In both contexts, we suggest that the law should play (and at times has played) a role in preserving a space for the activities of expressive altlaws and outlaws. There are several reasons why the law should be especially concerned about the increasing tendencies, both within technology and law, to drastically increase the cost of disobedience. In the following sections, we offer a variety of approaches that can help preserve the informational value that expressive disobedience offers.

Preserving the Signaling Value of Disobedience

As we suggested in chapter 5, intellectual property disobedience often takes one of two forms—activities that are clearly illegal (the outlaw) or activities that fall within a gray area of legality (the altlaw). But it is often very difficult to tell the difference between the two. Consider Matt Mason's description:

> So who exactly is a pirate?
>   That guy who sells bootleg DVDs on the corner;
>   Some dude with a beard and a parrot who might mug you if you go boating;

A guardian to free speech who promotes efficiency, innovation, and creativity, and who has been doing so for centuries.

The correct answer is all of the above. A pirate is essentially anyone who broadcasts or copies someone else's creative property without paying for it or obtaining permission.[20]

Intellectual property law reflects the same conflicting divergence—Is a pirate an outlaw or a freedom fighter? the law asks, unable to offer a comprehensive answer. Because the law has not always attempted to honor its obligation to protect both existing property rights and innovation, its mediation has resulted in a regime characterized by a high degree of variance in terms of how it responds to individual acts of disobedience. Although there are circumscribed areas of the law that clearly favor one interest over the other, it is often difficult to predict which approach courts will adopt. As a result, businesses and innovators rest in a difficult and unenviable position of trying to weigh their uncertain options while planning ahead to either raise or defend against allegations of piracy.

This confusion highlights why exploring the *reasons* for unauthorized activity can provide valuable insight into the desirability of possible responses to free-riding activity other than simple prohibition. Consider, again, *The Grey Album* and the Grey Tuesday protest that accompanied it. Grey Tuesday, and the discussions that it generated within cyberspace, suggested the need for a much greater degree of sophistication among those with an interest in copyright law in understanding the nature of and productive labor involved in musical sampling and in taking stock of sampling's distributive implications within the marketplace for recorded music.

Perhaps most importantly, Grey Tuesday illuminated the productive value of studying informal channels of communication outside the common institutions of intellectual property governance.[21] As Kembrew McLeod, a University of Iowa professor who was served with a cease-and-desist letter for his participation in Grey Tuesday's "day of coordinated civil disobedience," explained afterwards: "I risked a lawsuit because I felt a responsibility to show that fair use exists in practice, not just in theory. For me, it would have been ethically wrong to act as a detached academic while others took the fall, because if anyone could make a fair use case, it's me. As a professor who regularly teaches undergraduate and graduate courses on copyright, popular music, and pop culture, I think it is important to make certain copyrighted materials available without worrying about getting sued. It was in the spirit of promoting conversation and debate about an illegal artwork (and a broken copyright regime) that I engaged in this act of copyright civil disobedience."[22]

According to Sam Howard-Spink, the Grey Tuesday story represented a "new form of political engagement"; indeed, it led to the creation of an underground political economy in which the protestors became the distributors and the marketers of an artifact of cultural identity. Howard-Spink writes, "This is where cultural studies and political economy find a new area of common ground: audiences are not merely active in the sense of creating meanings; they are active in the evolution of the technological and economic structures of the music circulation system itself." He asserts that "either consciously or unwittingly, every person who has downloaded The Grey Album has been party to the fostering of an emergent form of political participation."[23]

We have already discussed the risk of overdeterrence, both from the law and from technological forms of control. Independently, and in concert, these can work to foreclose the opportunity for the periodic emergence of conflict necessary to the processes of deliberation and legal change we have been describing. And when this happens, the informational value of disobedience is lost. The DMCA's harsh penalties, for example, should cause us to question whether the criminal law is an appropriate tool for enforcing the complex and indeterminate norms of copyright. Consider this example. On October 31, 2005, the computer programmer Mark Russinovich broke the news that Sony had installed a "rootkit"—a program that "cloaks" computer files and registry keys from diagnostic and security software—on his computer. Rootkits are usually used by malware providers and hackers who seek to hide their identifying information in order to maintain control over a computer after invasion. In this case, Russinovich discovered the existence of a hidden directory, a series of device drivers, and a hidden application that surreptitiously communicated information to Sony for anti-piracy purposes. Attempting to remove the device would damage the computer's operating system and corrupt the files needed to operate the computer's CD player. But the presence of the program, in and of itself, actually made the computer far more vulnerable to control by other hackers who could use the rootkit to circumvent a variety of antivirus programs on the market.[24]

What should an ordinary consumer do in such a situation? Although the DMCA is notoriously difficult to parse, it does not seem to prohibit the consumer from removing the rootkit, as long as the consumer has lawful access to the "infected" CD. But unless the consumer is unusually sophisticated, that right will not be of much value, since the DMCA prohibits anyone from assisting the consumer in working around the DRM technology. Anyone who sells (or even provides, free of charge) a software tool to remove the harmful rootkit, that is, any third party who helps the consumer do what he or she has a legal right to do, might arguably violate the DMCA and could be subject to crippling civil penalties and, if such activities can somehow be construed as having been willful and undertaken for commercial gain, criminal prosecution.[25] Even though the DMCA creates a series of exceptions, supposedly to protect innocent research and other noninfringing efforts to circumvent DRM technology, its lack of clarity creates a penumbra of potential civil and criminal liability that inevitably chills a great deal of arguably lawful activities.[26] As one commentator has put it: "The [DMCA] makes it hard to understand what research you can perform when copyright protection is involved. I speak from personal experience: I once bought a copy-protected CD with the intent of breaking the (privacy-invading) software on it. As I started my research, and read the DMCA, I realized that I was unsure of the legal ground I was on. Talking to attorneys versed in this, it came down to 'How do you feel about being a test case?' I went away, and someone else solved the problem."[27] Because many of the exceptions to the DMCA are so unclear, and given the risks involved, most risk-averse individuals will opt not to challenge its boundaries. As a result, fewer and fewer disputes will even reach the courts. The opportunities for judicial intervention on the disobedient's behalf will thus be foreclosed, and the possibilities of informative communication will be limited.

There are a variety of specific substantive and procedural tools the law of intellectual property can use to preserve the signaling effect of the altlaw's activities in acquisitive and expressive scenarios. Many of these adjustments are procedural, and they aim to prod lawmakers or judges to consider the viability of crafting limited safe harbors for disobedient conduct. Consider, for example, the utility of expanding the use of declaratory judgments, such as those used in the *Diebold* case, which enable a party to seek in advance formal approval by a court of an activity that might otherwise carry the risk of legal liability. Other approaches to limiting the risk of overdeterrence might involve limiting criminal penalties—such as the anticircumvention penalties in the DMCA—for conduct that occurs in the "gray areas" of the law. Or they might involve making self-help measures more costly, both from a legal and technological perspective, for intellectual property owners. Or, more substantively, they might simply involve expanding notions of "fair use" to protect the informational benefits generated by some kinds of activities, like the production of unauthorized derivative works.

Fair Use, Again

In a recent article, James Gibson argues that there is a serious informational imbalance embedded within the copyright doctrine of fair use. This imbalance results from the doctrine's incorporation of existing market practices to evaluate whether a potentially infringing use is "fair" and therefore immune from copyright liability. Because of the test's unpredictability, the high costs of litigating a fair use defense to a successful conclusion, and the risk aversion of many users, copyright users have a strong incentive to err on the side of caution and obtain permission or pay for licenses from copyright owners even when there is a strong likelihood that their use would ultimately be deemed a fair one. This risk-averse practice creates markets for "fair uses," which the courts then cite as evidence that those who do not take advantage of these markets are not fair users but infringers. The result is a vicious feedback loop through which the domain of fair use steadily shrinks over time.

Outlaw and altlaw conduct have a crucial role to play in rebalancing the fair use defense. According to Gibson, risk-averse fair users frequently err on the side of caution, even when their chances of successfully establishing that their use is fair exceeds 50 percent. Let us assume that someone who thinks he or she has a high likelihood (say, more than an 80 percent chance) of being deemed a fair user is neither an altlaw nor an outlaw.

Those who think that, on balance, there is a substantial likelihood that they will be deemed to have infringed are altlaws, and those who think they are almost certain (say, more than 80 percent likely) to be deemed to have infringed are outlaws. If copyright users are risk neutral, they will copy without paying only if they think the odds are greater than even that their use will ultimately be deemed a fair use. And if, as Gibson argues, consumers are risk averse, they will require even better odds before they risk liability. Unless a sufficient number of people are willing to appropriate intellectual property even when they have a substantial likelihood of being deemed infringers, however, we can expect to see a steady shift toward voluntary licensing and, consequently, toward a narrower fair use doctrine. In other words, given the existing system, people we are describing as altlaws and outlaws play a crucial role in balancing the information on market practices to which courts look in determining whether a given use is a fair one. Indeed, in order to generate a stable fair use test that looks to actual market behavior, the law needs to encourage at least some altlaw and outlaw behavior. And, as Gibson points out, the costs of establishing fair use and the penalties for guessing wrong about the outcome of the test currently deter too many people from adopting the altlaw or outlaw course of action.

The most obvious way to restore balance to the fair use analysis is to find ways to encourage more risk taking among potential infringers. Gibson considers but rejects the prospect of making the fair use test more predictable. Another solution would be to reduce the sanctions for copyright infringement in order to lessen the risk for potential fair users of guessing wrong. As Gibson notes, the high likelihood of injunctive relief should infringement be found contributes greatly to risk-averse behavior among repeat fair users in the entertainment industry. Reducing penalties to a more compensatory level and making the award of injunctive relief less routine would go a long way toward reducing risk-averse refusals to assert fair use.[28]

Gibson's solution nicely complements Wendy Gordon's recommendation to draw on fair use in cases of market failure. In the *Diebold* case, Diebold, armed with the DMCA, used its purported copyright to impede the flow of information of vital public importance. Its motives can be analogized to those of a copyright owner who refuses to license its work due to the fear of criticism or parody.[29] In such situations, fair use is an appropriate remedy for the market failure and helps ensure that the law steps in to ensure that the public will continue to receive the benefits generated by the free flow of the information. Yet before a court can even make the determination that a use is a fair one, the use must occur and be litigated. In other words, for the fair use doctrine to function as a solution to market failure, copyright sanctions must be adjusted so that they do not overdeter potential fair uses from reaching a determination in their favor.

Expressive Necessity

We have already discussed the necessity defense in the context of tangible property and the narrowness of its application to situations of dire material need. But, as we have also observed, it might be appropriate to recognize a broader role for the necessity defense in situations in which expressive altlaws and outlaws lack alternative means of conveying their message.

In a variety of state-court proceedings, civil disobedients have successfully used the necessity defense in expressive contexts that did not bespeak physical need.[30] In 1984, for example, protestors who forcibly staged a sit-in at the Vermont office of Senator Robert Stafford to demand a public meeting on Central America were acquitted under a necessity defense after they demonstrated that they had attempted "every reasonable manner to communicate" with the senator.[31] There are many other examples. In some cases, juries apparently concluded that although defendants willfully violated the law, they did so without malice and for the public purpose of protest, and the juries acquitted as a result.[32] In others, the defendants were permitted to argue that they should be acquitted on the grounds that they believed that their protest would stop the clear and immediate threat of public harm[33]—from violations of human rights and international law in South Africa and Central America[34] to the threats posed by nuclear power plants.[35] The necessity defense has been applied in state courts to immunize acts of criminal trespass,[36] blocking traffic,[37] defacing tobacco billboards,[38] and supplying clean needles to drug users.[39] In all these circumstances, the law has been asked to mediate between the need to encourage law-abiding behavior and the occasional absence of expressive alternatives.

As in these cases, a broader conception of "expressive necessity" would permit expressive altlaws (particularly the expressive altlaws we have called "commentators") to make the case that their actions were justified because they were necessary to communicate a valuable public message. Indeed, one might argue that this is what happened in the *Diebold* case. The argument for such a broadened conception of necessity is particularly compelling in the context of expressive appropriations of intellectual property, since the nonrivalrous nature of information permits disobedients to gain access to the property they need without depriving the owner of it. Parodic uses of intellectual property are the most obvious example of unauthorized expressive uses. This is particularly obvious when the original intellectual property owner is the one being skewered and therefore has strong incentives to use its monopoly power to deny the parodist the material needed to communicate his or her message. In such cases, the owner's desire to avoid embarrassment might be just as strong as the parodist's desire to communicate a message.[40] Here, parody's status as a core example of fair use, even when the parodist's degree of appropriation and copying is extensive and even when the parodist's activities severely damage the market for the original work, partially confirms this intuition, and we might view at least some categories of fair use as justified uses under a doctrine of "expressive necessity" that already operates in the copyright context.

But expressive necessity goes beyond parody, and so should fair use. The *Diebold* case provides a good example of expressive necessity in the context of political speech. Even intellectual property violations motivated by public-health concerns can present examples of expressive necessity when the violator feels compelled to make HIV drugs, for example, more accessible in order to make a particular political point. Here, the distinction between acquisitive and expressive behavior can blur, but it tracks the distinction between those who feel compelled to violate patents primarily to facilitate "consumption" and those who infringe in order to spread their expressive message of distaste for the patent system to others. In some cases, as in the TAC defiance campaign, both motives may even be at work simultaneously.

The utilitarian case for a forced transfer in these expressive situations, while plausible, is more difficult to evaluate than in cases of physical need.

Provided that similar situations can be identified with some reliability, permitting such infringement may have only a marginal impact on intellectual property producers' incentives. Indeed, the costs will be limited to the risk that unworthy expressive altlaws and outlaws will be able to take advantage of the exception or that some of the material copied will find its way into the open market, supplanting "official" revenue-producing avenues of distribution. Although we do not mean to underestimate these risks, we think that they must be balanced with a strong consideration of the public benefits that flow from the permitted expression.

As the *Diebold* case clearly illustrates, the utility that consumers gain from having access to the information may tip the balance in favor of justifying the alleged "infringement" in at least some cases. The interests being compared here are not just those of the owner and the appropriator but include the interests of all potential consumers of the information. On this view, although Diebold's desire to keep information about its voting systems under wraps may have been as strong as the desire of the students to disseminate it, society as a whole was better served by having the information made public. And intellectual property owners can usually counter the unwanted speech with their own message. We therefore favor a broader doctrine of necessity, particularly for expressive commentators.

Copyright Misuse

Another possibility for harnessing the informational value of disobedience, one that could work in concert with fair use reform, would aim to raise the cost of asserting overbroad intellectual property rights. In the case of an expressive commentator, as in the *Diebold* case, a party seeks to use a protected work for some reason that is connected to discussion, commentary, or reporting, but faces the risk of censorship because of the intellectual property owner's control over information. In such circumstances, a productive free rider may choose to distribute the information despite the risk of civil or criminal liability. In these situations, a voluntary bargain frequently cannot be struck between the parties themselves (usually because of the critical nature of the commentary), but the circulation of the information creates positive externalities that benefit the public. In cases like *Diebold*, the law has intervened to protect access to the information, and rules of prohibitory restraint, at times, limit a property owner's overenforcement tendencies and the overextension of copyright through the doctrine of "copyright misuse."

Patent law already prohibits the false assertion that a product is protected by patent.[41] Anyone may assert a claim under the statute on behalf of the public interest, and claimants need not establish that anyone actually relied to their detriment on the false assertion of patent protection.[42] We support a similar cause of action in the copyright context. But we would go even further and impose penalties for the unreasonable assertion of intellectual property entitlements, as a means of leveling the playing field between copyright owners and consumers.

The existing doctrine of copyright misuse might provide a template. Copyright misuse is an equitable doctrine that stems from the notion of "unclean hands."[43] Although the doctrine has existed for half a century, misuse has taken on greater prominence in the last twenty years, mostly as a result of a series of high-profile cases involving the relationship between law, contractual agreements, and technology.[44] Copyright misuse arises in two basic circumstances: (1) when a copyright owner uses his or her entitlements in a way that violates federal antitrust law and (2) when a copyright owner attempts to extend copyright protection beyond the scope of the entitlement in a way that contradicts the governing public policy of copyright law.[45] In such circumstances, as in the context of fair use, the entitlement itself can be shifted to the altlaw, who may be granted the right to use the information or property without the intellectual property owner's interference and may be entitled to compensatory damages when the owner oversteps his or her rights and attempts to interfere with the use.

Rather than focusing on the behavior of the alleged infringer, this solution seeks to shift some of the risk of the fair use doctrine's uncertainty to the copyright owner, thereby modifying his or her *ex ante* calculus. For example, if a party accused of infringement successfully establishes a defense of fair use at a minimum along the lines of *Diebold* (where the court thought it was unreasonable for Diebold to assert its claim for copyright infringement), he or she could be awarded some quantum of damages that at least approaches the statutory damages for copyright infringement—damages for which the defendant would be liable if his or her assessment of the applicability and scope of the fair use defense turned out to be unreasonable. Of course, the precise quantum of damages would have to be studied further, but the overall approach is worth considering. Making such penalties payable to those who successfully assert a fair use defense against an unreasonable infringement action would provide incentives for fair users to assert their rights and, if the penalties were large enough, might even help mitigate litigation costs by encouraging the development of a contingent-fee-based market for legal services for copyright defendants. It would also inject some risk into the *ex ante* cost-benefit analysis of copyright owners, who presently stand to lose very little by aggressively overasserting the scope of their intellectual property rights. Altlaws would play a crucial role in the operation of this cause of action, since their willingness to engage in borderline uses of intellectual property (some of which might cross the line) would help maintain the stability of the boundary between fair use and infringement.

As Brett Frischmann and Dan Moylan have explained, the doctrine of copyright misuse serves several important functions. One of these functions, they argue, is corrective: the doctrine of copyright misuse allows courts to play a "gap-filling" function where statutory language is vague or absent. Another function involves "coordination": the doctrine enables courts to balance the entitlements of copyright with other related doctrines within both patent and antitrust law. And finally, Frischmann and Moylan argue, the doctrine of misuse plays a safeguarding function that enables courts to balance the equities when copyright holders misuse the terms of their property rights but such misuse doesn't rise to the level of a formal antitrust violation.[46] An expanded and more aggressive version of the doctrine of copyright misuse might be able to incorporate several of the reforms we are advocating.

The *Diebold* case demonstrates the utility of raising enforcement costs through the introduction of penalties for expansive assertions of intellectual property rights. The intellectual property altlaws in that case not only asserted a defense of fair use but also successfully invoked the doctrine of copyright misuse to impose sanctions on Diebold for its overly broad assertions. The effect was to create something akin to a (counter)property right in the successfully asserted fair use. According to the copyright scholar Justin Hughes, the boundaries of real property are fairly clear: "We may not know who the owner is, but we can readily see where the property starts, know that it does not belong to us, and assume that it belongs to someone else." In contrast, the boundaries of copyright are almost incomparably fuzzy—which is why the reasoning of the *Diebold* case becomes so important. By making a clear case for fair use rights to post the material, the court, in Hughes's eyes, draws clearer boundaries as precedents for future generations to follow. "If our analysis about X as a fair use is always an ad hoc balancing of social interests, it will be harder to say that counsel should have known activity X was a fair use," Hughes explains. "But if there is an edge, albeit a difficult one for laymen to see, it will be easier for the court to say, 'Counsel, it was your duty to see where the property stopped and the public domain began.'"[47] In this sense, Hughes is emphasizing how the court thus increased the odds that future litigants would tread carefully in attempting to use copyright to censor similarly expressive activities.

Even if the sorts of civil penalties we envision could not be made to fit into the doctrine of copyright misuse, we would support creating a standalone cause of action modeled on the patent law's statutory cause of action against those who falsely claim patent protection. Combined with liberal standing requirements, this new cause of action against intellectual property owners who unreasonably overestimate the scope of their intellectual property rights and thereby deter fair uses or other noninfringing conduct would represent a powerful tool to restore balance between intellectual property owners and consumers. As Jason Mazzone has argued, this cause of action might be enacted by federal statute or read into existing consumer-protection statutes at the state level. It might even be brought to bear against intellectual property owners through the common law of fraud, notwithstanding preemption issues.[48]

As we suggested in chapter 7, the willingness of the Swarthmore students to tread on Diebold's proprietary rights in its information sparked an important debate and allowed courts to consider the positive benefits associated with making the information at issue publicly available. The students also contributed to an important legal innovation in the form of the district court's novel use of the doctrine of copyright misuse. Through the interaction of the fair use defense and an expanded doctrine of copyright misuse, the law might create a dynamic balance in which altlaws constitute a crucial counterweight to the power of copyright owners that prevents the steady diminution of fair use that Gibson has correctly decried.

Private Acquiescence

Madhavi Sunder and Robert Merges have both referred to *The Grey Album* as an expression of cultural dissent.[49] But Merges, insightfully, warns us against over-romanticizing rebellion: "There is a sense in these writings of the need to 'fight fire with fire'—to actively reshape powerful cultural images, and 'take back our minds from the corporate interests that would dominate them,' if you will. These writings often describe the mass media as boringly conventional, socially conservative, or at least too 'vanilla' to be interesting. As a consequence, many of the stories told by strong public domain advocates feature romantic narratives of resistance and rebellion: the brave and lonely battle of the 'little guy' against the flat, metallic, and vapid forces of the corporate media machine." Merges pragmatically reminds us that the "remix culture" will not remake the world of intellectual property; if anything, it merely moves us further toward the availability of content whose owners actively encourage and permit remixing, but chides the disobedient remixer to remember that the need for self-expression must always be weighed against the legitimate claims of hard-working creators and to balance what is desired with the basic needs of others. "Remixers," he concludes, "despite their energy and their enthusiasm—are not immune from this basic fact of social life."[50]

Especially in the artistic context (what we are calling the domain of "expressive creators"), not all altlaws are successful, and sometimes even their lack of success in achieving accommodations from the law provides important informational benefits. In many of these situations, however, it is not clear at the outset whether the activity of a given expressive creator falls within the protections for fair use. In some situations, if the new creation supplants the market for the preexisting work, the substitutive effect of such activity may weigh in the other direction. One common example that falls loosely within this category involves derivative works, which, under copyright law, are works based on a preexisting copyrighted source: for example, if someone created a movie version of the novel *You Shall Know Our Velocity*, by best-selling author David Eggers, the resulting script would be considered a derivative work of Eggers's novel, and hence would violate his rights in the original work. Authors and creators of derivative works thus often risk being held liable for supracompensatory damages for borrowing from works without permission. And, as a result, they are likely to find themselves enjoined from distributing their own creative works.

In at least some cases, the law might want to take a middle course, awarding only compensatory damages to the owner of the original work, but allowing the expressive creator to distribute the derivative work. This would be especially appropriate in what Gordon calls "intermediate cases of market failure," where the market cannot be relied upon to generate all desirable exchanges between an author and the artist of a derivative work.[51] In such situations, Gordon writes, fair use might cause some injury to copyright incentives because fair use could substitute for purchase. The danger from enforcement of the property right means that the law might prevent desirable transfers; but the danger of treating the use as an uncompensated fair use means that incentives to create may be undermined in the process. To remedy this problem, Gordon advocates denying fair use if the absolute level of damages would be substantial to the defendant, even if the comparison of benefit and injury demonstrates that the defendant's use would create a net social benefit. According to Gordon, this recommendation would help preserve the incentive-based system of copyright. By providing some additional protection to copyright owners, this approach helps ensure that the system of fair use does not always work to disadvantage them permanently.[52]

Courts, however, have often failed to perform such complicated analyses, opting for a much more absolutist view of control over derivative works. For example, one court, when confronted with a loop of an eight- to ten-second sample song, starkly proclaimed in the first sentence of its opinion, "Thou shall not steal."[53] In that case, the defendant had sought permission to use the sample, but released the album before the copyright owner could respond. In assessing the evidence, the court observed, "One would not agree to pay to use the material of another unless there was a valid copyright! What more persuasive evidence can there be!"[54] The court even took the additional step of referring the matter to the U.S. attorney's office for further exploration of criminal penalties. Another case (decided very soon after Grey Tuesday) held that *all* musical samples, even those lasting only a few seconds—and even those that have been transformed beyond recognition—must be paid for by the artists who appropriate them.[55] In that case, the Sixth Circuit Court of Appeals simply stated, "Get a license or do not sample,"[56] reversing the lower court's decision that a two-second sample did "not rise to the level of a legally cognizable appropriation."[57] In response to these cases, a journalist from the *Boston Globe* observed, "Not since the early 1990s has a legal decision carried such potential for a chilling effect on hip-hop," drawing a parallel to a 1989 dispute involving a recognized sample by the Turtles used by the hip-hop band De La Soul.[58]

These cases often demonstrate the tendency of copyright, like other forms of property, to reflexively undervalue the labor-intensive forces at work among expressive creators in remixing works into something new.[59] For many samples in classic hip-hop, the *Boston Globe* article argued, samples were so "manipulated, fried, and compressed" that they became virtually unrecognizable—examples include samples by Public Enemy, the Dust Brothers, and Prince Paul, all of whom layered hundreds of samples to create transformative aural collages. Had these artists been required to license each of the samples, none of them would have been able to create their music.[60]

Even where the law is likely to respond dismissively to assertions of fair use, copyright owners at times display a willingness to tolerate the use rather than a desire to ban it altogether. Certainly, the prevalence of clips and videos on YouTube suggests a tendency for owners to tolerate certain unauthorized uses, a phenomenon Professor Wu has termed "tolerated use"— as opposed to "fair use." Wu explains: "Tolerated use is infringing usage of a copyrighted work of which the copyright owner may be aware, yet does nothing about."[61] In these situations, both owners and nonowners might derive utility from the unlicensed appropriation of a work, and such "tolerated uses" have created an important but often overlooked gray zone of legality. In such cases, there may be many reasons behind an owner's decision not to pursue legal action—laziness, enforcement costs, the desire to create goodwill, or even the conclusion that infringement might actually complement, rather than supplant, the demand for a copyrighted work.[62]

There are many examples of such tolerated uses on the Web—fan fiction, mashups, user-generated content—and all these uses, in one way or another, might plausibly infringe the copyright of an original work. Yet in many situations, the copyright owner opts to allow the use to flourish rather than stamp it out altogether. At the end of the day, for example, no legal action resulted from the Grey Tuesday protests or *The Grey Album* itself. In fact, one might argue that Grey Tuesday demonstrates that, in addition to the sorts of legal reforms we advocate, private acquiescence can enable communication between parties, even in the absence of formal legal change. In such cases, activism doesn't have to result in a clear legal change in order to have important and powerful effects. Instead, meaningful change can come through a variety of mechanisms—particularly privately sponsored means that provoke owners' acquiescence, rather than prohibition. Indeed, these stories demonstrate that private acquiescence is an important and underrecognized tool for preserving the space necessary for productive disobedience to occur.

We end the chapter with yet another story. In 2004, Jay-Z's *Black Album* was remixed by another disc jockey, Cheap Cologne, who mixed it with Metallica's *Black Album,* creating what he called *The Double Black Album*. He pressed three hundred copies of the album and distributed most of them for free. A short time later, however, Cheap Cologne received a cease-and-desist letter from the Recording Industry Association of America, which threatened him with jail time and a six-figure fine if he failed to comply with their demands to cease all distribution of the work. A few days later, Cheap Cologne discussed his plight on MTV, explaining that *Double Black* was meant to be a "joke." A day later, he received a phone call from the association, which retracted its threat and claimed that the letter had been a "mistake."[63]

CONCLUSION

It was January 20, 2004, when Gavin Newsom, the young, charismatic mayor of San Francisco, went to Washington, D.C., to attend the State of the Union address. As he sat in the audience, he heard George W. Bush proudly praise the Defense of Marriage Act, a federal law that bars federal recognition of same-sex marriages, proclaiming the need to "defend the sanctity of marriage . . . as a union of a man and a woman."[1] In his speech, President Bush announced a plan to go even further, and proposed a constitutional amendment to ban gay marriage.

Newsom found himself distinctly out of place. "At that point in my mind I realized the President was going to use this as a wedge issue to divide this country. I felt offended by it," he explained. "I'd just taken an oath as mayor of the most diverse city, where people are living together and prospering together across every conceivable difference. And for the President to try to deny millions of Americans the same rights that he and I have just didn't seem right."[2] He reported feeling sick as he walked out into the cold January air. That night, he called his chief of staff, a gay man, and asked him to look into the possibility of extending the right to marriage to same-sex couples—immediately.[3]

On February 10, 2004, Newsom drafted a formal letter to the San Francisco county clerk. The letter explained the following: since he, as mayor, had taken an oath to uphold the California Constitution's promise of equal protection of the laws, Newsom had decided that it was time to issue marriage licenses on a nondiscriminatory basis, without regard to gender or sexual orientation. The letter pointedly observed that other state supreme courts (in both Massachusetts and Hawaii) had found that their state constitutions prohibited discrimination against gay men and lesbians with respect to the rights and obligations flowing from marriage. "It is my belief," Newsom concluded, "that these [state court] decisions are persuasive and that the California Constitution similarly prohibits such discrimination."[4] But the point of the letter was not merely to summarize these decisions; it was to offer a new directive to the county clerk to start issuing marriage licenses immediately, one that would end up embroiling the city in a lengthy, costly, and groundbreaking legal battle.

On February 12, 2004, the city clerk began issuing marriage certificates to same-sex couples. The first couple to tie the knot were Phyllis Lyon and Del Martin, then seventy-nine and eighty-three years old, respectively—a couple that had been together for over fifty years—in a small, emotional ceremony at City Hall. Newsom spent much of that morning pacing the floor of his office. As he later explained to the *San Francisco Chronicle*, the City's plan had been to marry the couple before nine o'clock in the morning, because he and other officials were sure that the courts would immediately issue an injunction as soon as they opened. But the wedding didn't take place until eleven o'clock. "I was furious," Newsom later said. "I was upstairs because I didn't want to create a political melee, and I kept calling down, like, 'Guys, are you done yet?' I kept thinking it wasn't going to happen."[5]

If a court ordered the City to stop issuing licenses, the City planned to immediately obey. But on that day, nothing happened. In fact, the injunction didn't come until several weeks later. Meanwhile, thousands of people rushed to City Hall from all parts of the state and country (and even from abroad), camping out, sometimes overnight, to have the opportunity to wed. Just five days after the licensing began, San Francisco City Hall had married 2,200 couples.[6] By the time the city's efforts were brought to a halt, twenty-nine days later, over 4,000 couples had come to San Francisco's City Hall to be married. Within that short span of time, marriage had become a national rallying cry for civil rights and gay equality.

Newsom's actions were controversial, even among supporters of gay marriage. Some members of his staff, many of whom were openly gay, warned Newsom that he would be sacrificing his political career and that his actions could imperil John Kerry's bid for the presidency and could potentially have consequences for Massachusetts, where the high court had recently held that the state constitution required gay marriage.[7] One prominent Democrat asked Newsom if he was on Karl Rove's payroll.[8]

Newsom, however, remained steadfast. "I do not believe it's appropriate for me, as mayor of San Francisco, to discriminate against people," he said. "And if that means my political career ends, so be it."[9] A couple of days after the weddings began, Newsom's senior adviser, Michael Farrah (a groomsman in Newsom's own wedding), promptly canceled his plans for Valentine's Day, and he and his girlfriend performed weddings the entire day instead. "I was crying at the weddings of people I didn't even know. It was the most rewarding weekend in ten years of working in government," Farrah reported.[10] A few municipalities in New Mexico, Oregon, and New Jersey responded to the San Francisco example by performing same-sex marriages on their own.

Newsom, however, became the personal target of heated criticism. On Valentine's Day, a friend asked Newsom how his day had been. "It was good," Newsom responded. "I only got 300 death threats."[11] On election day, 2004, Senator Dianne Feinstein apparently "took him to the woodshed for a private tongue lashing," warning him that he had pushed too far and too quickly, and had thereby hurt the Democratic Party and contributed to Kerry's loss. "So you're saying I'm personally responsible for Kerry losing?" he responded during an interview on the radio station KQED. "That's a pretty big burden. I mean, come on. Maybe Democrats shouldn't have supported civil rights in the '60s."[12]

Newsom's actions also unleashed a torrent of legal challenges, one of which called Newsom's actions reminiscent of "municipal anarchy."[13] A conservative group filed suit against the City, trying to get it to stop performing weddings. "Gavin Newsom is a renegade, and the word equality is being misused to rob all the sacred things of their uniqueness," said Randy Thomasson, the founder of a family rights group opposed to gay marriage. "What's next? Legalized heroin? Prostitution? Polygamy? Incest?" he asked.[14] California's governor, Arnold Schwarzenegger, urged Newsom to back down and obey the law. "It's time for the city to stop traveling down this dangerous path of ignoring the rule of law," he said.[15] Even Barney Frank, an openly gay congressman, argued that Newsom's action was a mere "symbolic point" that only served to divert attention from the other issues plaguing the gay community.[16]

Two weeks after the weddings began, California's attorney general, Bill Lockyer, petitioned the state supreme court for an injunction to force the City of San Francisco to stop performing weddings. He argued that the same-sex marriages that had been performed were unlawful and had generated uncertainty and numerous problems for the state. The petition argued that the existing "conflict and uncertainty, and the potential for future ambiguity, instability, and inconsistent administration among various jurisdictions and levels of government, present a legal issue of statewide importance that warrants immediate intervention." The petition also urged the court to decide the issue of same-sex marriage directly, pointing out that the issue was ripe for the court's determination.[17]

Newsom told CNN that he was more than willing to sacrifice his political career and observed that the denial of marriage benefits for same-sex couples was tantamount to the denial of civil rights for racial minorities in the civil rights movement. "I do not believe in advancing separate but unequal status. . . . These were the same debates we were having on interracial relationships a few decades ago, where blacks couldn't marry whites."[18] Newsom often referred to Martin Luther King Jr.'s "Letter from a Birmingham Jail." He said, "I really believe people will support you if they believe you're doing what you think is right. If you show conviction."[19]

Many critics, even some who were sympathetic to the goal of gay marriage, asked why it was necessary for Newsom and the City of San Francisco to defy laws restricting marriage, rather than challenge them in court. But the San Francisco city attorney Dennis Herrera, for his part, had planned to do both. He had instructed his staff to prepare a lawsuit to be filed as soon as a court injunction stopped the weddings. "We knew we were going to have to address the constitutionality issue," Herrera said. "Essentially right when the court issued its decision [on the injunction], it was inviting us to file a lawsuit, and we were ready to move within an hour saying the marriage laws were unconstitutional."[20]

In what turned out to be just the first skirmish in a longer (and ongoing) battle over same-sex marriage in California, Newsom lost. The state supreme court held that Newsom had exceeded his authority by issuing the marriage licenses, and the court promptly invalidated all four thousand of them, in one fell swoop. In his opinion for the court, Chief Justice Ronald George asserted that public officials are not free to ignore their duty to follow the law solely because they think the law is unconstitutional. Otherwise, he argued, "any semblance of a uniform rule of law quickly would disappear."[21]

The reasons for the court's conclusion were threefold. First, the mayor's duty to enforce the existing laws regarding marriage was largely ministerial, and it did not afford him the ability to decide whether to alter the law itself. "A mayor has no authority to expand or vary the authority of a county clerk or county recorder to grant marriage licenses of register marriage certificates under the governing state statutes, or to direct those officials to act in contravention of those statutes," the chief justice wrote.[22] Because Newsom's responsibility to enforce the laws governing marriage did not involve any substantive oversight of the law, he lacked the authority, in the absence of a judicial determination, to refuse to enforce the marriage regulations on his own belief that they were unconstitutional. In the absence of a judicial determination of unconstitutionality, the mayor lacked the independent authority to refuse to enforce a particular statute, the court concluded.

Second, the court explained that what invalidated the marriages was not that the county clerk's actions were unauthorized; rather, what made the marriages invalid was a state law, enacted through a referendum in 2001— the so-called Knight initiative—that limited marriage to a man and a woman. "It is that substantive legislative limitation on the institution of marriage, and not simply the circumstance that the actions of the county clerk or county recorder were unauthorized, that renders the existing same-sex marriages invalid and void from the beginning," the court explained.[23]

Third, the court reasoned that the judiciary, rather than a lone mayor, was in the best position to assess complex constitutional questions. The city should not have questioned the constitutionality of the governing marriage statutes on its own, the court asserted. And instead of marrying thousands of couples, the court suggested, the city should have simply advised same-sex couples to seek direct redress in court. "Laws are presumed

to be, and must be treated and acted upon by subordinate executive func-
tionaries as[,] constitutional and legal, until their unconstitutionality or illegality has been judicially established, for, in all well regulated government, obedience to its laws by executive officers is absolutely essential, and
of paramount importance," the court concluded.[24]

The court's decision to invalidate the marriages that had already been
performed served several goals. On the practical level, by invalidating these
unions, the court neatly resolved the difficult legal conundrum that it
might have found within Newsom's decentralized legal interpretation. Had
the court allowed the marriages to stand, even briefly, there would have
been a conflict between the law—which proscribed these marriages—and
the marriages that had nonetheless been performed. In refusing to take this
path, the court, quite sensibly, reasoned that if every official were empow-
ered to act according to his or her judgment of the constitutionality of a
statute, statutes would be enforced on a haphazard basis, which would lead
to "confusion and chaos." On the more rhetorical level, however, the court
observed, to give every public official the right to disregard ministerial duties on the basis of the official's constitutional opinions would be "fundamentally inconsistent" with the vision, espoused by Founding Father John
Adams, that government action be determined by the rule of law instead of
the opinion of a governmental official. The court quoted the famous words
attributed to Thomas More in *A Man for All Seasons:*

> ROPER: So now you'd give the Devil benefit of law!
> MORE: Yes. What would you do? Cut a great road through the
> law to get to the Devil?
> ROPER: I'd cut down every law in England to do that!
> MORE: Oh? And when the last law was down, and the Devil
> turned round on you—where would you hide, Roper, the laws all
> being flat? This country's planted thick with laws from coast to
> coast—man's laws, not God's—and if you cut them down—and
> you're just the man to do it—d'you really think you could stand
> upright in the winds that would blow then? Yes, I'd give the Devil
> benefit of law, for my own safety's sake.[25]

Embracing disobedience, the court suggested, would be tantamount to
abandoning the rule of law, and would make society vulnerable to even

greater injustices as a result. In a final observation, the court noted that "history demonstrates that members of minority groups, as well as individuals who are unpopular or powerless, have the most to lose when the rule of law is abandoned—even for what appears, to the person departing from the law, to be a just end."[26] Disobedience of the rule of law, the court suggested, only paves the way to further inequality.

It may seem odd that a book devoted to the topic of property disobedience ends with a story about marriage. We raise it, however, to situate the phenomena we have been describing within a broader tradition of legal disobedience. Newsom's actions share many features with the property phenomena we have been discussing. In an article in the *Stanford Law Review*, Heather Gerken classifies Newsom's actions as an example of "dissenting by deciding." As she puts it, "disaggregated institutions create the opportunity for global minorities to constitute local majorities. They thus allow dissenters to decide, to act on behalf of the state. Dissenting by deciding occurs when would-be dissenters—individuals who hold a minority view within the polity as a whole—enjoy a local majority on a decision-making body and can thus dictate the outcome." In Gerken's view, dissenting by deciding differs from simply registering one's opinion in that it "express[es] disagreement not through a Web log, a protest, or an editorial, but by offering a real-life instantiation of [the dissenter's] views."[27]

The sort of "dissenting by deciding" in which Newsom engaged is obviously a close cousin of the property-outlaw activity we have discussed in this book. The phenomenon of the property outlaw, however, is both broader and narrower. It is broader in that it encompasses the dissenting activity of private parties, not just the governmental actors on which Gerken focuses. It is narrower in the sense that its focus is on the law of private ownership, an area in which we believe the need for such tactics is likely to be particularly acute. But, although our discussion in this book has been restricted to disobedient dissent within the law of property, our analysis of property outlaws and intellectual property altlaws complements and has obvious implications for the exploration of actions like Newsom's and for the mechanism of dissent that Gerken elaborates.

Both property outlaws and dissenting deciders provide lawmakers and deliberating citizens with tangible manifestations of the reality they hope to bring about. Thus, both help to overcome the sorts of imaginative deficits that can stand in the way of legal reform. Moreover, both sorts of dissent provide a powerful avenue of legal change for minorities who might otherwise be invisible to the majoritarian political process. Because of these similarities, the ways in which property law has responded to and, at times, embraced the conduct of outlaws can provide useful analogies for a broader discussion of disobedient dissent and of how the law should evaluate and respond to such activity.

The California Supreme Court's criticism of Gavin Newsom for undermining the rule of law is one that should be familiar to us by now, because it has been raised by contemporary observers in almost every episode of property lawbreaking that we have described in this book. Indeed, to our critics, our sympathetic interest in outlaws will be understood as nothing more than a paean to anarchy and lawlessness—a perverse effort to find virtue in legal defiance. It it true, as we have noted, that property disobedience—like Newsom's marriage disobedience—can, at first glance, appear to pose a foundational threat to the rule of law. But it is important to consider the precise extent of the threat. Is disobedience a threat to the rule of law generally, or to property law more specifically? In many of the property and intellectual property case studies we have explored thus far, the argument might readily be made that every time the law concedes to the violator of property rights, we weaken the right of property—and, seemingly, the rule of law itself. That argument was deployed with dramatic effects in response to the 1960 lunch-counter sit-in protests and has been raised again in debates surrounding intellectual property.

But there is another side to this cautionary tale. At several points in this book, we have referred to Robert Cover's classic essay "*Nomos* and Narrative." As Cover explored the conflicts within competing versions of "law," he began to outline a vision of law as a constant dialogue among competing interpretations of the law, both public and private. As Cover wrote, social movements faced with a hostile official legal regime have two options: they can either conform their behavior to the official "law" and protest that the law is wrong, or they can conform their behavior to their understanding of the law, thereby acting out the legal regime they wish to bring about.

Instead of discussing lawmaking through the singular lens of officially sanctioned legal interpretation, Cover instead viewed lawmaking—and lawbreaking—as a complex, dynamic (even messy) process emerging from a "genuine meeting, or clash, of distinct, independently legitimate, normative worlds."[28] In each of the chapters, through our stories of disobedience and, sometimes, legal transformation—stories of squatters, patent protesters, civil rights activists, bloggers, and remixers—we have offered a similarly dynamic reinterpretation of property law. Although it is tempting to join the California Supreme Court in viewing disobedience as necessarily antithetical to property's role as a guarantor of stable rights of possession, we have suggested that the actions of property outlaws and altlaws who challenge the boundaries of legality out of necessity or for purposes of expression can also be understood, somewhat paradoxically as strengthening and reinforcing property. Whether they intend this result or not, their aspirations to participate more fully in the system of ownership reaffirm its importance.

Moreover, the episodic reform that property outlaws of all types sometimes succeed in initiating helps keep the law up to date. Although violations of the law certainly can hurt the rights of both minorities and majorities in the process, the resulting conflicts can also help generate important opportunities for lawmakers to (re)evaluate the relative merits of arguments against the status quo. Outlaws and altlaws then, in their own way, illustrate how unauthorized activity challenges the law to develop. As we have suggested, the intentional (and unintentional) violation of property law plays an important, though underexamined, role in the development of law and policy. The law must therefore aim to strike a balance between protecting the stability of property and intellectual property norms—without such stability those norms would lose a great deal of their value—and permitting some degree of disobedience in order to keep this dynamic system in motion.

In 2004, public officials in San Francisco were unquestionably disheartened by the California Supreme Court's determination that the city had acted unlawfully by issuing marriage licenses to same-sex couples. Newsom said that he would abide by the decision, but he refused to apologize for his actions. "We decided to challenge the law," Newsom explained.

"We decided, more importantly, to put a human face on discrimination. We decided to give people a narrative, a story, and I'm proud that 4,037 couples from 46 states, eight different countries came to San Francisco to live their life out loud."[29]

The city then filed its own lawsuit, arguing that a state law that limited marriage to a man and a woman violated the equal protection clause of the California Constitution and that the court should step in and affirm the right of same-sex couples to marry. Since California already had a domestic-partnership law in place that afforded virtually the same protections and obligations to same-sex couples as married couples, the court focused on the narrower question whether the state constitution prohibited the state from treating same-sex couples differently from opposite-sex couples by designating same-sex partnerships as "domestic partnerships" rather than as "marriages."

In one of the most significant decisions in the history of the California Supreme Court, Newsom and his team won. After describing the right to marry as a "fundamental right whose protection is guaranteed to all persons by the California Constitution,"[30] the court concluded that this right is a component of the liberty, autonomy, and privacy protected by the state constitution. The court noted that marriage has historically been limited to a union between a man and a woman, but asserted that "constitutional concepts are not static. . . . In determining what lines are unconstitutionally discriminatory, we have never been confined to historic notions of equality, any more than we have restricted due process to a fixed catalogue of what was at a given time deemed to be the limits of fundamental rights."[31] Given the evolution in the understanding of the fundamental rights to which all persons are entitled regardless of sexual orientation, the Court wrote that "it is not appropriate to interpret [the privacy and due process] provisions in a way that, as a practical matter, excludes gay individuals from the protective reach of such basic civil rights."[32]

The court then went on to find that the prohibition against same-sex marriage amounted to discrimination on the basis of sexual orientation and impinged on a fundamental right guaranteed by the California Constitution. From that powerful vantage point, the court concluded that the existing domestic-partnership provisions, coupled with the denial of the nomenclature of "marriage," would inevitably create a caste system in which same-sex couples were branded with the mark of second-class citizenship. In a trenchant observation, the court wrote: "Although the understanding of marriage as limited to a union of a man and a woman is undeniably the predominant one, if we have learned anything from the significant evolution in the prevailing societal views and official policies toward members of minority races . . . it is that even the most familiar and generally accepted of social practices and traditions often mask an unfairness and inequality that frequently is not recognized or appreciated by those not directly harmed by those practices or traditions." The court closed by noting that "the interest in retaining a tradition that excludes an historically disfavored minority group from a status that is extended to all others—even when the tradition is long-standing and widely shared—does not necessarily represent a compelling state interest for purposes of equal protection analysis."[33] In stark contrast to the court's earlier opinion invalidating the marriage licenses granted by the City of San Francisco, this opinion mandated that state officials "take all actions necessary to effectuate our ruling" and guarantee same-sex couples the same right to marry as opposite sex couples.[34]

And so the right of marriage arrived once again at the doorstep of same-sex couples in San Francisco. Thousands gathered at the courthouse to celebrate; others celebrated in the streets. Stewart Gaffney and John Lewis, two San Francisco residents, wrapped themselves in an oversize California flag and stood outside the courthouse on the day of the decision. "Today the two of us can get married because of the wisdom of the court," Gaffney said. "The moment we heard the decision we felt elation. Boundless joy. Our hearts skipped beats. We took a long, deep breath and realized we were a couple in the eyes of the world. How good is that?" they asked.[35]

Not everyone, of course, agreed with the decision. Randy Thomasson, president of the Campaign for Children and Families, observed that the California Supreme Court "destroyed the civil institution of marriage between a man and a woman." Describing the opinion as "arrogant judicial activism" from "the rebel city of San Francisco," Thomasson asserted that "law-abiding Americans must condemn it in the strongest terms."[36] Los Angeles mayor Antonio Villaraigosa was much more enthusiastic, pledging to officiate as many same-sex marriages as he could perform. "This is about people and the right for people to love who they want. . . . I will stand with you," he said. "I will do everything in my power to keep this decision the law of the land."[37]

We chose to end our book with this story not because the struggle for gay marriage ended in victory, but *despite* the fact that the decision was ultimately overturned by the electorate in 2008 and affirmed by the California Supreme Court almost six months later. Opponents of same-sex marriage collected enough signatures to place a measure on the ballot, Proposition 8, that repudiated the supreme court's decision and the right of same-sex couples to marry by amending the California Constitution to limit marriage to the union of a man and a woman.

The day after the election, gay-rights advocates woke up to the news that Proposition 8 had passed by 52 percent of the vote, a margin of about half a million votes. A photograph from that day captured the emotion of the reversal: it showed a young lesbian couple, arms entwined, being turned away from San Francisco City Hall after requesting to be married.

Despite the outcome, Newsom's original act of disobedience played a crucial role in an ongoing evolution in our country's understanding of marriage. Immediately after the second California Supreme Court decision, voters overwhelmingly approved of same-sex marriage—California voters approved of the opinion by a margin of 51 to 42 percent.[38] This was a striking change from 2000, when over 60 percent of voters approved a referendum limiting marriage to opposite-sex couples. Just as in 2004, Del Martin and Phyllis Lyon were, again, the first same-sex couple to be married after the Supreme Court's decision, only three months before Del died at the age of eighty-seven. The carefully chosen picture of gay marriage looked a lot like every other marriage: two loving individuals choosing each other as partners for life in front of supporters, friends, and family.

Since November 2008, the reaction against Proposition 8 has become as significant as the proposition itself. Thousands of people have protested its passage in every major city in the United States, garnering tremendous support from people, gay and straight alike. Indeed, even though the California Supreme Court upheld Proposition 8, as many predicted it would, the lengthy opinion did little to stem the national tide that has turned in favor of legalizing gay marriage. A poll by ABC News and the *Washington Post* found that as of April 2009, a slim majority of Americans are in favor of gay marriage, from 49 percent in favor to 46 percent opposed.[39] Days earlier, a CBS News/*New York Times* poll had found that 42 percent favored gay marriage, a nine-point jump from the month before.[40] The battle over gay marriage has even entered the federal courts, as two of the most prominent lawyers in the country—former solicitor general Ted Olson and star lawyer David Boies, once on opposing sides in *Bush v. Gore*—announced that they had joined forces to file suit against Proposition 8 on behalf of two same-sex couples. "Mr. Olson and I are from different ends of the political spectrum," explained Boies, "But we are fighting this case together because Proposition 8 clearly and fundamentally violates the freedoms guaranteed to all of us by the Constitution. Olson, for his part, added, "Whatever discrimination California law now might permit, I can assure you, the United States Constitution does not."[41] In the weeks before this book went to press, the legislatures of three New England states (Maine, Vermont, and New Hampshire) voted to legalize gay marriage. Thus, rather than resolving, once and for all, the question whether same-sex marriage would be legalized, Proposition 8 simply constituted one more episode in an ongoing dialogue, both inside and outside the courts and legislature, between proponents and opponents of gay marriage, a dialogue for which Gavin Newsom's initial act of disobedience was an indispensable catalyst. The issue appears to be headed, once more, for the California ballot in 2012.

NOTES

Preface

1. *See* Troy Johnson et al., *American Indian Activism: Alcatraz to the Longest Walk* 27 (1997). It is also important to note that this was not the first time that Native Americans had drawn on civil disobedience to assert their claims. Tribal members participated, along with celebrities like Marlon Brando, in "fish-ins" to assert their on- and off-reservation right to fish in the 1960s. *See* Johnson, *supra*, at 14–15; Robert Odawi Porter, *Tribal Disobedience*, 11 Tex. J. on C.L. & C.R. 137 (2006).

2. *See* Johnson, *supra* note 1, at 27.

3. *See id.* at 32–33.

4. The documentary *Alcatraz Is Not an Island* provides an excellent account, also summarized at http://www.pbs.org/itvs/alcatrazisnotanisland/activism.html.

5. *See* Alvin M. Josephy et al., *Red Power: The American Indians Fight for Freedom* 101–109 (1999).

6. *See* Alcatraz Is Not an Island, http://www.pbs.org/itvs/alcatrazisnotanisland /activism.html.

7. For an excellent set of perspectives on Alcatraz, see the essays in Robert A. Rundstrom, *American Indian Placemaking on Alcatraz 1969–1971*, Am. Indian Culture & Res. J., Fall 1994, at 190, 204 (quoting Grace Thorpe and arguing that from the place of Alcatraz, "a people had to emerge"). Also, for a wider set of views on American Indian legal history, see the body of work by Vine Deloria Jr., including *Behind the Trail of Broken Treaties* (1994).

8. *See* Carol Rose, *Property and Persuasion* (1994).

9. *See* Eduardo M. Peñalver, *Homesteaders in the Hood*, Slate, Mar. 25, 2009, http://www.slate.com/id/2214544/.

10. For recent accounts of these movements, see Chris Carlsson, *Nowtopia: How Pirate Programmers, Outlaw Bicyclists, and Vacant-Lot Gardeners Are Inventing the Future Today* (2008); Jeff Ferrell, *Tearing Down the Streets: Adventures in Urban Anarchy*

(2001); and Matt Mason, *The Pirate's Dilemma: How Youth Culture Reinvented Capitalism* (2008). For related accounts, see Yochai Benkler, *The Wealth of Networks* (2006); Clay Shirky, *Here Comes Everybody: The Power of Organizing without Organizations* (2008); and Lawrence Lessig, *Remix: Making Art and Commerce Thrive in a Hybrid Economy* (2008).

11. *See Mohawk Protester Brant Gets Light Penalty for Blockades,* CBCNews, Sept. 29, 2008, http://www.cbc.ca/canada/story/2008/09/29/brant-charges.html (summarizing protests led by Shawn Brant, a Mohawk activist).

Introduction

1. Marvin Sykes, *Negro College Students Sit in at Woolworths Lunch Counter,* Greensboro Record, Feb. 2, 1960.

2. *N.C. Stores Close Down Counters,* Greensboro Record, Feb. 10, 1960.

3. Eric Sorrentino, *Rare Civil Rights Film, "Eyes on Prize" Shown Tonight,* U. Daily Kansan, Feb. 8, 2005, http://www.kansan.com/stories/2005/feb/08/news_campus_film.

4. DeNeen L. Brown and Hamil R. Harris, *A Struggle for Rights: "Eyes on the Prize" Mired in Money Battle,* Wash. Post, Jan. 17, 2005, at C1, *available at* http://www.washingtonpost.com/wp-dyn/articles/A14801-2005Jan16.html.

5. This account of Downhill Battle's protest and Blackside's response is drawn from Sheigh Crabtree and Chris Marlowe, *"Eyes" Campaign Spurs New Civil Disobedience,* Hollywood Rep., Feb. 3, 2005.

6. Brown and Harris, *supra* note 4 (quoting Lawrence Guyot).

7. Eyes on the Screen: Direct Action to Save Eyes on the Prize, Posting of Cory Doctorow to BoingBoing, http://boingboing.hexten.net/2005/01/26/eyes-on-the-screen-d.html (Jan. 26, 2005, 9:26 a.m.) (quoting a Downhill Battle announcement).

8. Catherine Foster, *"Eyes" Fight Focuses on Rights,* Boston Globe, Feb. 5, 2005, *available at* http://www.boston.com/ae/tv/articles/2005/02/05/eyes_fight_focuses_on_rights (quoting Lawrence Guyot).

9. *See* Crabtree and Marlowe, *supra* note 5, and Foster, *supra* note 8 (quoting Blackside's lawyers).

10. It Doesn't Matter If the Cause Is Just, Sharp Tools, http://www.sharptools.net/archives/000191.html (Jan. 26,2005).

11. *Negro Minister Criticizes Student Movement,* Greensboro Record, Feb. 10, 1960.

12. Jakob Schiller, *In Defiance of Copyright Law Viewers Keep "Eyes on the Prize,"* Berkeley Daily Planet, Feb. 11, 2005, http://www.berkeleydailyplanet.com/issue/2005-02-11 (quoting Bruce Hartford).

13. *Oxford English Dictionary Online,*http://www.oed.com (trespass) (subscription required).

14. Tom Stephenson et al. *Forbidden Land: The Struggle for Access to Mountain and Moorland* 89 (1989); *see also Ilott v. Wilkes,* (1820) 106 Eng. Rep. 674, 676 (K.B.).

15. *See, e.g.,* Michelle Jones, Trespassers Will Be Shot, http://blessingsforlife.com/southernliving/trespassers.htm (last visited September 10, 2008).

16. *See Lingle v. Chevron USA, Inc.,* 125 S. Ct. 2074, 2082 (2005); *Loretto v. Teleprompter Manhattan CATV Corp.,* 458 U.S. 419, 435 (1982); Henry E. Smith, *Exclusion and Property Rules in the Law of Nuisance,* 90 Va. L. Rev. 965, 972 (2004); Thomas W. Merrill, *The Landscape of Constitutional Property,* 86 Va. L. Rev. 885, 970–974 (2000).

17. Abraham Bell and Gideon Parchomovsky, *A Theory of Property,* 90 Cornell L. Rev. 531, 552 (2005).

18. *See, e.g.,* Nicholas Blomley, *Law, Property, and the Geography of Violence: The Frontier, the Survey, and the Grid,* 93 Annals Ass'n Am. Geographers 121, 125–133 (2003) (discussing property as a locus of repeated violence and resolution).

19. Jeremy Waldron, *The Right to Private Property* 32 (1988).

20. Larry D. Kramer, *The People Themselves: Popular Constitutionalism and Judicial Review* 25–27 (2004).

21. Jim Pope, *Worker Lawmaking, Sit-Down Strikes, and the Shaping of American Industrial Relations 1935–1958,* 24 Law & Hist. Rev. 45, 84 (2006).

22. On this subject, see James Boyle, *The Second Enclosure Movement and the Construction of the Public Domain,* 66 Law & Contemp. Probs. 33 (2003).

23. *See, e.g.,* Richard A. Posner, *A Theory of Negligence,* 1 J. Legal Stud. 29 (1972).

24. *See, e.g.,* Stuart Banner, *Transitions Between Property Regimes,* 31 J. Legal Stud. 359, 368–369 (2002); William Michael Treanor, *The Original Understanding of the Takings Clause and the Political Process,* 95 Colum. L. Rev. 782 (1995).

25. *See* Eric Kades, The Law and Economics of Civil Disobedience 20–21 (2006) (unpublished manuscript, on file with authors).

26. *See, e.g., State v. Shack,* 277 A.2d 369 (N.J. 1971).

27. *See, e.g.,* Stuart Banner, *How the Indians Lost Their Land: Law and Power on the Frontier* 242 (2005) (discussing the encroachment on Navajo property by white trespassers).

28. We do not use the term "civil disobedience," so as to avoid any confusion about the broader scope of our discussion, which encompasses lawbreaking activity that would not normally be understood as civil disobedience.

1. Why <u>Property</u> Outlaws?

1. Augustine, *De Libero Arbitrio,* 1.5.

2. Thomas Aquinas, *Summa Theologiae* 1-2.93.3.

3. Robert P. George, *Kelsen and Aquinas on the Natural-Law Doctrine,* 75 Notre Dame L. Rev. 1625, 1640–1643 (1999).

4. Ronald Dworkin, *A Matter of Principle* 108–110 (1985).

5. *See* John Rawls, *A Theory of Justice* (1972), 365, 372; Michael Walzer, *Obligations: Essays on Disobedience, War, and Citizenship* 20 (1970).

6. Daniel Markovits, *Democratic Disobedience,* 114 Yale L.J. 1897, 1921–1928, 1934–1948 (2005).

7. Robert M. Cover, *The Supreme Court 1982 Term—Foreword:* Nomos *and Narrative,* 97 Harv. L. Rev. 4 (1983).

8. See, for example, *City of Raleigh v. Forbes* (N.C. Super. Ct. Wake County, Apr. 22, 1960), cited in Civ. Liberties Docket, June 1960, at 68, in which a North Carolina court reversed the convictions of forty-three protesters for trespassing on a private stretch of sidewalk outside a shopping center.

9. *See* Margaret Jane Radin, *Property and Personhood*, 34 Stan. L. Rev. 957 (1982). Radin argues that "to achieve proper self-development . . . an individual needs some control over resources in the external environment." *Id.* at 957.

10. Jeremy Waldron articulates this view in *The Right to Private Property* 353–357, 372–375 (1988). Waldron notes Hegel's thesis, which is "that by appropriating, owning, and controlling objects, a person can establish his will as an objective feature of the world." *Id.* at 356.

11. Nicholas Blomley, *Law, Property, and the Geography of Violence: The Frontier, the Survey, and the Grid,* 93 Annals Ass'n Am. Geographers 121, 131 (2003).

12. These views are expressed, respectively, by Radin, *supra* note 9, at 1007–1008, and Joseph William Singer, *The Ownership Society and Takings of Property: Castles, Investments, and Just Obligations,* 30 Harv. Envtl. L. Rev. 309 (2006). Singer quotes a University of Texas economist as saying that he favored private property so much that he "want[ed] everyone . . . to have some." *Id.* at 310.

13. Jeremy Waldron, *Homelessness and the Issue of Freedom,* 39 UCLA L. Rev. 295, 318 (1991). Waldron argues that because society makes freedoms dependent on having property on which to exercise those freedoms, any ban on public activities has disproportionate implications for the freedom of the homeless.

14. *See* Claude S. Fischer, *To Dwell among Friends: Personal Networks in Town and City* 252–253 (1982); Amitai Etzioni, *Liberals and Communitarians, in A Responsive Society: Collected Essays on Guiding Deliberate Social Change* 127, 140 (1991).

15. 301 U.S. 1 (1937).

16. Jim Pope, *Worker Lawmaking, Sit-Down Strikes, and the Shaping of American Industrial Relations, 1935–1958,* 24 Law & Hist. Rev. 45, 61 (2006).

17. *Id.* at 73.

18. Robert Morss Lovett, *A G.M. Stockholder Visits Flint,* Nation, Jan. 30, 1937, at 124 (quoted in Drew D. Hansen, *The Sit-Down Strikes and the Switch in Time,* 46 Wayne L. Rev. 49, 93 (2000)).

19. Abraham Bell and Gideon Parchomovsky, *A Theory of Property,* 90 Cornell L. Rev. 531, 551 (2005) (emphasis added); *see also* Carol M. Rose, *Seeing Property, in Property and Persuasion: Essays on the History, Theory, and Rhetoric of Ownership* 267, 272 (1994).

20. *See, e.g.,* Thomas W. Merrill and Henry E. Smith, *Optimal Standardization in the Law of Property: The* Numerus Clausus *Principle,* 110 Yale L.J. 1, 8 (2000); Thomas W. Merrill and Henry E. Smith, *The Property/Contract Interface,* 101 Colum. L. Rev. 773, 778–779 (2001).

21. Margaret Jane Radin, The Colin Ruagh Thomas O'Fallon Memorial Lecture on Reconsidering Personhood, *in* 74 Or. L. Rev. 423, 429–431 (1995).

22. Holly Doremus, *Takings and Transitions,* 19 J. Land Use & Envtl. L. 1, 1–5, 11–

12 (2003). Doremus comments, "Regulatory takings claims are all about change." *Id.* at 11.

23. *See, e.g.*, Ralph W. Aigler, *The Operation of the Recording Acts*, 22 Mich. L. Rev. 405, 406 (1924) (noting that competing claims are settled on the basis of time, not notice).

24. For example, in *Escobar v. Cont'l Baking Co.*, 597 N.E.2d 394, 398 (Mass. App. Ct. 1992), the court unsympathetically told the plaintiff, "'No one can move into a quarter over to foundries and boiler shops and demand the quiet of a farm'" (quoting the earlier case *Stevens v. Rockport Granite Co.*, 104 N.E. 371, 373 (Mass. 1914)). And even in the more plaintiff-friendly case *Spur Indus. v. Del E. Webb Dev. Co.*, 494 P.2d 700, 706–708 (Ariz. 1972), the court held that a developer who "came to a nuisance" could enjoin the nuisance but also had to indemnify the property owner.

25. *See, e.g.*, Daniel Kahneman et al., *Experimental Tests of the Endowment Effect and the Coase Theorem*, 98 J. Pol. Econ. 1326 (1990).

26. *See, e.g.*, Doug Bond, *Nonviolent Direction Action and the Diffusion of Power, in Justice Without Violence* 59, 66 (Heidi Burgess and Guy M. Burgess eds., 1994) (defining violence as violence targeting persons).

27. Model Penal Code § 3.02 (1962).

28. *See* Joshua Getzler, *Use of Force in Protecting Property*, 7 Theoretical Inquiries L. 131, 143 (2005) ("Night-time intruders can more likely expect to confront the inhabitants, and a prepared and watchful intruder might easily prevail against sleepy and surprised dwellers.").

29. Cover, *supra* note 7, at 47–48.

30. Charles M. Payne, *I've Got the Light of Freedom: The Organizing Tradition and the Mississippi Freedom Struggle* 78 (1995) (internal quotation marks and footnote omitted).

31. John Hart Ely, *The Supreme Court 1977 Term—Foreword: On Discovering Fundamental Values*, 92 Harv. L. Rev. 5, 35 (1978) (quoting Alexander Bickel, *The Least Dangerous Branch* 267 (1962)).

32. Heather K. Gerken, *Dissenting by Deciding*, 57 Stan. L. Rev. 1745, 1754–1759 (2005). In many ways, property-outlaw behavior is the private-law analog to what Gerken has, in the public-law context, called "dissenting by deciding." In both cases, the acting out of legal dissent provides decision makers with an especially vivid understanding of the alternative legal conception that the dissenter is inviting decision makers to embrace.

33. *See* Martha Nussbaum, *The Fragility of Goodness: Luck and Ethics in Greek Tragedy and Philosophy* 300–301 (1986) ("Principles . . . fail to capture the fine detail of the concrete particular, which is the subject matter of ethical choice.").

34. Miles Wolff, *Lunch at the Five and Ten: The Greensboro Sit-Ins: A Contemporary History* 152 (1970).

35. James Kilpatrick, Editorial, Richmond Daily News, Feb. 22, 1960.

36. Editorial, *Some Racial Facts and Fallacies*, Wall St. J., Mar. 25, 1960, at 8.

2. Property and Intellectual Property

1. John Perry Barlow, A Declaration on the Independence of Cyberspace, http://homes.eff.org/~barlow/Declaration-Final.html (last visited May 10, 2009).

2. John Perry Barlow, *The Economy of Ideas*, Wired, Mar. 1994, http://www.wired.com/wired/archive/2.03/economy.ideas.html.

3. *See* Jessica Litman, *Digital Copyright: Protecting Intellectual Property on the Internet* (2001); Lawrence Lessig, *The Future of Ideas: The Fate of the Commons in a Connected World* (2001); Siva Vaidhyanathan, *Copyrights and Copywrongs: The Rise of Intellectual Property and How It Threatens Creativity* (2001).

4. Jessica Litman, *The Exclusive Right to Read,* 13 Cardozo Arts & Ent. L.J. 29, 51 (1994).

5. *See* John Logie, *Peers, Pirates & Persuasion* 14 (2006).

6. For an excellent series of views on this question, see Jack Goldsmith and Tim Wu, *Who Controls the Internet? Illusions of a Borderless World* (2006).

7. Robert P. Merges et al., *Intellectual Property in the New Technological Age* 2 (4th ed. 2007).

8. *Id.* at 2.

9. For an excellent discussion of these comparisons, see Mark A. Lemley, *Property, Intellectual Property, and Free Riding,* 83 Tex. L. Rev 1031, 1031–1046 (2005).

10. *See generally* Peter Menell and Suzanne Scotchmer, *Intellectual Property, in Handbook of Law and Economics* (Mitchell Polinsky and Steven Shavell eds., 2007). A draft of the chapter is available at http://papers.ssrn.com/sol3/papers.cfm?abstract_id=741424.

11. *See, e.g.,* Willam Patry, *The Fair Use Privilege* (1985) (discussing copyright law's fair-use defense); *Nimmer on Copyright* § 13.05 (2005) (same).

12. Jed Rubenfeld, *The Freedom of Imagination: Copyright's Constitutionality,* 112 Yale L.J. 1, 11 (2002) (describing the speech-restricting effects of copyright's enlargement).

13. *See, e.g., Sega Enter., Ltd. v. Accolade, Inc.,* 977 F.2d 1510, 1527 (9th Cir. 1993) (finding that the disassembly or decompilation of a computer program to produce a noninfringing program is a fair use); *see also* Pamela Samuelson and Suzanne Scotchmer, *The Law and Economics of Reverse Engineering,* 111 Yale L.J. 1575 (2002) (providing a comprehensive overview of the reverse-engineering issue).

14. *See, e.g.,* Paul Goldstein, *International Copyright: Principles, Law, and Practice* 309-10 (2001) (discussing compulsory licenses, which "reflect the legislator's judgment that to extend an exclusive right [to a copyright holder] would hamper socially important uses").

15. *See* Lessig, *supra* note 3, at 94–95 (discussing the nonrivalrous nature of intellectual property); Douglas G. Baird, *Common Law Intellectual Property and the Legacy of* International News Service v. Associated Press, 50 U. Chi. L. Rev. 411, 413 (1983) (discussing the distinction between information and tangible products).

16. Clarissa Long, *Information Costs in Patent and Copyright,* 90 Va. L. Rev. 465, 472, 483–84 (2004).

17. *Id.* at 483–484.

18. *Id.* at 484.

19. *Id.* at 486.

20. *Id.* at 484.

21. For a discussion of the former position, see Stephen L. Carter, *Does it Matter Whether Intellectual Property Is Property?*, 68 Chi.-Kent L. Rev. 715, 723 (1993), summarizing parallels between intellectual property and property and minimizing role of tangibility; Richard Epstein, *Liberty versus Property? Cracks in the Foundations of Copyright Law*, 42 San Diego L. Rev. 1, 28 (2005), concluding that a system of copyright that conceptually mirrors real property is the "lesser of two evils"; and Pamela Samuelson, *Information as Property: Do* Ruckelshaus *and* Carpenter *Signal a Changing Direction in Intellectual Property Law?*, 38 Cath. U. L. Rev. 365, 368 (1989), questioning the "necessity and wisdom" of treating information as property.

22. *See* Lemley, *supra* note 9, at 1044 (summarizing this view).

23. *See* Merges et al., *supra* note 7, at 2.

24. *See* Lemley, *supra* note 9, at 1069–1075.

25. For an example of this approach, see Timothy Wu, *Copyright's Communications Policy*, 103 Mich. L. Rev. 278 (2004) (theorizing the evolution of liability rules in copyright).

26. Lemley, *supra* note 9, at 1058–1064.

27. *See* Stuart Sterk, *Intellectualizing Property: The Tenuous Connections between Land and Copyright*, 83 Wash. U. L.Q. 417, 446 (2005).

28. *Id.*

29. *See* Michael A. Carrier, *Cabining Intellectual Property through a Property Paradigm*, 54 Duke L.J. 1 (2004); Richard Epstein, *The Property Rights Movement and Intellectual Property*, Regulation, Winter 2008, at 58 (responding to Peter S. Menell, *The Property Rights Movement's Embrace of Intellectual Property: True Love or Doomed Relationship* (U.C. Berkeley Public Law Research Paper No. 965083, 2007), *available at* http://ssrn.com/abstract=965083).

30. *See* Sterk, *supra* note 27, at 417.

31. *See* Lemley, *supra* note 9, at 1042–1043; Brett M. Frischmann and Mark A. Lemley, *Spillovers*, 107 Colum L. Rev. 257 (2007).

32. *See generally* Lemley, *supra* note 9. For a strident response to Lemley's piece on property and free riding, see John F. Duffy, *Intellectual Property Isolationism and the Average Cost Thesis*, 83 Tex. L. Rev. 1077 (2005).

33. *See* Lemley, *supra* note 9, Harold Demsetz, *Toward a Theory of Property Rights*, 57 Am. Econ. Rev. 347, 356 (1967); Henry E. Smith, *Exclusion versus Governance: Two Strategies for Delineating Property Rights* 31 J. Legal Stud. 453, 453–456, 467–478 (2002).

34. Demsetz, *supra* note 33, at 354–356.

35. Lemley, *supra* note 9, at 1046–1047.

36. *See id.* at 1032.

37. See, for example, Mark Lemley's critique of the overuse thesis in *Ex Ante Versus*

Ex Post Justifications for Intellectual Property, 71 U. Chi. L. Rev. 129 (2004), and in Lemley, *supra* note 9, at 1050–1052.

38. *See* Lemley, *supra* note 9, at 1050 ("There is no tragedy of the commons in intellectual property.").

39. *See* Mark A. Lemley, *Reply—What's Different about Intellectual Property?*, 83 Tex. L. Rev. 1097, 1098–1099 (2005).

40. Stacey L. Dogan, *Code versus the Common Law*, 2 J. on Telecomm.& High Tech. L. 73, 83–84 (2003).

41. *Id.* at 84.

42. *Id.*

43. *See In re Aimster*, 334 F.3d 643, 647 (7th Cir. 2003).

44. *See* Carrier, *supra* note 29, at 4.

45. *See* James Boyle, *A Nondelegation Doctrine for the Digital Age*, 50 Duke L.J. 5 (2000).

46. *See* Neil Netanel, *Market Hierarchy and Copyright in Our System of Free Expression*, 53 Vand. L. Rev. 1879 (2000); *see also* Carrier, *supra* note 29, at 100; Christina Bohannan, *Reclaiming Copyright*, 23 Cardozo Arts & Ent. L.J. 867 (2006).

47. *See* Netanel, "Market Hierarchy," *supra* note 46, at 1904.

48. *See* Jack Balkin, *Digital Speech and Democratic Culture: A Theory of Freedom of Expression for the Information Society*, 79 N.Y.U. L. Rev. 1, 6–13 (2004).

49. *See* Dan L. Burk, *Legal and Technical Standards in Digital Rights Management Technology*, 74 Fordham L. Rev. 537 (2005); Julie Cohen, Lochner *in Cyberspace: The New Economic Orthodoxy of "Rights Management,"* 97 Mich. L. Rev. 462 (1998); Pamela Samuelson, *DRM {and, or, vs.} the Law*, Comm. ACM April 2003, at 41, *available at* http://www.sims.berkeley.edu/~pam/papers/acm_v46_p41.pdf.

50. *See Eldred v. Ashcroft*, 537 U.S. 186 (2003).

51. *See* Stewart E. Sterk, *Rhetoric and Reality in Copyright Law*, 94 Mich. L. Rev. 1197, 1217 (1996).

52. *See* Carrier, *supra* note 29, at 18.

53. *See, e.g.*, Lemley, *supra* note 9, at 1101 (discussing the indeterminacy of "boundaries" in intellectual property).

54. Carrier, *supra* note 29, at 12.

55. *See, e.g.*, *Davidson & Assoc. v. Jung*, 422 F.3d 630 (8th Cir. 2005) (finding defendant's assent to shrink-wrap license waived fair-use defense to no-reverse-engineering clauses).

56. *See generally* Dan L. Burk, *DNA Rules: Legal and Conceptual Implications of Biological "Lock-Out" Systems*, 92 Cal. L. Rev. 1553 (2004).

57. *See* Burk, *supra* note 56, at 1564.

58. *See* Carrier, *supra* note 29, at 14.

59. *See* Dan L. Burk, *Anticircumvention Misuse*, 50 UCLA L. Rev. 1095 (2003).

60. *See* Burk, *supra* note 56, at 1567 ("To the extent that the DMCA appears to legitimate technological controls over copyrighted works without regard to their effect on public policy, the statute effectively grants rubber-stamp approval to such private 'legislation.'"); *see also* Niza Elkin-Koren, *The Privatization of Information Policy*, 2

Ethics & Info. Tech. 201 (2001); Charles R. McManis, *The Privatization (or "Shrink-Wrapping") of American Copyright Law,* 87 Cal. L. Rev. 173 (1999).

3. Acquisitive Outlaws: The Pioneers

1. For a comprehensive account of the history of public land law, see Paul W. Gates, *History of Public Land Law Development* (1979).

2. *See* John G. Sprankling, *An Environmental Critique of Adverse Possession,* 79 Cornell L. Rev. 816, 843–844 (1994).

3. *See* Mary E. Young, *Congress Looks West: Liberal Ideology and Public Land Policy in the Nineteenth Century, in The Frontier in American Development,* 74, 110 (David M. Ellis ed., 1969).

4. *See* Gates, *supra* note 1, at 145.

5. *See* Daniel Feller, *The Public Lands in Jacksonian Politics* 77 (1984); Young, *supra* note 3, at 79; Donald J. Pisani, *The Squatter and Natural Law in Nineteenth-Century America,* 81 *Agricultural Hist.* 443 (2007). David Schorr has found a similar resort to moral claims in his examination of the origins of frontier water laws. David B. Schorr, *Appropriation and Agrarianism: Distributive Justice in the Creation of Property Rights,* 32 Ecology L.Q. 3, 25–33 (2005).

6. Gregory H. Nobles, *Breaking into the Backcountry,* 46 Wm. & Mary Q., 3d ser. 642, 655 (1989) (quoting a 1798 pamphlet by Maine settler and pamphleteer James Shurtleff).

7. Paul Wallace Gates, *The Wisconsin Pine Lands of Cornell University: A Study in Land Policy and Absentee Ownership* 74 (1943).

8. *See* Gates, *supra* note 1, at 219.

9. *See id.* and Paul W. Gates, *Landlords and Tenants on the Prairie Frontier: Studies in American Land Policy* (1973), on the treatment of public lands during this period.

10. In March 1804, Congress enacted a statute authorizing the army forcibly to eject squatters from public lands and imposing severe fines and even imprisonment on squatters. *See* Act of Mar. 26, 1804, 2 Stat. 283. In 1807, as the squatter problem continued unabated, Congress made the penalties even more severe. *See* Act of Mar. 3, 1807, 2 Stat. 445, 445–446. The consequences of this legislation are discussed in Gates, *supra* note 1.

11. Act of Mar. 26, 1804, 2 Stat. 289.

12. Alfred Brunson, *A Methodist Circuit Rider's Horseback Tour from Pennsylvania to Wisconsin, 1835, quoted in* Gates, *supra* note 1, at 154.

13. *See* Gates, *supra* note 1, at 145–56, 161, 164; Richard White, *"It's Your Misfortune and None of My Own": A History of the American West* 140–142 (1991). White comments, "Such extralegal modifications changed the [land] system more effectively than legal changes could have done." *Id.* at 141–142.

14. Gates, *supra* note 1, at 223.

15. Feller, *supra* note 5, at 17.

16. Cong. Globe, 25th Cong., 1st Sess., 142–143, app. at 134 (1838) (statement of Senator Henry Clay) (quoted in Gates, *supra* note 1, at 233).

17. *See* 8 Reg. Debates 2268–2271 (1832).

18. Gates, *supra* note 7, at 68.

19. *See* Gates, *supra* note 1, at 173, 220; Henry Cohen, *Vicissitudes of an Absentee Landlord, in The Frontier in American Development, supra* note 3, at 192, 215.

20. Arthur J. Larson, *Crusader and Feminist: Letters of Jane Grey Swisshelm* 153 (1934).

21. Gates, *supra* note 7, at 68.

22. Cong. Globe, 31st Cong., 2d Sess. 442 (1851) (statement of Senator George Jones) (quoted in Gates, *supra* note 7, at 69).

23. Cong. Globe, 31st Cong., 2d Sess. 1251–1253 (1850) (statement of Senator Jim Lane) (quoted in Gates, *supra* note 9, at 156).

24. *See* Gates, *supra* note 9, at 108–110.

25. *See* Gates, *supra* note 1, at 235.

26. Cohen, *supra* note 19, at 202.

27. *See* Gates, *supra* note 1, at 267.

28. For discussion of tax titles and their significance for absentee-owned property, see Gates, *supra* note 1, at 267–268; Gates, *supra* note 9, at 23–25, 42–47; and Cohen, *supra* note 19, at 201–202.

29. *See* Cohen, *supra* note 19, at 203. Cohen notes that absentee owners took great care to stay out of state courts, which often sympathized with local settlers.

30. *See* Gates, *supra* note 9, at 30–40.

31. Gates, *supra* note 7, at 86.

32. *See, e.g.,* Morton J. Horwitz, *The Transformation of American Law 1780–1860* (1977); Sprankling, *supra* note 2, at 844.

33. *See* John G. Sprankling, *The Antiwilderness Bias in American Property Law,* 63 U. Chi. L. Rev. 519, 538–540 (1996); Sprankling, *supra* note 2, at 816. Sprankling argues that nineteenth-century Colorado law was designed to favor the "actual settler" over "absentee speculators and corporations controlled by eastern and European investors." *Id.* at 816. Schorr contends that the modern doctrine of adverse possession evolved as part of a "predevelopment nineteenth-century ideology that encourages and legitimates economic exploitation." Schorr, *supra* note 5, at 25–26.

34. *See, e.g.,* 3 *American Law of Property* § 15.1, at 755 (1952); Percy Bordwell, *Disseisin and Adverse Possession,* 33 Yale L.J. 10 n.78 (1923) (observing that the majority position is not to require good faith on the part of the adverse possessor). This point has no bearing, and is not affected by, the well-known debate between R. H. Helmholz and Roger Cunningham over the significance of good faith in modern adverse-possession case law. *See* R. H. Helmholz, *Adverse Possession and Subjective Intent,* 61 Wash. U. L.Q. 331 (1983) [hereinafter Helmholz, *Subjective Intent*]; Roger A. Cunningham, *Adverse Possession and Subjective Intent: A Reply to Professor Helmholz,* 64 Wash. U. L.Q. 1 (1986); R. H. Helmholz, *More on Subjective Intent: A Response to Professor Cunningham,* 64 Wash U. L.Q. 65 (1986). Even assuming that Helmholz is correct that subjective intent has become a relevant inquiry in adverse-possession cases, he limits his claims to "recent cases" published between 1966 and 1983. Helmholz, *Subjective Intent, supra,* at 332–333. Nothing in his analysis casts doubt on the accuracy of the

scholarly consensus that the "older cases" unanimously agreed that the "'claim of right' [necessary for an adverse possessor to prevail] is equally efficacious whether it is asserted in 'good faith' or 'bad faith.'" Cunningham, *supra*, at 23.

35. *See* William Sternberg, *The Element of Hostility in Adverse Possession*, 6 Temp. L.Q. 207, 213 (1932). The principal alternative to the Maine rule was not a rule requiring that the adverse possessor occupy the land in good faith, but rather the so-called Connecticut rule, which holds that the adverse possessor's state of mind is irrelevant to the adverse-possession inquiry. *Id*. at 214–215.

36. For discussion of Maine public lands and squatters' claims before and after Maine's break from Massachusetts, see Frederick J. Allis Jr., *The Maine Frontier, in A History of Maine: A Collection of Readings on the History of Maine 1600–1976* 141, 142, 149 (Ronald F. Banks ed., 4th ed. 1976). See also Alan Taylor, *Liberty Men and Great Proprietors* (1990), for a comprehensive history of squatter resistance against landowners in the years leading up to Maine's break from Massachusetts.

37. David C. Smith, *Maine and its Public Domain, in The Frontier in American Development, supra* note 3, at 114, 119–122 (describing Maine's efforts to lure settlers to its northern frontier and the limiting effects of absentee ownership on its population growth).

38. Gates, *supra* note 1, at 268.

39. *Id*. at 175.

40. *Id*.

41. For an account of this shift in federal policy through successive presidential administrations, see *id*. at 129, 162, 175, 225, 236. Gates notes that Congress enacted twenty-four special preemption acts before 1820 and fifteen between 1820 and 1837, all of which were retroactive in effect. *Id*. at 129, 162, 225.

4. Expressive Outlaws: Civil Rights Sit-Ins

1. John Lewis with Michael D'Orso, *Walking with the Wind: A Memoir of the Movement* 114 (1998); *see also* Robert Weisbrot, *Freedom Bound: A History of America's Civil Rights Movement* 37 (1998) (noting that "since its founding in 1910," the NAACP and its "predominantly middle-class, professional leadership had fought its most protracted struggles in court chambers and congressional anterooms").

2. *See* Aldon D. Morris, *The Origins of the Civil Rights Movement: Black Communities Organizing for Change* 188–194 (1984). The Greensboro sit-ins were not the first time intentional trespass had been employed in the civil rights movement. Civil rights groups had experimented with the tactic a generation earlier. Clusters of sit-ins also had erupted during the 1950s, albeit without the national media attention that catapulted the Greensboro sit-ins to iconic status. The earlier sit-ins had established the property right of owners to exclude selectively on the basis of race. *See, e.g., Solicitor Says Race Incidents Unnecessary*, Greensboro Daily News, Feb. 10 1960, at A4 (describing a 1957 sit-in at a North Carolina ice-cream parlor). The Greensboro sit-ins were different both because of the national attention they received and because, as a consequence of that attention, they inspired countless sit-ins across the South in the

weeks that followed. *See, e.g., First Sitdown Staged in Deep South,* Greensboro Daily News, Feb. 26, 1960, at A3; *Negroes' Protests Still Spreading,* Greensboro Daily News, Feb. 12, 1960, at A10.

3. *See* Jack M. Bloom, *Class, Race, and the Civil Rights Movement* 159 (1987); Lewis, *supra* note 1, at 93–107.

4. *See, e.g.,* Morris, *supra* note 2, at 197 ("In the South during the 1950s segregation laws prohibited blacks and whites from eating together.").

5. *See Bell v. Maryland,* 378 U.S. 226, 271–78 (1964) (Douglas, J., concurring) (providing a review of cases where "the testimony of corporate officers shows that the reason [for segregation] was either a commercial one or, which amounts to the same thing, that service to Negroes was not in accord with local custom").

6. William H. Chafe, *Civilities & Civil Rights: Greensboro, North Carolina, and the Black Struggle for Freedom* 116 (1980) (quoting a protestor).

7. *Id.* at 139.

8. Bloom, *supra* note 3, at 171.

9. *Id.* at 172; *see also* Chafe, *supra* note 6, at 117 n.* ("The national NAACP criticized the sit-in tactic and refused legal or moral support for some time."); Morris, *supra* note 2, at 198 ("The national office of the NAACP and many conservative ministers refused to back the Greensboro sit-ins.").

10. Mary L. Dudziak, *Working towards Democracy: Thurgood Marshall and the Constitution of Kenya,* 56 Duke L.J. 763–764 (2006) (quoting Derrick Bell, *An Epistolary Exploration for a Thurgood Marshall Biography,* 6 Harv. BlackLetter L.J. 51, 55 (1989)).

11. Chafe, *supra* note 6, at 120.

12. Guy Munger, *Sit-In Protests Are Assailed by Governor,* Greensboro Daily News, Mar. 11 1960, at A1.

13. Weisbrot, *supra* note 1, at 24.

14. 106 Cong. Rec. 4, 5211 (1960)

15. 106 Cong. Rec. 6, 7764 (1960).

16. *See, e.g.,* Eugene A. Hood, Letter to the Editor, *Police Protection,* Greensboro Daily News, Feb. 15, 1960, at A6 (condemning the Greensboro police for failing to enforce property rights in the face of sit-ins); W. N. Jefferies, Letter to the Editor, *It Is Disgusting,* Greensboro Daily News, Mar. 18, 1960, at A8 ("It is disgusting that the white citizens of the State of North Carolina will even consider 'negotiations' with these arrogant lawbreakers and trespassers who are ruining private businesses."); Letter to the Editor, *A Christian Movement?,* Greensboro Daily News, Feb. 17, 1960, at A8 (calling the sit-in participants "covetous," "selfish," and unchristian); Marian S. Patterson, Letter to the Editor, *Work of the Devil,* Greensboro Daily News, Feb. 22, 1960, at A4 (calling sit-in participants "rioters" and the sit-ins "the work of the devil"); Readsville Reader, Letter to the Editor, *Lost a Friend?,* Greensboro Daily News, Feb. 18, 1960, at A6 ("Those seeking equal rights at the lunch counter, in my opinion, went about it in a way of the belligerent.").

17. T. W. Chandler, Letter to the Editor, *Un-American?,* Greensboro Daily News, Feb. 24, 1960, at A8; *see also id.* ("Those who show so much concern about the rights of the invaders of private property apparently have no concern whatsoever about the

rights of those who own property, which to me is a strange, un-American and unchristian attitude.").

18. *See, e.g.*, Miles Wolff, *Lunch at the Five and Ten: The Greensboro Sit-Ins: A Contemporary History* 82 (1970) (noting that "the editorial pages of [local papers] supported the students, although not without some reservations"); Editorial, *Of Civil Rights and Civilities,* Greensboro Daily News, Mar. 2, 1960, at A6 ("Somewhere a Southern community must find a way to deal with civilities as well as civil rights. Such an answer will not be found while the management is under the gun. It will be found only where both sides are able to sit down and work out an answer unimpeded by the threat of force or the worry of economic reprisal.").

19. Editorial, *Lunch Counters and Private Property,* Greensboro Daily News, April 23, 1960, at A6.

20. Wolff, *supra* note 18, at 115 (quoting Harry Truman).

21. President's News Conference on Domestic and Foreign Matters (Mar. 16, 1960), *in* N.Y. Times, Mar. 17, 1960, at 16.

22. *See, e.g., 26 Sitdowners Given Suspended Sentences,* Greensboro Daily News, April 5, 1960, at A5; *43 Students Convicted in Raleigh,* Greensboro Daily News, Mar. 29, 1960, at A1; *Judge Finds 22 Guilty of Sitdown Trespass,* Greensboro Daily News, Mar. 3, 1960, at A1; *Two Sentenced for Trespassing,* Greensboro Daily News, April 27, 1960, at A4.

23. *Negroes Plan Tests on Legal Fronts,* N.Y. Times, Mar. 20, 1960, at E8; *see also Anti-Sitdown Bills Passed,* Greensboro Daily News, Feb. 25, 1960, at B14 (describing three trespassing bills passed by the Virginia Senate prohibiting "any person who has been forbidden to do so from going into or staying on property" after they had been given notice).

24. For accounts of judicial and law-enforcement responses to the protests, see Morris, *supra* note 2, and Weisbrot, *supra* note 1. For example, Morris describes Judge J. Robert Elliott's "sweeping injunction, which barred Albany's Negroes from unlawful picketing, congregating or marching in the streets, and from any act designed to promote breaches of the peace." Morris, *supra* note 2, at 247. Weisbrot refers to the "use of chains, knives, and attack dogs" to quiet antisegregation protesters. Weisbrot, *supra* note 1, at 39. See also *Stricter Laws of Trespass Approved,* Greensboro Daily News, Feb. 26, 1960, at A3, which describes legislation enacted in response to the protests, stating, "[The laws] would protect the rights of the private property owner to conduct his business as he might legally choose. . . . The property owner could serve either or both races segregated or integrated as he saw fit."

25. *See Bell v. Maryland,* 378 U.S. 226, 271–278 (1964) (Douglas, J., concurring) (listing refusals by several companies in southern communities to serve blacks at their lunch counters).

26. Arthur I. Waskow, *From Race Riot to Sit-In, 1919 and the 1960s: A Study in the Connections between Conflict and Violence* 228 (1966).

27. Our description of the movement's accomplishments draws on accounts in Weisbrot, *supra* note 1, at 39; Wolff, *supra* note 18, at 167–173; Morris, *supra* note 2, at 272; and *Lunch-Counter Mixing Is Voted in Winston,* Greensboro Daily News, May 24, 1960, at A1.

28. *See* Chafe, *supra* note 6, at 61 (describing Greensboro school board chairman John Foster's belief that most blacks were also doubtful about the merits of integration).

29. *See* Wolff, *supra* note 18, at 66–67; *see also* T. F. Webster, Letter to the Editor, *Folly of Their Ways,* Greensboro Daily News, Apr. 4, 1960, at A8 ("Although these demonstrating students steadfastly declare this to be a spontaneous move, I am inclined to believe they have been indoctrinated, brainwashed and regimented by Negro leaders of their race from the pulpit on down through many organizations, mostly originating in the North.").

30. James E. Brown Sr., Letter to the Editor, *An Injustice,* Greensboro Daily News, Feb. 27, 1960, at A6.

31. *See* Chafe, *supra* note 6, at 79 ("The notion of an angry white crowd about to rebel appears to have been as much a political creation of [North Carolina Governor Luther] Hodges as a fearsome social reality.").

32. *Stores Begin Desegregated Lunch Service,* Greensboro Daily News, May 26, 1960, at A1.

33. Wolff, *supra* note 18, at 150.

34. Lewis, *supra* note 1, at 108.

35. Morris, *supra* note 2, at 267.

36. Clifford M. Lytle, *The History of the Civil Rights Bill of 1964,* 51 J. Negro Hist. 275, 282–283 (1966).

37. *See* Weisbrot, *supra* note 1, at 45, 87 (noting that "Kennedy's presidency—and his martyrdom—had made civil rights an issue no successor could safely defuse").

38. Civil Rights Act of 1964, Pub. L. No. 88-352, tit. 2, § 201, 78 Stat. 241, 243.

39. Lytle, *supra* note 36, at 285.

40. *See* Waskow, *supra* note 26, at 231.

5. Property Outlaws and Property Altlaws

1. Alexandra Samuel, Hacktivism and the Future of Political Participation 165 (Sept. 2004) (unpublished Ph.D. dissertation, Harvard University), *available at* http://www.alexandrasamuel.com/dissertation/pdfs/Samuel-Hacktivism-entire.pdf.

2. *See Universal Studios, Inc. v. Corley,* 273 F.3d 429, 437–438 (2d Cir. 2001).

3. Samuel, *supra* note 1, at 166.

4. *See Universal Studios,* 273 F.3d at 439.

5. *See DVD Copy Control Ass'n v. Bunner,* 116 Cal. App. 4th 241, 248 (Ct. App. 2004).

6. *Id.* at 247.

7. *Universal Studios,* 273 F.3d at 439.

8. *See* 17 U.S.C. § 1201(a)–(b) (2000) (anticircumvention provisions); *Universal Studios,* 273 F.3d at 441.

9. *DVD Copy Control Ass'n v. Bunner,* 75 P.3d 1, 8 (Cal. 2003) (quoting trial court's order for a preliminary injunction).

10. *DVD Copy Control Ass'n v. Bunner,* 116 Cal. App. 4th 241, 248 (Ct. App. 2004).

11. *Universal Studios, Inc. v. Corley,* 273 F.3d 429, 441 (2d Cir. 2001).

12. *See* Gallery of CSS Descramblers, http://www.cs.cmu.edu/~dst/DeCSS/Gallery (last visited Mar. 21, 2008).

13. *Universal City Studios, Inc. v. Reimerdes,* 111 F. Supp. 2d 294, 345. (S.D.N.Y. 2000).

14. *Universal Studios, Inc. v. Corley,* 273 F. 3d 429, 457 (2d Cir. 2001).

15. Writing about the decision on Findlaw.com, journalist Julie Hilden dryly observed, "We should think long and hard about whether it makes sense, under the First Amendment, to make journalists liable for 'trafficking' in code upon which they comment, or to which they link. In the past, we have used loose concepts of trafficking to go after drug dealers and those who make their living from stolen goods. Journalists, even those on the web, are a far cry from these malfeasors." Julie Hilden, *The Dubious Logic of Prohibiting Journalists from Posting or Even Linking to Code that Circumvents Copyright Protection Measures,* FindLaw, Dec. 13, 2001, http://writ.news.findlaw.com /hilden/20011213.html.

16. Although the industry subpoenaed about five hundred other individuals, including a T-shirt maker, Bunner was one of only three people who actually answered the subpoena, believing that he had done nothing wrong. *See* Susan Kuchinskas, *Calif. Court Rules Against DVD Code Poster,* internet news.com, Aug. 26, 2003, http://www .internetnews.com/ent-news/article.php/3069011.

17. *See DVD Copy Control Ass'n v. Bunner,* 75 P.3d 1 (Cal. 2003).

18. *DVD Copy Control Ass'n v. Bunner,* 10 Cal. Rptr. 3d. 185, 193 (Ct. App. 2004).

19. *See* Nina Berglund, *Prosecutors Let DVD-Jon's Victory Stand,* Aftenposten, Jan. 5, 2004, http://www.aftenposten.no/english/local/article702236.ece; Nina Berglund, *DVD-Jon Wins New Legal Victory,* Aftenposten, Dec. 22, 2005, http://www.aften posten.no/english/local/article696330.ece.

20. Robert M. Cover, *The Supreme Court 1982 Term—Foreword:* Nomos *and Narrative,* 97 Harv. L. Rev. 4, 45 (1983).

21. Mark A. Lemley, *Reply—What's Different about Intellectual Property?,* 83 Tex. L. Rev. 1097, 1100–1101 & n.9 (2005) (citing Dan L. Burk and Mark A. Lemley, *Quantum Patent Mechanics* 9 Lewis & Clark L. Rev. 29, 33 (2005)).

22. 334 U.S. 1 (1948); *see also* Christopher W. Schmidt, The Sit-Ins and the Failed State Action Revolution (Dec. 8, 2008) (unpublished manuscript, on file with authors).

23. *See, e.g., Black v. Cutter Laboratories,* 351 U.S. 291 (1956).

24. *Cf.* Martin Luther King Jr., Letter from a Birmingham Jail (Apr. 16, 1963), *in I Have a Dream: Writings and Speeches That Changed the World* 83 (James M Washington ed., 1992).

25. Dimitri Skylarov and his employer, Elcomsoft, were famously targeted by criminal authorities for creating a program, "The Advanced eBook Processor," that enabled owners of an Adobe eBook to translate the format from a secure version into a more common format, the portable document format (PDF) by unlocking its encrypted content. In the end, the government lost its case, however. Merely selling a program that could be used to violate copyright protection was not enough to show that they had "willfully" intended to violate the law. *See* Free Dmitry Skylarov!, http://www.free sklyarov.org (last visited Mar. 21, 2008); Lisa M. Bowman, *ElcomSoft Verdict: Not*

Guilty, CNET News, Dec. 17, 2002, http://www.news.com/2100-1023-978176 .html; Alex Salkever, *Digital Copyright: A Law Defanged?,* BusinessWeek, Dec. 19, 2002, http: //www.businessweek.com/technology/content/dec2002/tc20021219 _4518.htm. A copy of the indictment is available at http://cryptome.org/dmitry-indict.htm (last visited Mar. 21, 2008).

26. Lawrence Liang and Achal Prabhala, *Reconsidering the Pirate Nation: Notes from South Africa and India,* InfoChange News and Features, Nov. 2006, http://info changeindia.org/200611096076/Trade-Development/Intellectual-Property-Rights/Reconsidering-the-pirate-nation-Notes-from-South-Africa-and-India.html (quoting Lawrence Lessig, *Free Culture* (2004)). For a related approach, see Rebecca Tushnet, *Copy This Essay: How Fair Use Doctrine Harms Free Speech and How Copying Serves It,* 114 Yale L. J. 535 (2004).

27. *See* Ravi Sundaram, *Recycling Modernity: Pirate Electronic Cultures in India, in Sarai Reader 01: The Public Domain* 93 (Shudhabrata Sengupta and Geert Lovink eds., 2001), *available at* http://www.sarai.net/publications/readers/01-the-public-domain /093-099piracy.pdf.

28. *See* Raqs Media Collective, *X Notes on Practice: Stubborn Structures and Insistent Seepage in a Networked World, in DATA browser02: Engineering Culture* 209, 220 (Geoff Cox and Joasia Krysa eds., 2005), *available at* http://www.data-browser.net/ 02/DB02/Raqs2.pdf.

29. Lawrence Liang, *Porous Legalities and Avenues of Participation, in Sarai Reader 05: Bare Acts* 6, 10–11 (Monica Narula et al. eds., 2005), *available at* http://www .sarai.net/publications/readers/05-bare-acts/02_lawrence.pdf.

30. McKenzie Wark, *A Hacker Manifesto,* 176 (2004).

31. *See, e.g.,* Hakim Bey, *The Temporary Autonomous Zone, Ontological Anarchy, Poetic Terrorism* (1991), *available at* http://www.hermetic.com/bey/taz_cont.html.

32. For an excellent discussion, *see* Samuel, *supra* note 1, at 2 (citing Dorothy E. Denning, *Activism, Hacktivism, and Cyberterrorism: The Internet as a Tool for Influencing Foreign Policy, in Networks and Netwars: The Future of Terror, Crime, and Militancy* 239, 241 (John Arquilla and David F. Ronfeldt eds., 1999)).

33. *Id.* at 41 (quoting Steven Levy, *Hackers: Heroes of the Computer Revolution* 40 (1984)).

34. *Id.* at 2 (citing Dorothy E. Denning, *Activism, Hacktivism, and Cyberterrorism: The Internet as a Tool for Influencing Foreign Policy, in Networks and Netwars: The Future of Terror, Crime, and Militancy* 239, 241 (John Arquilla and David F. Ronfeldt eds., 1999)).

35. *Id.* at 2 (quoting Tim Jordan and Paul A. Taylor, *Hacktivism: Informational Politics for Informational Times* (2004)).

36. *Id.* at 51.

37. Wark, *supra* note 30, at 20, 21 (citing Arthur Kroker and Michael A. Weinstein, *Data Trash: The Theory of the Virtual Class* 6 (1994)).

38. *Id.* at 32.

39. *Id.* at 176.

40. *Id.* at 36.

41. *Id.* at 253.

42. Brian Martin, *Information Liberation* 33, 53 (1998), *available at* http://www
.uow.edu.au/arts/sts/bmartin/pubs/98il/ilo3.pdf.

43. *See* Quinn Norton, *Secrets of the Pirate Bay,* Wired, Aug. 16, 2006, http://www
.wired.com/science/discoveries/news/2006/08/71543.

44. *Id.*

45. Wikipedia, Pirate Party, http://en.wikipedia.org/wiki/Pirate_Party (last visited Mar. 18, 2008).

46. Press Release, Motion Picture Association of America, Swedish Authorities Sink
Pirate Bay (May 31, 2006), *available at* http://www.mpaa.org/press_releases/2006
_05_31.pdf.

47. Norton, *supra* note 43.

48. *See* Eric Pfanner, *Four Convicted in Sweden in Internet Piracy Case,* N.Y. Times,
Apr. 18, 2009, at B2.

49. *Id.*

50. *See* Kristin R. Eschenfelder et al., *The Ethics of DeCSS Posting,* Info. Res., July
2006, http://informationr.net/ir/11-4/paper273.html (drawing a similar distinction).

6. Acquisitive Altlaws: The Treatment Action Campaign, Patents, and Public Health

1. James Thuo Gathii has written eloquently and at great length on this topic in the
context of public health. *See, e.g.,* James Thuo Gathii, *Rights, Patents, Markets, and the
Global AIDS Pandemic,* 14 Fla. J. Int'l. L. 261, 276 (2002); James Thuo Gathi, *The Legal Status of the Doha Declaration on TRIPS and Public Health Under the Vienna Con-
vention on the Law of Treaties,* 15 Harv. J.L. & Tech. 291 (2002).

2. 383 U.S. 519, 534 (1966).

3. *See* Michael A. Carrier, *Cabining Intellectual Property through a Property Paradigm,* 54 Duke L.J. 1, 45 (2004) ("Money that would have remained in the pockets of
consumers, had the work been priced at the level at which the marginal cost of producing it equaled the demand for it, will now go into the pocket of the copyright or patent
holder." (quoting William W. Fisher III, *Reconstructing the Fair Use Domain,* 101
Harv. L. Rev. 1659, 1701–1702 (1988))).

4. Christopher S. Yoo, *Copyright and Product Differentiation,* 79 N.Y.U. L. Rev.
212, 230 (2004).

5. For a discussion of this view, see Amy Kapczynski, *The Access to Knowledge Mo-
bilization and the New Politics of Intellectual Property,* 117 Yale L.J. 804, 828 (2008).

6. *See* Debora Halbert, *Globalized Resistance to Intellectual Property* (2005),
http://globalization.icaap.org/content/v5.2/halbert.html.

7. *Id.*

8. *See* Tshimanga Kongolo, *Public Interest versus the Pharmaceutical Industry's
Monopoly in South Africa,* 4 J. World Intell. Prop. 609, 611 (2001) (quoting the Medicines and Related Substances Control Amendment Act 90 of 1997).

9. *See* Medicines and Related Substances Control Amendment Act 90 of 1997,

available at http://www.info.gov.za/view/DownloadFileAction?id570836. For an excellent, thoughtful summary of how TAC successfully merged grassroots work with judicial challenges in South Africa, see Ronen Shamir, *Corporate Responsibility and the South African Drug Wars: Outline of a New Frontier for Cause Lawyers, in The World Cause Lawyers Make* 39 (Austin Sarat and Stuart A. Scheingold eds., 2005).

10. *Id.* at 39–40.

11. *See* Donald G. McNeil Jr., *South Africa's Bitter Pill for World's Drug Makers,* N.Y. Times Mar. 29, 1998, § 3, at 1.

12. *Id.*

13. *Id.*

14. *Id.*

15. *Id.*

16. *See, e.g.,* Kongolo, *supra* note 8 (discussing the specific provisions of the 1997 act, specifically section 15C, which provides measures to ensure the supply of more affordable medicines, section 22F, which addresses the role of pharmacists, section 22C, which contains licensing provisions, and section 22G, which addresses pricing matters).

17. *See* Jayashree Watal, *Pharmaceutical Patents, Prices, and Welfare Losses: Policy Options for India under the WTO TRIPS Agreement,* 23 *World Economy* 733 (2000) (observing that compulsory licensing is expected to be used in rare occasions); Carlos Correa, *Integrating Public Health Concerns into Patent Legislation in Developing Countries* 94 (2002) (citing UNAIDS at 2 (1999)), *available at* http://www.southcentre.org/index.php?option=com_content&task=view&id=69&Itemid=67.

18. *See* Correa, *supra* note 17, at 79–80.

19. Agreement on Trade-Related Aspects of Intellectual Property Rights art. 8; *see also id.* art. 27, 31. To invoke the compulsory licensing provision, a country was required, among other things, to make efforts to obtain authorization from the patent holder and to provide for "adequate renumeration."

20. *See* Duane Nash, *South Africa's Medicines and Related Substances Control Act of 1997,* 15 Berkeley Tech L.J. 485, 487 (2000) (discussing provisions).

21. *See* U.S. Department of State, *U.S. Government Efforts to Negotiate the Repeal, Termination, or Withdrawal of Article 15(c) of the South African Medicines and Related Substances Act of 1965* (1999), available at http://www.cptech.org/ip/health/sa/stdept-feb51999.html.

22. *See* Shamir, *supra* note 9, at 42.

23. McNeil, *supra* note 11.

24. *See* Shamir, *supra* note 9, at 42 (citing *U.S. State Department on U.S. Efforts to Negotiate the Repeal, Suspension, or Termination of South African Law on Essential Medicines,* IPHealth, Apr. 9, 1999, http://lists.essential.org/info-policy-notes/msg00013.html).

25. *See id.* at 42 (citing Letter from Sir Leon Brittan, Vice President of the European Commission, to Thabo Mbeki, Vice President of South Africa (Mar. 23, 1998)).

26. *See, e.g.,* Sheryl Gay Stolberg, *Africa's AIDS War,* N.Y. Times, Mar. 10, 2001, at

A1; Rachel A. Swarns, *Drug Makers Drop South Africa Suit over Aids Medicine,* N.Y. Times, April 20, 2001, at A1.

27. *See* Applicant's Notice of Motion, *Pharm. Mfrs. Ass'n of South Africa v. President of the Republic of South Africa,* No. 4183/98 (S. Afr. Feb. 18, 1998), *available at* http://www.cptech.org/ip/health/sa/pharmasuit.html.

28. *See* Shamir, *supra* note 9, at 40.

29. *See, e.g.,* Editorial, *Drugs for Aids in Africa,* N.Y. Times, Aug. 23, 1999, at A24 ("While defending intellectual property is important, the narrowness of the Administration's views is dismaying. Pharmaceutical companies would lose little if they found legal and controllable ways to let poor countries—which offer scant markets anyway—reproduce drugs or buy them cheaply.").

30. *See* Steven Lee Myers, *South Africa and U.S. End Dispute over Drugs,* N.Y. Times, Sept. 18, 1999, at A8.

31. *See* Donald G. McNeil Jr., *As Devastating Epidemics Increase, Nations Take on Drug Companies,* N.Y. Times, July 9, 2000, http://partners.nytimes.com/library/world/global/070900drug-prices.html.

32. Samantha Power, *The AIDS Rebel; An Activist Fights Drug Companies, the Government, and His Own Illness,* New Yorker, May 19, 2003, at 54 (quoting Zackie Achmat).

33. *See id.* at 56.

34. *Id.*

35. *See* Jordi Trullen and William B. Stevenson, *Strategy and Legitimacy: Pharmaceutical Companies' Reaction to the HIV Crisis,* 45 Bus. & Soc'y 178, 187 (2006).

36. Apparently, Pfizer had authorized distribution only for patients who suffered from cryptococcal meningitis, and not systemic thrush, which is the more common disease faced by HIV-positive individuals. *See* TAC, Defiance Campaign Intro, http://www.tac.org.za/Documents/DefianceCampaign/defiancecampaign.htm (last visited Mar. 10, 2008).

37. *See* Sanjay Basu, *Punting Patents: Drug Smuggling and the War over Generic Medicines,* Thistle, June–July 2001, http://web.mit.edu/thistle/www/v13/4/drugs.html.

38. *Defying the Drug Cartel: The South African Campaign for Access to Essential Medicines, an Interview with Zachie Achmat* [hereinafter *Interview with Zachie Achmat*], Multinational Monitor, Jan.–Feb. 2001, *available at* http://www.multinationalmonitor.org/mm2001/01jan-feb/interview.html.

39. *Id.*

40. *See* TAC, *supra* note 36.

41. *See, e.g.,* D.S.K. Culhane, *No Easy Talk: South Africa and the Suppression of Political Speech,* 17 Fordham Int'l L.J. 896, 903 (1994) (discussing South Africa's nationwide defiance campaign).

42. *See Interview with Zachie Achmat, supra* note 38.

43. *See* Power, *supra* note 32.

44. *See* Tony Karon, *South African AIDS Activist Zackie Achmat,* Time, Apr. 19, 2001, http://www.time.com/time/pow/article/0,8599,106995,00.html.

45. Press Release, TAC, TAC Announces the Christopher Moraka Defiance Campaign against Patent Abuse (Oct. 17, 2000), *available at* http://lists.essential.org/pipermail/ip-health/2000-October/000566.html.

46. John S. James, *South Africa: Historic "Defiance Campaign" Imports Generic Fluconazole-Treatment Action Committee Imports Fluconazole for HIV Treatment,* Bnet Business Network, Oct. 20, 2000, http://findarticles.com/p/articles/mi_mo HSW/is_2000_Oct_20/ai_68872348/print.

47. *See* Karon, *supra* note 44.

48. *See* Power, *supra* note 32; *see also* Judith Soal, *Rebels Show Smuggled Drugs Cost R100 Less,* IOL, Oct. 17, 2000, http://www.iol.co.za/index.php?click_id=79&art_id =ct20001017215504113D625260.

49. *Interview with Zachie Achmat, supra* note 38.

50. Basu, *supra* note 37 (quoting Zachie Achmat).

51. *See Interview with Zachie Achmat, supra* note 38.

52. Judith Soal, *Actor from Save our Souls Is "Saving" Role with HIV Tablets,* Cape Times, Jan. 15, 2001, *available at* http://lists.essential.org/pipermail/ip-health/2001-January/000772.html.

53. *See* Power, *supra* note 32.

54. *See* Karon, *supra* note 44.

55. *See Interview with Zachie Achmat, supra* note 38.

56. *See* Shamir, *supra* note 9, at 44.

57. Naomi A. Bass, Note, *Implications of the TRIPS Agreement for Developing Countries: Pharmaceutical Patent Laws in Brazil and South Africa in the 21st Century,* 34 Geo. Wash. Int'l L. Rev. 191, 212–213 (2002).

58. *Id.*

59. Swarns, *supra* note 26.

60. *See* Press Release, Médecins Sans Frontières et al., Generic AIDS Drugs Offer New Lease on Life to South Africans: Importation of Generics Cuts Price in Half (Jan. 29, 2002), *available at* http://www.tac.org.za/community/node/2484.

61. TAC, Questions and Answers about TAC and MSF Importing Generic Medicines from Brazil, http://www.tac.org.za/documents/DefianceCampaign/Q_A_ImportBrazil.htm (last visited May 10, 2009).

62. *Groups Import Generic Drugs into South Africa, Flouting Patent Laws,* U.N. Wire, Jan. 30, 2002, http://www.unwire.org/unwire/20020130/23423_story.asp. TAC decided to mount a formal campaign of civil disobedience to draw attention to the need for treatment, and the group organized a series of high-profile protests. *See* Power, *supra* note 32. Although TAC suspended the campaign after receiving assurances from the government that a treatment plan would soon be forthcoming, it voted to restart the campaign a year later, in February 2003, after the government failed to move forward in developing a comprehensive plan. Over ten thousand people marched on the opening of parliament to demand access to antiretrovirals. Toward the year's end, the government once again changed its position and began distributing the medicines. *See* Robert J. Thomson, Identity Politics in South Africa: Lessons from the Peo-

ple 11 (Mar. 14, 2006) (unpublished manuscript), *available at* http://www.nu.ac.za/ccs/files/Identity%20politics%20revised%20RJT%202006%2003%2014.pdf.

63. *See* Jane Galvão, *Access to Antiretroviral Drugs in Brazil*, 360 Lancet 1862, 1862 (2002), *available at* http://image.thelancet.com/extras/01art9038web.pdf; Pascual Ortells, *Brazil's Response to AIDS: A Model for the South,* Cooperation South, 2003, at 63; Indira A. R. Lakshaman, *Drug Costs Imperil Brazil AIDS Fight,* Boston Globe, Jan. 3, 2007, at A1 (discussing Brazil's success).

64. Constituição Federal art. 196 (right to health).

65. *See* Jillian Clare Cohen and Kristina M. Lybecker, *AIDS Policy and Pharmaceutical Patents: Brazil's Strategy to Safeguard Public Health,* 28 World Economy 211, 213 (2005).

66. *See id.* at 212.

67. *See* Jorge Bermudez et al., Access to Drugs, the WTO TRIPS Agreement, and Patent Protection in Brazil: Trends, Perspectives, and Recommendations to Help Find Our Way 212 (Feb. 9, 2002) (unpublished paper, on file with authors). The agreement entered into force in January 1995, with a timeline of eleven years till full implementation, and makes patent protection mandatory for all inventions that meet its subject-matter requirements, with few exceptions. *Id.*

68. Ortells, *supra* note 63, at 65. Some of the remaining drugs were already being produced domestically, since Brazil had begun manufacturing them before it decided to comply with TRIPS. *Id.* at 63.

69. Presidential Decree No. 3.201 of Oct. 6, 1999, *available at* http://www.wipo.int/clea/en/details.jsp?id=516.

70. Cohen and Lybecker, *supra* note 65, at 219.

71. Ortells, *supra* note 63 (quoting Brazil's response).

72. Press Release, TAC et al., "Discrimination in Media Reporting on Brazil," Say NGOs (Aug. 31, 2000), *available at* http://www.healthgap.org/press_releases/01/030501_MOT_PS_BRA_CL_Nelf.html.

73. Cohen and Lybecker, *supra* note 65, at 220. Indeed, Brazil represented one of the top ten markets for pharmaceuticals in the world. *Id.*

74. *Id.*

75. *Id.* (citing Miriam Jordan, *Brazil to Break Roche's Patent on AIDS Drug,* Wall St. J., Aug. 23, 2001, at A3).

76. Merck offered discounts of 59 percent and 60 percent on its drugs. *See* Jennifer L. Rich and Melody Petersen, *Brazil Will Defy Patent on HIV/AIDS Drugs Made by Roche,* N.Y. Times, Aug. 23, 2001, at C6; Cohen and Lybecker, *supra* note 65, at 222.

77. In September 2003, Brazil issued a decree that enabled it to produce or import antiretrovirals without the consent of the patent holder; the announcement was made after Brazil had attempted to obtain significant discounts from a variety of pharmaceutical companies. Once again, after the announcement was made, the pharmaceutical industry relented, and the sides reached agreement. *See* Racist and Ignorant Reactions on Thailand Compulsory License, Posting of James Love to Huffington Post, http://www.huffingtonpost.com/james-love/racist-and-ignorant-react_b_39618.html (Jan. 25, 2007, 2:01 p.m.) (listing international examples of compulsory licenses).

78. *See* Michael Astor, *Both Sides Declare Victory in Brazil's Patent Battle with U.S. Pharmaceutical Company,* Associated Press, July 11, 2005.

79. 151 Cong. Rec. E1435 (daily ed. June 30, 2005) (statement of Representative Tom Feeney). Another commentator claimed that compulsory licensing was just a polite way to refer to theft. *See* 151 Cong. Rec. E1435–1436 (2005) (reprinting James Pinkerton, *Richman, Beggarman, Thief?,* Tech Central Station, June 29, 2005).

80. *See* Natasha Metzler, *Brazil Uses Compulsory License Threat in Negotiations,* Pharmaceutical Executive, July 18, 2005.

81. *See* Mary Anastasia O'Grady, *Brazil Mulls Drug Patent Theft as AIDS Antidote,* Wall St. J., June 24, 2005, at A13. The economics of the pharmaceutical industry are a subject of widespread attention in the literature. *See, e.g.,* Joseph DiMasi et al., *The Cost of Innovation in the Pharmaceutical Industry,* 10 J. Health Econ. 107 (1991); Bruce Lehman, *Intellectual Property and Compulsory Licensing, Pharmaceuticals and the Developing World (Akin Gump Strauss Hauer & Feld, White Paper, 2005), available at* http://jobfunctions.bnet.com/whitepaper.aspx?&docid=142303.

82. The Brazilian government declared Merck's drug a "public interest medicine," which gave Merck seven days to negotiate lower prices or face a compulsory license. *See* Michael Astor, *Brazil's HIV-Drug Talks Break Down,* Associated Press, May 3, 2007.

83. Ministry of Public Health and the National Health Security Office, Thailand, *Facts and Evidences [sic] on the Ten Burning Issues Related to the Government Use of Patents on Three Patented Essential Drugs in Thailand* (2007), *available at* http://www.moph.go.th/hot/White%20Paper%20CL-EN.pdf.

84. Editorial, *Abbott's Bad Precedent,* Wall St. J., April 30, 2007, at A13.

85. Peter J. Pitts, *Drug Patent Theft Carries High Price,* Balt. Sun, Feb. 20, 2007, at A11.

86. Editorial, *Abbott in Thailand,* Chi. Trib. May 10, 2007, at 26.

87. *See Abbott's Bad Precedent, supra* note 84.

88. Cohen and Lybecker, *supra* note 65, at 226.

89. *See* Sonia K. Katyal, *Making Patents Public,* FindLaw, Oct. 11, 2001, http://writ.news.findlaw.com/commentary/20011011_katyal.html.

90. *See* Frederick M. Abbott, *The TRIPS-Legality of Measures Taken to Address Public Health Crises: A Synopsis,* 7 Widener L. Symp. J. 71, 72 (2001).

91. *See, e.g.,* CPtech, Examples of Health Related Compulsory Licenses, http://cptech.org/ip/health/cl/recent-examples.html (last visited Mar. 14, 2008).

92. *See* Galv{{atilde}}o, *supra* note 63, at 3.

93. *See id.* at 3.

94. *See* CPtech, *supra* note 91.

95. The Doha declaration also extended the deadline for developing countries to harmonize to 2017.

96. World Trade Organization, Ministerial Declaration of 14 November 2001, WT/MIN(01)/DEC/2, ¶ 4, 41 I.L.M. 746 (2002), *available at* http://www.wto.org/English/thewto_e/minist_e/min01_e/mindecl_trips_e.htm.

97. *Id.* ¶ 5(c).

98. The new rules allowed countries to suspend the patents on particular drugs so

long as the rules would be "used in good faith to protect public health . . . not [as] an instrument to pursue industrial or commercial policy objectives." *WTO Votes to Bypass Patents on Medicines; Cheap Generics to Poor Nations,* Wash. Post, Aug. 31, 2003, at A16.

99. *See Cipla Gets Malaysian Node for AIDS Drugs; In a Trailblazing Move, Malaysia Has Issued A Compulsory License,* Our Bureau New Dehli, Feb. 25, 2006, *available at* http://www.deolhonaspatentes.org.br/media/file/Casos/Malasia/comentarios _cptech.PDF.

100. *See* CPtech, *supra* note 91; Kevin Outterson, *Pharmaceutical Arbitrage: Balancing Access and Innovation in International Prescription Drug Markets,* 5 Yale J. Health Pol'y L. & Ethics 193, 259 (2005).

101. Cohen and Lybecker, *supra* note 65, at 226; *see also* Brendan Case and Laurence Iliff, *Mexico Seeks Remedy for High Drug Costs: Proposal to Relax Protection on Patents Touches Off Debate,* Apr. 9, 2003, Dallas Morning News, at A7.

102. Tina Rosenberg, *Look at Brazil,* N.Y. Times, Jan. 28, 2001, at A6.

7. Expressive Altlaws: Copyright and the New Liberation of Information

1. For an excellent account from which much of this chapter is drawn, see Mary Bridges, *Diebold vs. The Bloggers* (Berkman Center for Internet & Society, Berkman Briefing, Oct. 3, 2004), http://cyber.law.harvard.edu/briefings/dvb. *See also* Jonathan Zittrain, *A History of Online Gatekeeping,* 19 Harv. J.L. & Tech. 253, 266–267 (2006).

2. *See* Andrea L. Foster, *Voting-Machine Producer Retreats on Threats to Colleges and Students,* Chron. Higher Educ., Dec. 12, 2003; Bridges, *supra* note 1.

3. *See* Paul Roberts, *Diebold Voting Case Tests DMCA,* PCWorld, Nov. 4 2003, http://www.pcworld.com/article/113273/diebold_voting_case_tests_dmca.html.

4. *See* John Palfrey, *Electronic Voting and Copyright?,* CNET News, Oct. 5, 2004, http://www.news.com/Electronic-voting-and-copyright/2010-1028_3-5395784 .html; Kim Zetter, *California Bans E-Vote Machines,* Wired, Apr. 30, 2004, http://www .wired.com/politics/security/news/2004/04/63298.

5. *See* Bridges, *supra* note 1.

6. Palfrey, *supra* note 4; Bridges, *supra* note 1.

7. Bridges, *supra* note 1.

8. *See* Robert S. Boynton, *The Tyranny of Copyright?,* N.Y. Times, Jan. 25, 2004, § 6 (Magazine), at 40.

9. *See Online Policy Group v. Diebold, Inc.,* 337 F. Supp. 2d 1195, 1198–1199 (N.D. Cal. 2004).

10. Kathy Hamlin, *Diebold Wants Internal Memos Concealed,* Amherst Student, Nov 12., 2003, http://amherststudent.amherst.edu/current/news/view.php?year= 2003-2004&issue=11&section=news&article=01.

11. 17 U.S.C. § 512(c)(3)(v) (1999).

12. *See* Mark A. Lemley and R. Anthony Reese, *Reducing Copyright Infringement*

without Restricting Innovation, Stan. L. Rev. 1345, 1369 (2004) ("Congress enacted the [DMCA] safe harbors in response to concerns expressed by online service providers about their potentially overwhelming liability for copyright infringement committed by their users."); Jennifer M. Urban and Laura J. Quilter, *Efficient Process of "Chilling Effects"? Takedown Notices under Section 412 of the Digital Millennium Copyright Act,* 22 Santa Clara Computer & High Tech. L.J. 621, 631–641 (2006) (discussing at length the rationale behind section 512); Zittrain, *supra* note 1, at 264–266 (discussing the history of the DMCA safe-harbor provisions).

13. Sonia K. Katyal, *The New Surveillance,* 45 Case W. Res. L. Rev. 297, 328 (2004) (discussing the notice-and-takedown provision of the DMCA).

14. *See* Bridges, *supra* note 1, § 5.0.

15. Roberts, *supra* note 3.

16. Doris Estelle Long, *Electronic Voting Rights and the DMCA: Another Blast from the Digital Pirates or a Final Wake Up Call for Reform?,* 23 J. Marshall J. Computer & Info. L. 533, 538 (2005).

17. 17 U.S.C. § 512(g)(3); *see also* Urban and Quilter, *supra* note 12, at 628.

18. *See* Urban and Quilter, *supra* note 12, at 639.

19. Roberts, *supra* note 3 (quoting John Palfrey).

20. *See, e.g.,* Letter from Diebold to William Doherty, Online Policy Group (Oct. 10, 2003), *available at* http://www.chillingeffects.org/linking/notice.cgi?NoticeID =911.

21. John Schwartz, *File Sharing Pits Copyright against Free Speech,* N.Y. Times, Nov. 3, 2003, at C1 (quoting David Bear).

22. *Id.* (quoting Nelson Pavlovsky).

23. *See* Kim Zetter, *E-Vote Protest Gains Momentum,* Wired, Oct. 29, 2003, http://www.wired.com/news/politics/0,1283,61002,00.html; *see also* Press Release, Swarthmore College, Dean Gross Statement on Student Action in Diebold Memo Case (Oct. 29, 2003), *available at* http://www.swarthmore.edu/news/releases/03/ diebold2.html.

24. *See* Declan McCullagh, *Students Buck DMCA Threat,* CNET News, Nov. 3, 2003, http://news.cnet.com/Students-buck-DMCA-threat/2100-1028_3-5101623.html (quoting Alfred Bloom).

25. Zetter, *supra* note 23.

26. *Id.* (quoting Robert Gross)

27. *See* Bridges, *supra* note 1; Swarthmore Coalition for the Digital Commons, Diebold Hear This: We Won't Rest, http://scdc.sccs.swarthmore.edu/diebold/ (last visited Mar. 1, 2008) (distributing and highlighting contested memos); Why War?, Targeting Diebold with Electronic Civil Disobedience, http://www.why-war.com/features/2003/10/diebold.html (last visited Mar. 1, 2008) (observing on October 23, 2003, that students from over 50 schools had joined the campaign).

28. Siva Vaidhyanathan, Between Pragmatism and Anarchism: The American Copyright Revolt Since 1998, at 5 (2005) (draft manuscript, cited with permission), *available at* http://papers.ssrn.com/sol3/papers.cfm?abstract_id=791024.

29. *See* Roberts, supra note 3 (quoting John Palfrey).

30. Posting of Wendy Seltzer to Freedom to Tinker, http://www.freedom-to-tinker.com/blog/felten/swarthmore-students-re-publish-diebold-memos (Oct. 23, 2003, 3:28 p.m.).

31. Posting of I.R.A. Darth Aggie to Freedom to Tinker, http://www.freedom-to-tinker.com/blog/felten/swarthmore-students-re-publish-diebold-memos (Oct. 24, 2003, 2:53 a.m.).

32. Posting of Jon Stanley to Freedom to Tinker, http://www.freedom-to-tinker.com/blog/felten/swarthmore-students-re-publish-diebold-memos (Oct. 26, 2003, 4:11 a.m.).

33. *See* Why War?, *supra* note 27.

34. *See* Palfrey, *supra* note 4.

35. *See* Why War?, *supra* note 27.

36. *See id.*

37. *Id.* (statement of Micah White).

38. Kim Zetter, *Students Fight E-Vote Firm,* Wired, Oct. 21, 2003, http://www.wired.com/print/techbiz/media/news/2003/10/60927 (quoting Luke Smith).

39. Paul Roberts, *Dispute Tests Limits of Free Speech Online,* PCWorld, Nov. 5, 2003, http://www.pcworld.com/article/id,113301-page,1/article.html.

40. *Id.*

41. *See* Schwartz, *supra* note 21.

42. *See* Roberts, *supra* note 39 (quoting John Palfrey)

43. See John P. Mello, *Activists Seek Damages from Diebold over Copyright Abuse,* Tech News World, Feb. 10, 2004, http://www.technewsworld.com/story/32812.html?welcome=1204404096.

44. *Id.* (quoting Eric A. Prager).

45. *See* Paul Festa, *Diebold Retreats; Lawmaker Demands Inquiry,* CNET News Dec. 1, 2003, http://www.news.com/2100-1028-5112430.html.

46. Congressman Dennis Kucinich, Stopping False Copyright Claims, http://kucinich.house.gov/Issues/Issue/?IssueID=1572#Privatized%20Voting,%20Private%20Interests (last visited May 10, 2009); Weblog of Dan Fingerman, Kucinich Slaps Diebold, http://danfingerman.com/dtm/archives/000069.html (Nov. 19, 2003, 10:42 p.m.) (quoting Dennis Kucinich).

47. *See* Festa, *supra* note 45.

48. Kim Zetter, *Diebold Loses Key Copyright Case,* Wired, Sept. 30, 2004, http://www.wired.com/politics/security/news/2004/09/65173 (quoting David Bear).

49. Hamlin, *supra* note 10 (quoting Nelson Pavlovsky).

50. *See Lasercomb Am., Inc. v. Reynolds,* 911 F.2d 970, 978 (4th Cir. 1990).

51. *Online Policy Group v. Diebold, Inc.,* 337 F. Supp. 2d 1195, 1198–1204 (N.D. Cal. 2004).

52. *See* 17 U.S.C. § 512(f) (1999).

53. *Online Policy Group,* 337 F. Supp. 2d at 1203–1204.

54. *See, e.g.,* Urban and Quilter, *supra* note 12, at 683–693; Electronic Frontier Foundation, *Unsafe Harbors: Abusive DMCA Subpoenas and Takedown Demands* (2003), *available at* http://www.eff.org/IP/P2P/20030926_unsafe_harbors.php;

Malla Pollack, *Rebalancing Section 512 to Protect Fair Users from Herds of Mice-Trampling Elephants, or A Little Due Process Is Not Such a Dangerous Thing,* 22 Santa Clara Computer & High Tech. L.J. 547, 566 (2006).

55. Bridges, *supra* note 1, § 5.0.

56. Vaidhyanathan, *supra* note 28, at 6.

57. *Id.*

58. Bridges, *supra* note 1, § 5.0(quoting Derek Slater).

8. Two Perspectives on Property Outlaws

1. This risk is present whether one adopts a more formalist approach in which the outlaw is viewed as having broken an existing legal rule, with the law sometimes changing in response, or a more pluralist approach in which, as Cover might have said, the outlaw (or perhaps, for the pluralist, the altlaw), merely insists on his or her own interpretation of the extant law, which the organs of official legal interpretation sometimes adopt as their own.

2. *See* Keith N. Hylton, *Optimal Law Enforcement and Victim Precaution,* 27 RAND J. Econ. 198 (1996).

3. *See, e.g.,* Jules L. Coleman, *Crimes, Kickers, and Transaction Structures, in Nomos XXVII: Criminal Justice* 314 (J. Ronald Pennock and John W. Chapman eds., 1985).

4. Gary S. Becker, *Crime and Punishment: An Economic Approach,* 76 J. Pol. Econ. 169, 201 (1968).

5. *See id.* at 201; Hylton, *supra* note 2, at 198–199; A. Mitchell Polinksy and Steven Shavell, *The Optimal Tradeoff between the Probability and Magnitude of Fines,* 69 Am. Econ. Rev. 880 (1979).

6. *See, e.g.,* Richard A. Epstein, *Skepticism and Freedom* 98–100 (Chicago: University of Chicago Press 2003) (explaining the private necessity doctrine); Lee Anne Fennell, *Efficient Trespass: The Case for "Bad Faith" Adverse Possession,* 100 Nw. U. L. Rev. 1037 (2006) (arguing that adverse possession should be understood as a "doctrine of efficient trespass").

7. Michael S. Moore, *The Moral Worth of Retribution, in Responsibility, Character, and the Emotions: New Essays in Moral Psychology* 179 (Ferdinand Schoeman ed., 1987).

8. *See, e.g.,* Gordon Tullock, *The Welfare Costs of Tariffs, Monopolies, and Theft,* 5 W. Econ. J. 224, 231 (1967).

9. *See* Stewart Schwab, *Coase Defends Coase: Why Lawyers Listen and Economists Do Not,* 87 Mich. L. Rev. 1171, 1178–1179 (1989) (reviewing Ronald Coase, *The Firm the Market and the Law* (1988), and discussing wealth effects).

10. *See* Richard L. Hasen and Richard H. McAdams, *The Surprisingly Complex Case against Theft,* 17 Int'l Rev. L. & Econ. 367, 370 (1997).

11. *See* Fennell, *supra* note 6, at 1040.

12. See generally Marion Shoard, *A Right to Roam* (1999), and Tom Stephenson, Ann Holt, and Mike Harding, *Forbidden Land* (1989), for a detailed discussion of the history of the British "right to roam" movement.

13. Ronald Dworkin, *Law's Empire* 286–287 (1986).

14. *See, e.g.,* Tom R. Tyler, *Why People Obey the Law* 65 (1990); Amitai Etzioni, *The Moral Dimension: Toward a New Economics* 58–63, 77 (1988).

15. *See* Tyler, *supra* note 14, at 22; Dan M. Kahan, *What Do Alternative Sanctions Mean,* 63 U. Chi. L. Rev. 591, 603–604 (1996) (discussing the ways in which criminal law affects preferences for obedience to the law).

16. See Bradley R. E. Wright et al., *Does the Perceived Risk of Punishment Deter Criminally Prone Individuals? Rational Choice, Self-Control, and Crime,* 41 J. Res. Crime & Delinquency 180 (2004).

17. Tom Tyler has argued in a similar vein that willingness to break the law correlates strongly with views about the justice of society's distribution of wealth as well as views about legal legitimacy. Tyler, *supra* note 14, at 96, 107–108.

18. On the first effect, see Frank I. Michelman, *Property, Utility, and Fairness: Comments on the Ethical Foundations of "Just Compensation" Law,* 80 Harv. L. Rev. 1165, 1214 (1967). On the second and third effects, see *Southwark v. Williams,* [1971] 2 All E.R. 175, 179, 180 (A.C.). Michelman's account of the failure to invest attributes the effect to something like the "demoralization" that he says is a likely result of uncompensated takings. In part, however, the effect may result from genuine uncertainty about the contours of property rights in a regime that ratifies the actions of acquisitive outlaws. *See, e.g.,* Henry E. Smith, *Self-Help and the Nature of Property,* 1 J.L. Econ. & Pol'y 69, 88–91 (2005).

19. The broken-windows thesis was first raised in James Q. Wilson and George L. Kelling, *Broken Windows,* Atlantic Monthly, Mar. 1982, at 29. The body of literature supporting the thesis is large, rapidly growing, and somewhat controversial. *Compare* Robert C. Ellickson, *Controlling Chronic Misconduct in City Spaces: Of Panhandlers, Skid Rows, and Public-Space Zoning,* 105 Yale L.J. 1165, 1171, 1182 (1996) (arguing that public crime and public begging will lead to disorder through additional crime), *with* Bernard E. Harcourt and Jens Ludwig, *Broken Windows: New Evidence from New York City and a Five-City Social Experiment,* 73 U. Chi. L. Rev. 271, 314–316 (2006) (concluding, after empirical analysis, that increased police attention to eliminate disorder and misdemeanor violations does not reduce crime).

20. Frank I. Michelman, *Ethics, Economics, and the Law of Property, in Nomos XXIV: Ethics, Economics, and the Law* 3, 26–27 (Ronald Pennock and John W. Chapman eds., 1982); *see also* Smith, *supra* note 18, at 89 ("Ultimately, of course, the size of these various effects is an empirical question.").

21. *See* Tyler, *supra* note 14, at 96, 107–08; Franklin E. Zimring and Gordon J. Hawkins, *Deterrence: The Legal Threat in Crime Control* 220–221 (1973). As Zimring and Hawkins observe, the threat of punishment for behavior widely viewed as justified within a particular community can lead to an overall deterioration of respect for the rule of law.

22. *See* Paul W. Gates, *History of Public Land Law Development* 235 (1979).

23. Hernando de Soto, *The Other Path: The Invisible Revolution in the Third World* 19–26 (1989).

24. *Id.* at 55.

25. Robert Neuwirth, *Shadow Cities: A Billion Squatters, a New Urban World* 256–257 (2006).

26. *Id.* at 295–297.

27. *See* Joseph William Singer, *Property Law: Rules, Policies, and Practices* 25–26 (4th ed. 2006).

28. De Soto, *supra* note 23, at 27–29.

29. *See, e.g.*, Christopher Mele, *Selling the Lower East Side: Culture, Real Estate, and Resistance in New York City* 197 (2000); Seth Borgos, *Low-Income Homeownership and the ACORN Squatters Campaign, in Critical Perspectives on Housing* 428, 428–429, 433–436 (Rachel G. Bratt et al. eds., 1986). Borgos describes neighborhood support for ACORN Housing's squatting actions, which helped clean up otherwise derelict housing. A similar story can be told about the Green Guerrillas, 1970s activists who trespassed on abandoned, rubble-strewn properties in New York City to create community gardens. *See* Liz Christy Community Garden, http://www.lizchristygarden.org (last visited Mar. 23, 2007) (describing the creation of one community garden in New York by the Green Guerrillas).

30. *See* Ronald Dworkin, *A Matter of Principle* 108–110 (1985) [hereinafter, Dworkin, *Principle*]; Ronald Dworkin, *Taking Rights Seriously* 206–216 (1977).

31. *See* Charles Avila, *Ownership: Early Christian Teaching* 55 (1983).

32. John Chrysostom, *John Chrysostom on Wealth and Poverty* 55 (Catherine P. Roth trans., 1984).

33. *See* Thomas Aquinas, *Summa Theologiae* 2-2.66.7, *reprinted in On Law, Morality, and Politics* 187 (William P. Baumgarth and Richard J. Regan eds., 1988).

34. *See* Jean Porter, *Nature as Reason: A Thomistic Theory of the Natural Law* 357 (2005); Brian Tierney, *The Idea of Natural Rights: Studies on Natural Rights, Natural Law and Church Law, 1150–1625,* at 69–72 (1997); Brian Tierney, *Medieval Poor Law* 125–127 (1959).

35. Donald J. Pisani, *The Squatter and Natural Law in Nineteenth Century America,* 81 Agricultural Hist. 443, 444–450 (2007).

36. Jeremy Waldron, *Liberal Rights: Collected Papers, 1981–1991,* at 240–241 (1993).

37. This is not to say that the lawbreaker's subjective intent is absolutely irrelevant. *See, e.g.*, Mitchell N. Berman, *Lesser Evils and Justification: A Less Close Look,* 24 Law & Phil. 681, 701–704 (2005) (discussing the problem of mistaken necessity).

38. For newspaper articles describing deaths of homeless persons from exposure, see Juliet V. Casey, *Homeless in Las Vegas: On a Mission of Mercy,* Las Vegas Rev. J., Aug. 15, 2005, at 1B; Greg Garland, *Two Homeless Dead After Overnight Exposure,* Balt. Sun, Dec. 4, 2005, at B1; *Helping the Helpless,* Ariz. Republic, Sept. 7, 2005, at B8; Robert F. Moore and Bill Hutchinson, *The Killer Chiller,* Daily News (N.Y.), Jan. 19, 2005, at 5; Michelle O'Donnell and Anahad O'Connor, *Wind and Cold Are Blamed in Three Deaths,* N.Y. Times, Jan. 16, 2006, at B1; Paul Rubin, *Crying Shame,* Phoenix New Times, Oct. 6, 2005, http://www.phoenixnewtimes.com/2005-10-06/news/crying-shame; Annie Sweeney, *Lightning Strikes Thrice as Weather Gets Weird,* Chi. Sun-Times, Jan. 13, 2005, at 8.

39. Neuwirth, *supra* note 25, at 9.

40. *See* Martha Nussbaum, *Nature, Function, and Capability: Aristotle on Political Distribution, in Oxford Studies in Ancient Philosophy* 145, 149–150, 157 (Julia Annas and Robert H. Grimm eds., 1988); Adam Smith, *The Wealth of Nations* bk. V, ch. ii, pt. 2 (Edwin Cannan ed., Random House, 1937) (1776); Amartya Sen, *Resources, Values, and Development* 325–345 (1984); Elizabeth S. Anderson, *What Is the Point of Equality?*, 109 Ethics 287 (1999).

41. Waldron, *supra* note 36, at 246–247.

42. Smith, *supra* note 40, at 821–822.

43. Sen, *supra* note 40, at 336–337.

44. *Id.* at 336. Sen states, "For a richer community . . . the nutritional and other physical requirements . . . are typically already met, and the needs of communal participation . . . will have a much higher demand in the space of commodities and that of resources."

45. For an example of the "necessity" of telephone service, see Julia Sommerfeld, *Voice-Mail Service for Homeless Will Expand,* Seattle Times, Sept. 8, 2003, at B3.

46. *See* Singer, *supra* note 27, at 716–718 (discussing actions tenants are entitled to take when landlords fail to maintain their property).

47. *Id.* at 715 (describing circumstances that can give rise to this right of self-help).

48. Eric Kades, The Law and Economics of Civil Disobedience 22–25 (2006) (unpublished manuscript, on file with authors).

49. *See id.*

50. *See id.;* Steven M. Bauer and Peter J. Eckerstrom, Note, *The State Made Me Do It: The Applicability of the Necessity Defense to Civil Disobedience,* 39 Stan. L. Rev. 1173, 1189–1191 (1987).

51. *See Two Sentenced for Trespassing,* Greensboro Daily News, Apr. 27, 1960, at A4; *see also* John Lewis with Michael D'Orso, *Walking with the Wind: A Memoir of the Movement* 110 (1998) (describing the strategic importance of actually going to jail rather than paying a fine).

52. Kades, *supra* note 48, at 35. Kades also tells the story of one southern mayor who "secretly paid Martin Luther King, Jr.'s fine for trespass, and busted him from jail against his will." *Id.* at 35 n.99.

53. *See id.* at 29–36.

54. Dworkin, *Principle, supra* note 30, at 105.

55. *Id.* at 107–114 (contrasting "integrity-based" civil disobedience, which most agree justifies lawbreaking, with "justice-based" and "policy-based" civil disobedience, which are more problematic).

56. Daniel Markovits, *Democratic Disobedience,* 114 Yale L.J. 1897, 1927–1941 (2005).

57. Robert M. Cover, *The Supreme Court 1982 Term—Foreword:* Nomos *and Narrative,* 97 Harv. L. Rev. 4, 15–17, 32–35 (1983).

58. *See* Hannah Arendt, *Understanding and Politics,* 20 Partisan Rev. 377 (1953).

59. *Cf.* Guido Calabresi, *A Common Law for the Age of Statutes* 16–30 (1982) (describing strategies for coping with "legal petrification").

9. Responding to Property Outlaws

1. *See, e.g.,* N.Y. Penal Law §§ 140.10, 140.15 (McKinney 1999) (defining most criminal trespass violations as misdemeanors in New York).

2. For these U.K., U.S. state, and U.S. federal practices and statutes, see, respectively, Howard Hill, *Freedom to Roam* 67–68 (1980); N.Y. Penal Law § 70.15 (McKinney 2009); 18 U.S.C. § 1382 (2000).

3. 538 U.S. 63 (2003).

4. *See* Dan M. Kahan, *Social Influence, Social Meaning, and Deterrence,* 83 Va. L. Rev. 349, 377–382 (1997).

5. *See* Franklin E. Zimring and Gordon J. Hawkins, *Deterrence: The Legal Threat in Crime Control* 221 (1973).

6. *See* A. Mitchell Polinksy and Steven Shavell, *The Optimal Tradeoff between the Probability and Magnitude of Fines,* 69 Am. Econ. Rev. 880, 880–881, 884–885 (1979). Polinsky and Shavell note the potential unfairness of fining individuals "far in excess of the external cost they impose on society." *Id.* at 881.

7. *See* Kahan, *supra* note 4, at 349–352, 379.

8. *See, e.g.,* Jeremy Waldron, *Liberal Rights: Collected Papers, 1981–1991,* at 244–245 (1993).

9. *See* Frances Fox Piven and Richard A. Cloward, *Regulating the Poor: The Functions of Public Welfare* 4–6, 33–41 (1993).

10. Robert N. Bellah et al., *Habits of the Heart: Individualism and Commitment in American Life* 29 (1985).

11. 3 Am. Jur. 2d *Adverse Possession* § 10 (2002).

12. Lee Anne Fennell, *Efficient Trespass: The Case for "Bad Faith" Adverse Possession,* 100 Nw. U. L. Rev. 1037 (2006).

13. *See, e.g.,* Henry Cohen, *Vicissitudes of an Absentee Landlord, in The Frontier in American Development* 192, 201–204 (David M. Ellis ed., 1969).

14. *See* Kevin Gray and Susan Francis Gray, *Elements of Land Law* § 6.39, at 372 (4th ed. 2005) ("Statistically the most significant adverse possessor is one who claims that a minute sliver of land formally titled in his neighbour has been inaccurately fenced in his own favour or has been the subject of a mistaken double conveyance to himself.").

15. *See* Haya El Nasser and Paul Overberg, *No One Home: 1 in 9 Housing Units Vacant,* USA Today, Feb. 13, 2009.

16. *See* Susan Saulny, *Banks Starting to Walk Away on Foreclosures,* N.Y. Times, Mar. 29, 2009.

17. *See* Restatement (Second) of Torts § 197 (1965) (private necessity); Henry E. Smith, *Self-Help and the Nature of Property,* 1 J.L. Econ & Pol'y 69, 89–91 (2005) (describing "the right of one facing necessity" as a situation in which it would make sense to "delineate a stand-alone right to engage in self-help").

18. *See* Shaun P. Martin, *The Radical Necessity Defense,* 73 U. Cin. L. Rev. 1527, 1532 (2005) (recognizing the necessity defense as a long-standing part of Anglo-American jurisprudence). For an opposing view, see 2 Paul H. Robinson, *Criminal Law Defenses*

§ 124(a), at 45 (1984) (noting that only half of American jurisdictions recognize the necessity defense).

19. Martin, *supra* note 18, at 1535–1536.

20. Restatement (Second) of Torts § 197 (1965) (private necessity).

21. Martin, *supra* note 18, at 1567–1589 (describing the requirements for the necessity doctrine to apply: imminence, causation, and the absence of legal alternatives).

22. *See* Maria Foscarinis, *Downward Spiral: Homelessness and Its Criminalization,* 14 Yale L. & Pol'y Rev. 1, 16–26 (1996) (discussing cities' efforts to criminalize survival behavior by the homeless). Our analysis suggests not only that such conduct should be immune from sanction but that efforts to interfere with behavior necessary for survival, such as panhandling and sleeping in public, may well give rise to a civil remedy, such as that afforded in *Ploof v. Putnam,* 71 A. 188, 188–189 (Vt. 1908). Summarizing the law in this area, Richard Epstein has said that the "owner who casts away the stranger in need can be sued for the harm that follows." Richard A. Epstein, *Skepticism and Freedom* 98–100 (2003).

23. *See, e.g., State v. Gann,* 244 N.W.2d 746, 752–753 (N.D. 1976); *Harris v. State,* 486 S.W.2d 573, 574 (Tex. Crim. App. 1972); *State v. Moe,* 24 P.2d 638, 640 (Wash. 1933).

24. *See, e.g., Pottinger v. City of Miami,* 810 F. Supp. 1551, 1564 (S.D. Fla. 1992) ("An individual who loses his home as a result of economic hard times or physical or mental illness exercises no more control over these events than he would over a natural disaster."); *see also* John Augustine Ryan, *A Living Wage: Its Ethical and Economic Aspects* 297–298 (1906).

25. *See* Thomas Aquinas, *Summa Theologiae* 2-2.66.7, *reprinted in On Law, Morality, and Politics* 187 (William P. Baumgarth and Richard J. Regan eds., 1988).

26. *Mayfield v. State,* 585 S.W.2d 693 (Tex. Crim. App. 1979); *see also* J. Thomas Sullivan, *The Defense of Necessity in Texas: Legislative Invention Comes of Age,* 16 Hous. L. Rev. 333, 346–347 (1979).

27. *Southwark v. Williams,* [1971] Ch. 734, 744 (A.C.).

28. Under certain circumstances, or even in entire categories of cases, dire need might be so clear as to justify a judge in granting prospective injunctive relief or determining that enforcement of a particular law would, as a matter of law, violate the principle of necessity. A similar intuition may underlie the conclusions of some courts that the enforcement of laws prohibiting unavoidable behavior by the homeless, such as sitting or sleeping in public, constitutes cruel and unusual punishment in violation of the Eighth Amendment. *See, e.g., Jones v. City of Los Angeles,* 444 F.3d 1118, 1136 (9th Cir. 2006).

29. *See, e.g.,* Michael Kozura, *We Stood Our Ground: Anthracite Miners and the Expropriation of Corporate Property, 1930–41, in "We Are All Leaders": The Alternative Unionism of the Early 1930s* 199, 215 (Staughton Lynd ed., 1996) (discussing how juries "composed of friends and neighbors" aligned themselves with miners and unions to make "the cost of legal repression prohibitive for coal companies"); *see also* Jim Pope, *Worker Lawmaking, Sit-Down Strikes, and the Shaping of American Industrial Relations, 1935–1958,* 24 Law & Hist. Rev. 45, 84 (2006).

30. Robert C. Ellickson, *Controlling Chronic Misconduct in City Spaces: Of Panhandlers, Skid Rows, and Public-Space Zoning,* 105 Yale L.J. 1165 (1996).

31. *See* Kenneth W. Simons, *Exploring the Intricacies of the Lesser Evils Defense,* 24 L. & Phil. 645, 677 (2005) (arguing that trial fact finders are better equipped than legislatures to determine when the "lesser evils defense" should be accepted, since they are "appropriately sensitive to [the] special circumstances" underlying specific cases).

32. *Modderklip East Squatters v. Modderklip Boerdery (Pty) Ltd.,* 2004 (8) BCLR 821 (SCA), *discussed in* Gregory S. Alexander, *The Global Debate over Constitutional Property: Lessons for American Takings Jurisprudence* 192–196 (2006); *see also* Andre J. van der Walt, The State's Duty to Protect Property Owners v. The State's Duty to Provide Housing: Thoughts on the *Modderklip* Case (2006) (unpublished manuscript, on file with authors).

33. Van der Walt, *supra* note 32, at 18.

34. *See generally* Louis Kaplow and Steven Shavell, *Why the Legal System Is Less Efficient Than the Income Tax in Redistributing Income,* 23 J. Legal Stud. 667 (1994).

35. Ellickson, *supra* note 30, at 1190. Ellickson further comments, "Lawmakers would be unwise to abandon otherwise appropriate rules-of-the-road simply to provide aid to street people." *Id.* at 1190.

36. *See, e.g.,* Piven and Cloward, *supra* note 9, at 4–6, 33–41.

37. *See* Nat'l Coalition for the Homeless and Nat'l Ctr. on Homelessness & Poverty, *A Dream Denied: The Criminalization of Homelessness in U.S. Cities* (2006), *available at* http://www.nationalhomeless.org/publications/crimreport/report.pdf.

38. *See* Foscarinis, *supra* note 22, at 15.

39. See *id.* at 51–53, for a presentation of such survey results.

40. *See Southwark v. Williams,* [1971] 2 All E.R. 175, 179 (A.C.) ("Necessity would open a door which no man could shut. . . . There would be [those] who would imagine that they were in need, or would invent a need, so as to gain entry.").

41. But only to *some* extent. As already discussed, this deterrent mechanism operates most forcefully with respect to a small subset of the population, which is assumed to be generally law abiding. Moreover, as theorists have noted, minor changes in the extent or likelihood of criminal sanctions are unlikely to have an appreciable effect on crime rates. *See* Zimring and Hawkins, *supra* note 5, at 195.

42. *Cf. id.* at 195–196.

43. *See* Andre J. van der Walt, Exclusivity of Ownership, Security of Tenure, and Eviction Orders pt. II.b (2006) (unpublished manuscript, on file with authors).

44. *See* Steven M. Bauer and Peter J. Eckerstrom, Note, *The State Made Me Do It: The Applicability of the Necessity Defense to Civil Disobedience,* 39 Stan. L. Rev. 1173 (1987); Robert F. Schopp, *Verdicts of Conscience: Nullification and Necessity as Jury Responses to Crimes of Conscience,* 69 S. Cal. L. Rev. 2083 (1996).

45. *See* Heather K. Gerken, *Dissenting by Deciding,* 57 Stan. L. Rev. 1745, 1754–1759 (2005).

46. *Marsh v. Alabama,* 326 U.S. 501 (1946).

47. 391 U.S. 308 (1968).

48. *Lloyd Corp. v. Tanner,* 407 U.S. 551 (1972); *see also State v. Kolcz,* 276 A.2d 595 (N.J. Super. 1971).

49. 424 U.S. 507 (1976).

50. *See Pruneyard Shopping Center v. Robins,* 447 U.S. 74 (1980).

51. *New Jersey Coalition against War in the Middle East v. J.M.B. Realty Corp.,* 650 A.2d 757 (N.J. 1994).

52. *See Hamm v. City of Rock Hill,* 379 U.S. 306 (1964); *Bell v. Maryland,* 378 U.S. 226 (1964).

53. *Hamm,* 379 U.S. at 314. Justice Black, dissenting in *Hamm,* condemned the judicial excusal of the protesters' "lawless conduct," *id.* at 319 (Black, J., dissenting), and Justice Harlan blasted it as a "revolutionary" perversion of precedent, *id.* at 324 (Harlan, J., dissenting).

10. The Informational Value of Intellectual Property Disobedience

1. Larry Downes, *Why Johnny Can't Stop Sharing Files,* CIO Insight, Jan. 6, 2006, http://www.cioinsight.com/article2/0,1397,1913768.00.asp. The case Downes was referring to was *Metro-Goldwyn-Mayer Studios Inc. v. Grokster, Ltd.,* 545 U.S. 913 (2005), in which the Supreme Court held several peer-to-peer file-sharing networks liable for copyright infringement.

2. Downes, *supra* note 1 (quoting Pew Internet and American Life Project study). Downes also cited the Pew study finding that seven million adults had copied a file from an iPod or other MP3 device, and a July 2006 study finding that over 90 percent of all teenagers used the Internet. Admittedly, although all these observations might be subjected to empirical discussion, Downes's more general point still suggests the lack of control that copyright law has, so far, had over the illegal sharing of files.

3. *See id.*

4. *See, e.g.,* Johnny Continues to Ignore Copyright, Posting of Joel Alleyn to Slaw, http://www.slaw.ca/2006/04/27/johnny-continues-to-ignore-copyright (Apr. 27, 2006); Rob Hyndman, Copyright Is Effectively Dead, http://www.robhyndman.com/2006/04/28/copyright-is-effectively-dead (Apr. 28, 2006, 11:01 a.m.); Is Copyright Still Respected? Posting of Tad Mcilwraith to FieldNotes, http://www.anthro blog.tadmcilwraith.com/2006/04/28/is-copyright-still-respected (Apr. 28, 2006).

5. *See* Adam Sherwin, *How Much Is Radiohead's Online Album Worth?,* Times (London), Oct. 11, 2007.

6. *See* Jeff Leeds, *Radiohead Finds Sales, Even After Downloads,* N.Y. Times, Jan. 10, 2008.

7. For example, the most recent expansion of the term limits for copyright, first under the Copyright Term Extension Act and then under the Supreme Court's analysis in *Eldred v. Ashcroft,* 537 U.S. 186 (2003), has engendered widespread opposition among both copyright scholars and activists throughout the country. *See* Siva Vaidhyanathan, *The State of Copyright Activism,* First Monday, Apr. 2004, http://firstmonday.org/ht-bin/cgiwrap/bin/ojs/index.php/fm/article/view/1133/1053.

8. For excellent commentary on various aspects of contemporary intellectual property, see Lawrence Lessig, *Remix: Making Art and Commerce Survive in a Hybrid Economy* (2008); James Boyle, *The Public Domain: Enclosing the Commons of the Mind* (2008); Yochai Benkler, *The Wealth of Networks* (2007); and Jonathan Zittrain, *The Future of the Internet and How to Stop It* (2009).

9. *See* H. L. A. Hart, *Bentham and Beccaria, in Essays on Bentham: Jurisprudence and Political Theory* 40 (1982).

10. *See* Daniel Markovits, *Democratic Disobedience*, 114 Yale L.J. 1897, 1898–1899 (2005).

11. Elliot Zashin, *Civil Rights and Civil Disobedience: The Limits of Legalism*, 52 Tex. L. Rev. 285, 285 (1974).

12. John Rawls, *A Theory of Justice* 371–376 (1971).

13. *Id.* at 372.

14. *See* 17 U.S.C. § 504(c)(2) (2006).

15. *See* 17 U.S.C. § 504(c)(1) (2006).

16. *See* 17 U.S.C. § 506 (2006).

17. *See* Gideon Parchomovsky and Kevin Goldman, *Fair Use Harbors*, 93 Va. L. Rev. 1483 (2007).

18. *See generally* Timothy B. Lee, *Circumventing Competition: The Perverse Consequences of the Digital Millennium Copyright Act* (Cato Institute Policy Analysis No. 564, 2006), *available at* http://www.cato.org/pubs/pas/pa564.pdf.

19. *See* John Tehranian, *Infringement Nation*, 2007 Utah L. Rev. 537 (2007).

20. *See* Madhavi Sunder, *IP3*, 59 Stan. L. Rev. 257 (2006).

21. Tehranian, *supra* note 19, at 547.

22. *Id.*

23. *See* 17 U.S.C. § 1201 (2006).

24. Dan L. Burk, *Anticircumvention Misuse*, 50 UCLA L. Rev. 1095, 1101–1102 (2003).

25. *See* Jason Mazzone, *Copyfraud*, 81 N.Y.U. L. Rev. 1026 (2006); Jacqueline Palank, *Content Makers Are Accused of Exaggerating Copyright*, N.Y. Times, Aug. 2, 2007, at C2.

26. Mazzone, *supra* note 25, at 1041–1042, 1047.

27. *See id.*, at 1058–1071; *see also* James Gibson, *Risk Aversion and Rights Accretion in Intellectual Property Law*, 116 Yale L.J. 882 (2007).

28. Transcript of Oral Argument at 11, *Metro-Goldwyn-Mayer Studios, Inc. v. Grokster, Ltd.*, 545 U.S. 913 (2005) (No. 04-480), *available at* http://www.supremecourtus.gov/oral_arguments/argument_transcripts/04-480.pdf; *see also* Posting of Andrew Raff to IPTAblog, http://www.iptablog.org/2005/03/30/grokster_more_important_than_god.html (Mar. 30, 2005).

29. *See Sony Corp. of America v. Universal City Studios, Inc.*, 464 U.S. 417 (1984) (approving the consumer practice of "time shifting" media material); *Recording Indus. Ass'n of Am. v. Diamond Multimedia Sys., Inc.*, 180 F.3d 1072, 1079 (9th Cir. 1999) (describing the "space shifting" of music using a Rio MP3 player as "paradigmatic non-

commercial personal use"); *A&M Records, Inc. v. Napster, Inc.*, 239 F.3d 1004, 1019 (9th Cir. 2001) (distinguishing *Sony* and *Diamond* to hold that space shifting that makes materials accessible to the general public is not a fair use).

30. RIAA Says Ripping CDs to your iPod is NOT Fair Use, Posting of Fred von Lohman to Electronic Frontier Foundation DeepLinks Blog, http://www.eff.org/deeplinks/archives/004409.php (Feb. 15, 2006) (quoting RIAA filing); *cf.* Recording Industry Association of America, Ask the RIAA, http://www.riaa.com/issues/ask/default.asp#stand (last visited Mar. 22, 2008) ("If you choose to take your own CDs and make copies for yourself on your computer or portable music player, that's great. It's your music and we want you to enjoy it at home, at work, in the car and on the jogging trail.").

31. Lawrence Liang, *Beyond Representation: The Figure of the Pirate* 5 (2005) (unpublished paper), *available at* http://www.altlawforum.org/PUBLICATIONS/Beyond%20Representation.doc.

32. Julie E. Cohen, *The Place of the User in Copyright Law,* 74 Fordham L. Rev. 347, 351 (2005).

33. Liang, *supra* note 31, at 5–6.

34. *See* Clarissa Long, *Information Costs in Patent and Copyright,* 90 Va. L. Rev. 465, 484 (2004).

35. *See* Jennifer Rothman, *The Questionable Use of Custom in Intellectual Property,* 93 Virginia L. Rev. 1899, 1902 (2007).

36. *See id.* at 1912; *see also* Patricia Aufderheide and Peter Jaszi, *Untold Stories: Creative Consequences of the Rights Clearance Culture for Documentary Filmmakers* (2004), *available at* http://www.centerforsocialmedia.org/rock/backgrounddocs/printable_rightsreport.pdf.

37. *See* Rothman. *supra* note 35, at 1912–1913.

38. *See* Gibson, *supra* note 27.

39. *See* Emanuela Carbonara et al., *Unjust Laws and Illegal Norms* (Minnesota Legal Studies Research Paper No. 08-03), *available at* http://papers.ssrn.com/sol3/papers.cfm?abstract_id=1088742 (describing how laws that do not correspond with broadly accepted social norms can lead to an increase in lawbreaking); Ben DePoorter and Sven Vanneste, *Norms and Enforcement,* 84 Or. L. Rev. 1127 (2005) (describing the possibility of a norm backlash from the overenforcement of intellectual property rights).

40. Jessica Litman, *Digital Copyright* 195 (2001).

11. Responding to Acquisitive Altlaws

1. *See* Adolph A. Berle, *Property, Production, and Revolution,* 65 Colum. L. Rev. 1 (1965).

2. *See* John O'Neill, *Ecology, Policy, and Politics: Human Well-Being and the Natural World* 168–169 (1993)

3. *See id.;* Adam Smith, *An Enquiry into the Nature and Causes of the Wealth of Nations* 1 (Penguin 1997) (1776); Karl Marx, *The Grundrisse, in The Marx Engels Reader*

221, 256–257 (Robert C. Tucker ed., 2d ed. 1978); Karl Polanyi, *The Great Transformation* 55 (1944).

4. *See Neda Ulaby, French File-Sharing Law Would Cut Internet Access,* NPR, May 14, 2009, http://www.npr.org/templates/story/story.php?storyId=104114922&ft=1&f=1019.

5. The principle of fair use, according to Wendy Gordon's influential article, is a mode of judicial response to market failure. Wendy Gordon, *Fair Use as Market Failure,* 82 Colum. L. Rev. 1600 (1982); *see also* Glynn S. Lunney Jr., *Fair Use and Market Failure: Sony Revisited,* 82 B.U. L. Rev. 975 (2002); Lydia Pallas Loren, *Redefining the Market Failure Approach to Fair Use in an Era of Copyright Permission Systems,* 5 J. Intell. Prop. L. 1, 26 (1997); Pamela Samuelson, *Foreword to the Digital Content Symposium,* 12 Berkeley Tech. L.J. 1 (1997).

6. 510 U.S. 569, 575 (1994).

7. 17 U.S.C. § 107 (2006).

8. *Id.*

9. Gordon, *supra* note 5, at 1615.

10. *Id.* at 1615–1616.

11. *Id.* at 1601–1620.

12. *Id.* at 1616–1633.

13. *Sony Corp. of Am. v. Universal City Studios, Inc.,* 464 U.S. 417, 418 (1984).

14. *Id.* at 442.

15. *See* Tim Wu, *Intellectual Property, Innovation, and Decision Architectures,* 92 Va. L. Rev. 123, 143–444 (2006).

16. A few introductory principles are necessary in order for one to understand the dynamics of reverse engineering software. Computer programs are generally written in "object code," which is unreadable by humans. Individuals use one of two processes—either "decompilation" or "disassembly"—to reverse engineer object code and to translate object code into "source code," which is then readable by humans. Object code, for example, contains only two numerals, 0 and 1, in particular combinations that represent the alphanumeric characters within source code. An "assembler" or "compiler" is therefore required to translate the object code into source code, where it is then imprinted onto a silicon chip for distribution. Devices known as "disassemblers" or "decompilers," which are widely used within the industry, can read, store, and then convert object code into source code for this purpose. The resulting source code is then used to create other compatible software products. For a further explanation of this process, see *Sega Enter. Ltd. v. Accolade, Inc.,* 977 F.2d 1510, 1519 (9th Cir. 1992); Robert P. Merges et al., *Intellectual Property in the New Technological Age* 989 (2003); and Michael Carrier, *Cabining Intellectual Property through a Property Paradigm,* 54 Duke L.J. 1, 84 (2004).

17. *See Sega Enter.,* 977 F.2d at 1519 (noting that making a copy can still violate the copyright owner's exclusive rights, irrespective of whether the end product is itself infringing).

18. *See* Carrier, *supra* note 16, at 89; Julie E. Cohen and Mark A. Lemley, *Patent Scope and Innovation in the Software Industry,* 89 Cal. L. Rev. 1 (2001).

19. *See generally* Pamela Samuelson and Suzanne Scotchmer, *The Law and Economics of Reverse Engineering,* 111 Yale L.J. 1575 (2002).

20. *See* Pamela Samuelson et al., *A Manifesto Concerning the Legal Protection of Computer Programs,* 94 Colum. L. Rev. 2308, 2375 (1994).

21. 977 F.2d 1510 (9th Cir. 1992).

22. In reverse engineering Sega's Genesis console, Accolade wired a decompiler into the console circuitry, and then proceeded to generate printouts of the resulting source code. Accolade then loaded the disassembled code back into a computer to determine the interface specifications for the console by modifying the program and noting the results of those modifications. *Id.* at 1515.

23. *Id.* at 1527.

24. "In order to enjoy a lawful monopoly over the idea or functional principle underlying a work," the court wrote, "the creator of the work must satisfy the more stringent standards imposed by the patent laws." *Id.* at 1526.

25. *Id.* at 1523.

26. Kevin A. Goldman and Gideon Parchomovsky, *Fair Use Harbors,* 93 Va. L. Rev. 1483, 1496 (2007).

27. *See id.* at 1504

28. (1551) 75 Eng. Rep. 1, 29 (K.B.).

29. *See* Carrier, *supra* note 16, at 122–123, 125.

30. *See* Gordon, *supra* note 5, at 157.

31. *Id.* at 159 n.23.

32. *Id.* at 155.

33. *Id.* at 152.

34. *Id.* at 161–165, 193–94.

35. *See* Amy Harmon, *Fighting for a Last Chance at Life,* N.Y. Times, May 16, 2009.

36. Richard A. Epstein, *AIDS Drugs: Are Property Rights and Human Rights in Conflict?,* FT.com, May 7, 2007, http://us.ft.com/ftgateway/superpage.ft?news_id =ftoo51520070841096219.

37. Peter J. Pitts, *Drug Patent Theft Carries High Price,* Balt. Sun, Feb. 20, 2007, at 11A. Yet another academic, Gary Hull, echoed similar sentiments in 2003: "We should not be fooled into thinking that it is 'practical' or 'necessary' or 'humane' to violate another person's right, or a corporation's right, to property." Gary Hull, Editorial Commentary, *Patent Piracy,* Barron's, June 2, 2003, at 46, *available at* http://www.duke .edu/~hull/Barrons%2703.pdf.

38. Epstein, *supra* note 36.

39. Michael A. Heller and Rebecca S. Eisenberg, *Can Patents Deter Innovation?* Science, May 1, 1998, at 698.

40. *See* Peter F. Hammer, *Differential Pricing of Essential AIDS Drugs: Markets, Politics and Public Health,* 5 J. Int'l Econ. L. 883, 888 (2002); *see also* Aditi Bagchi, *Compulsory Licensing and the Duty of Good Faith in TRIPS,* 55 Stan. L. Rev. 1529, 1545 (2003).

41. *See* Timothy Wu, *Copyright's Communications Policy,* 103 Mich. L. Rev. 278, 294 (2004).

42. *See* Timothy Wu, *Intellectual Property, Innovation, and Decentralized Decisions,* 92 Va. L. Rev. 123 (2006).

43. *See* Fred von Lohmann, *Fair Use as Innovation Policy,* 23 Berkeley Tech. L.J. 1 (2008).

44. *See* Timothy Wu, *supra* note 41, at 294.

45. *See* Mark Lemley, *The Economics of Improvement in Intellectual Property Law,* 75 Tex. L. Rev. 989 (1997).

46. *See* Joe Liu, *Regulatory Copyright,* 83 N.C. L. Rev. 87, 104–105 (2004).

47. Wu, *supra* note 41, at 298.

48. *Id.*

49. *Id.* at 299 (quoting John Philip Sousa).

50. *Id.* at 298.

51. 209 U.S. 1 (1908).

52. *Id.* at 14.

53. Wu, *supra* note 41, at 303. "Why settlement? . . . [By] this time both challengers and incumbents began to represent a serious threat to one another. Following *White-Smith,* composers and publishers risked an ongoing decay of their profitability because of their inability to extract income from the recording industry. Conversely, the recording industry still faced some possibility that publishers would succeed in their efforts to extend copyright to mechanical recordings and use this power against them." *Id.*

54. *See* Liu, *supra* note 46, at 98.

55. Jane C. Ginsburg, *Copyright and Control over New Technologies,* 101 Colum. L. Rev. 1613, 1630 (2001).

56. *Id.* (discussing the Digital Performance Right in Sound Recordings Act, Pub. L. 104-39, 109 Stat. 336 (1995) (codified in scattered sections of 17 U.S.C.)).

57. *See Herbert v. Shanley Co.,* 242 U.S. 591 (1917); Wu, *supra* note 43, at 307–322.

58. *See* William Fisher, *Promises to Keep: Technology, Law, and the Future of Entertainment* (2004); Neil Winstock Netanel, *Impose a Noncommercial Use Levy to Allow Free Peer-to-Peer File Sharing,* 17 Harv. J.L. & Tech. 1 (2003).

59. *CBS Songs Ltd v. Amstrad Consumer Elecs.,* [1988] 2 W.L.R. 1191, 1209 (H.L.).

60. *Id.*

61. Tim Wu tells a similar story of courts and Congress brokering settlements by instituting a compulsory-licensing regime with respect to cable retransmissions. In that instance, starting in the 1950s and continuing onward, the broadcast industry accused cable operators of "signal piracy," which culminated in the complex compulsory-licensing solution enacted by Congress in 1976. Wu, *supra* note 41, at 313; (citing House Comm. on the Judiciary, 89th Cong., *Copyright Law Revision Part 6: Supplementary Report of the Register of Copyrights on the General Revision of Copyright Law: 1965 Revision Bill* 42 (Comm. Print 1965)); *see also* Liu, *supra* note 46, at 110; 17 U.S.C. § 111(d) (1978).

62. *See* Stacey L. Dogan, *Code versus the Common Law,* 2 J. on Telecomm. & High Tech. L. 73, 100–101 (2003).

63. *See, e.g.*, Kimberly M. Thomas, *Protecting Academic and Nonprofit Research*, 23 Santa Clara Computer & High Tech. L.J. 347 (2006–2007).

64. *See, e.g.*, *Long v. Dilling Mech. Contractors, Inc.*, 705 N.E.2d 1022 (Ind. Ct. App. 1999) ("An intention to abandon property . . . may be inferred as a fact from the surrounding circumstances, and it can be shown by acts and conduct clearly inconsistent with any intention to retain and continue the use or ownership of the property." (internal quotation marks omitted)); *id.* at 1025 (quoting *Right Reason Publications v. Silva*, 691 N.E. 2d 1341, 1351 (1998)).

65. *See id.* at 1025.

66. *See* 1 Am. Jur. 2d *Abandoned, Lost, and Unclaimed Property* § 59 (2008); *see also Wiggins v. 1100 Tons, More or Less, of Italian Marble*, 186 F. Supp. 452, 456 (E.D. Va. 1960).

67. *See Pocono Springs Civic Ass'n v. Mackenzie*, 667 A.2d 233 (Pa. Super. Ct. 1995).

68. Steven Kurutz, *Not Buying It*, N.Y. Times, June 21, 2007, at F1.

69. For example, Creative Commons uses an independent system of copyright protection. *See* Creative Commons, http://www.creativecommons.org.

70. *See, e.g.*, Dan Mitchell, *Lots of Froth but No Bubble*, N.Y. Times, June 8, 2008, at C5.

71. *See generally* Randal C. Picker, The Google Books Search Settlement: A New Orphan Works Monopoly? 12–14 (April 2009) (unpublished manuscript, on file with authors); Legally Speaking: The Dead Souls of Google's Booksearch Settlement, Posting of Pamela Samuelson to O'Reilly Radar, http://radar.oreilly.com/2009/04/legally-speaking-the-dead-soul.html (Apr. 17, 2009).

72. S. 2913, 110th Cong. (as passed by Senate, Sept. 26, 2008, and referred to House Comm. on the Judiciary).

73. Lawrence Lessig, Op-Ed, *Little Orphan Artworks*, N.Y. Times May 20, 2008, at A23.

12. Responding to Expressive Altlaws

1. *See* Noah Schactman, *Copyright Enters a Gray Area*, Wired, Feb. 14, 2004, http://www.wired.com/entertainment/music/news/2004/02/62276; Joseph Patel, *Grey Tuesday Group Says 100,000 Downloaded Jay-Z/Beatles Mix*, MTV, Mar. 5, 2004, http://www.mtv.com/news/articles/1485593/20040305/jay_z.jhtml; Wikipedia, The Grey Album, http://en.wikipedia.org/wiki/The_Grey_Album (lasted visited May 11, 2009). Apparently, Jay-Z's record label, Roc-A-Fella, released an a capella version of his Black Album in order to encourage remixes. See Posting of greyalbum to LiveJournal, http://greyalbum.livejournal.com/1199.html (Feb. 24, 2004, 11:54 a.m.) (quoting greytuesday.org).

2. *See* Sam Howard-Spink, *Grey Tuesday, Online Cultural Activism, and the Mashup of Music and Politics*, First Monday, July 2005, http://firstmonday.org/htbin/cgiwrap/bin/ojs/index.php/fm/article/view/1460/1375; Ben Greenman, *The Mouse That Remixed*, New Yorker, Feb. 9, 2004, *available at* http://www.newyorker.com/

archive/2004/02/09/040209ta_talk_greenman ("[Dangermouse spent] two and a half weeks in his room. 'Those were fifteen-hour days, easily,' he said.").

3. *See* Posting of duckfood to The Crusade.net, http://www.thecrusade.net/forums /index.php?showtopic=2315&mode=linearplus (Feb. 11, 2004, 2:22 p.m.). His main worry was whether Jay-Z, Ringo, and Paul would like his work. "If they say that they hate it," he observed, "and that I messed up their music, I think I'll put my tail between my legs and go." Greenman, *supra* note 2 (quoting DJ Danger Mouse).

4. *See* Posting of duckfood to The Crusade.net, *supra* note 3.

5. Howard-Spink, *supra* note 2 (citing a Downhill Battle press release).

6. *See id.*

7. *See id.*

8. *See* Peter Manuel, *Cassette Culture: Popular Music and Technology in North India* (1993).

9. *See, e.g.,* Elizabeth Armstrong, *Suppressed Album Finds Voice on Web,* Christian Science Monitor, Mar. 1, 2004, at 11, *available at* http://www.csmonitor.com/2004/ 0301/p11s01-almp.html (quoting Danger Mouse as saying, "I did this project because I love the Beatles and Jay-Z. . . . I knew when I produced the Grey Album that there might be questions and issues this project would bring up, but I really don't know the answers to many of them").

10. Howard-Spink, *supra* note 2 (quoting Paul Morley, *Words and Music* (2003))

11. Howard-Spink, *supra* note 2.

12. EMI records controls the sound recordings for the Beatles on behalf of Capitol Records, and the compositions themselves are owned by Sony Music/ATV Publishing, a venture between Sony Music and Michael Jackson. *See* Joseph Patel, *Producer of* The Grey Album, *Jay-Z/Beatles Mash-Up, Gets Served,* MTV, Feb. 10, 2004, http://www.mtv.com/news/articles/1484938/02102004/jay_z.jhtml. For a great discussion about EMI's ownership of the copyrights in question, see Electronic Frontier Foundation, Grey Tuesday: A Quick Overview of the Legal Terrain, http://w2 .eff.org/IP/grey_tuesday.php (last visited Mar. 30, 2008).

13. *See Grey Album Goes Gold,* P2PNet, Feb. 25, 2004, http://p2pnet.net/story/ 843.

14. *See, e.g., Newton v. Diamond,* 349 F.3d 591 (9th Cir. 2003); *Bridgeport Music Inc. v. Dimension Films,* 410 F.3d 792 (6th Cir. 2005).

15. Armstrong, *supra* note 9 (quoting Jeanne Meyer, a spokeswoman for EMI).

16. Howard-Spink, *supra* note 2 (quoting a Downhill Battle press release).

17. Response to EMI's Cease and Desist Letter, http://www.downhillbattle.org/ ?p=225 (Feb. 23, 2004, 7:56 p.m.).

18. Howard-Spink, *supra* note 2 (quoting a Downhill Battle press release).

19. *Id.*

20. Matt Mason, *The Pirate's Dilemma: How Youth Culture Is Reinventing Capitalism* 36 (2008).

21. Howard-Spink, *supra* note 2.

22. Kembrew McLeod, *Confessions of an Intellectual (Property): Danger Mouse, Mickey Mouse, Sonny Bono, and My Long and Winding Path as a Copyright Activist–*

Academic, 28 Popular Music & Soc'y 79, 80 (2005), *available at* http://www.mickey
mousestore.com/Mickey_Mouse_Mickey_mouse_theme_song_disney_157604
.html; *see also* Kembrew.com, U of Iowa Professor Served Cease and Desist for Copyright Civil Disobedience, http://kembrew.com/news/GreyCease.html (last visited
Sept. 25, 2008).

23. Howard-Spink, *supra* note 2.

24. *See* Mark's Blog, Sony Rootkits and Digital Rights Management Gone Too Far,
http://blogs.technet.com/markrussinovich/archive/2005/10.aspx (Oct. 31, 2005,
11:04 a.m.); *see also* Brian Krebs, *Study of Sony Anti-Piracy Software Triggers Uproar,*
Wash. Post, Nov. 2, 2005, at D1. Sony admitted that "this rootkit was designed to hide
a legitimate application, but it can be used to hide other objects, including malicious
software." Bruce Schneier, *Real Story of the Rogue Rootkit,* Wired, Nov. 17, 2005,
http://www.wired.com/news/privacy/0,1848,69601,00.html; Joris Evers, *Microsoft
Will Wipe Sony's "Rootkit,"* CNET News, Nov. 13, 2005, http://news.com.com/
Microsoft+will+wipe+Sonys+rootkit/2100-1002_3-5949041.html.

25. *See* David Nimmer, *A Riff on Fair Use in the Digital Millennium Copyright Act,*
148 U. Penn. L. Rev. 673, 689–690 (2000).

26. *See* Timothy B. Lee, *Circumventing Competition: The Perverse Consequences of
the Digital Millennium Copyright Act* 8–9 (Cato Institute Policy Analysis No. 564,
2006).

27. Sony's Rootkit and the DMCA, Posting of Adam Shostack to Emergent Chaos,
http://www.emergentchaos.com/archives/2005_11.html (Nov. 17, 2005, 9:40 a.m.).

28. *See generally* James Gibson, *Risk Aversion and Rights Accretion,* 116 Yale L.J 882
(2007).

29. Wendy Gordon, *Fair Use as Market Failure,* 82 Colum. L. Rev. 1600, 1633
(1982).

30. *See* William P. Quigley, *The Necessity Defense in Civil Disobedience Cases: Bring
in the Jury,* 38 New Eng. L. Rev. 3, 32–36 (2003–2004).

31. *See id.* at 30 (discussing *Vermont v. Keller,* No. 1372-4-84 CNCR (Vt. Dist. Ct.
Nov. 17, 1984)).

32. *See id.* at 31 (discussing *Michigan v. Largrou,* Nos. 85-000098, 85-000099, 85-
000100, 85-000102 (Oakland Co. Dist. Ct. 1985)); id. at 27 n.87 (discussing *People v.
Gray,* 571 N.Y.S.2d 851, 861 (N.Y. Crim. Ct. 1991)).

33. *See id.* at 32–33 (discussing *Massachusetts v. Carter,* No. 86-45 CR 7475 (Hampshire. Dist. Ct. 1987)).

34. *See id.* at 31 (discussing *People v. Jarka,* Nos. 002170, 002196, 002212, 00214,
00236, 00238 (Ill. Cir. Ct. Apr. 15, 1985)).

35. *See id.* at 33 (discussing *State v. McMillan,* No. D 00518 (Cal. Mun. Ct. San Luis
Obispo Jud. Dist. Oct. 13, 1987)).

36. *See id.* at 27; *see also State v. Mouer* (Or. Dist. Ct. Columbia Co. Dec. 12–16,
1977).

37. *See* Quigley, *supra* note 30, at 27 n.87 (discussing *People v. Gray,* 571 N.Y.S.2d
851 (N.Y. Crim. Ct. 1991)).

38. *See id.* at 35.

39. *See id.*

40. This dynamic appears to be at work in the copyright disputes revolving around the Church of Scientology. That church has used (and arguably abused) its copyright over the written works of L. Ron Hubbard to silence critics and dissidents. *See, e.g., Religious Tech. Ctr. v. Lerma,* 908 F. Supp. 1362 (E.D. Va. 1995).

41. Under federal law, "whoever marks upon, or affixes to, or uses in advertising . . . the word 'patent' . . . for the purpose of deceiving the public . . . shall be fined not more than $500 for every such offense." 35 U.S.C. § 292(a).

42. *See* 35 U.S.C. § 292(a)–(b); *see also* Jason Mazzone, *Copyfraud,* 81 N.Y.U. L. Rev. 1026, 1075–1076 (2006).

43. *See* Kathryn Judge, *Rethinking Copyright Misuse,* 57 Stan. L. Rev. 901, 902 (2004).

44. *See id.; see also Lasercomb America v. Reynolds,* 911 F.2d 970 (4th Cir. 1990).

45. Judge, *supra* note 43, at 902–904; *see also DSC Commc'ns Corp. v. DGI Tech. Inc.,* 81 F.3d 597 (5th Cir. 1996) (sustaining the defense of copyright misuse as an antitrust violation); Aaron Xavier Fellmeth, *Copyright Misuse and the Limits of the Intellectual Property Monopoly,* 6 J. Intell. Prop. L. 1, 34–36 (1998).

46. *See* Brett Frischmann and Dan Moylan, *The Evolving Common Law Doctrine of Copyright Misuse: A Unified Theory and Its Application to Software,* 15 Berkeley Tech. L.J. 865, 874–876 (2000).

47. Justin Hughes, *Copyright and Incomplete Historiographies: Of Piracy, Propertization, and Thomas Jefferson,* 79 S. Cal. L. Rev. 993, 1081–1082 (2006).

48. *See* Mazzone, *supra* note 42.

49. *See* Robert P. Merges (discussing Madhavi Sunder), *Locke Remixed ;-),* 40 U.C. Davis L. Rev. 1259, 1261 (2007).

50. *Id.* at 1266–1267, 1269.

51. Gordon, *supra* note 29, at 1618.

52. *Id.* at 1619–1620.

53. *Grand Upright Music, Ltd. v. Warner Bros. Records,* 780 F. Supp. 182, 183 (S.D.N.Y. 1991).

54. *Id.* at 184.

55. *See Bridgeport Music, Inc. v. Dimension Films,* 410 F.3d 792 (6th Cir. 2005). In response, Downhill Battle organized a new protest, requesting musicians to create thirty-second songs made exclusively from the same sample that inspired the litigation. Within less than a week, its Web site hosted forty-one songs. *See* Howard-Spink, *supra* note 2.

56. *Bridgeport Music,* 410 F.3d at 801.

57. *Bridgeport Music Inc, v. Dimension Films,* 230 F. Supp. 2d. 830, 841 (M.D. Tenn. 2002).

58. Renee Graham, *Will Ruling on Samples Chill Rap?,* Boston Globe, Sept. 14, 2004, at D1.

59. *See* Max V. Mathews, *The Technology of Computer Music* 2 (1969); *see also* Note, *A New Spin on Music Sampling: A Case for Fair Pay,* 105 Harv. L. Rev. 726 (1992).

60. *See* Graham, *supra* note 58. Consider the case of legendary creator DJ Shadow,

who created the critically acclaimed album *Endtroducing,* entirely from samples, and who has been an outspoken critic of clearance culture's effect on creativity. *See* www .djshadow.com.

61. *See* Tim Wu, *Tolerated Use,* 31 Colum. J.L. & Arts 617 (2008).

62. *Id.* at 619.

63. Cheap Cologne, The Double Black Album, http://www.iamcheapcologne.com /black.html.

Conclusion

1. Pub. L. No. 104-199, 110 Stat. 2419 (codified at 1 U.S.C. § 7 and 28 U.S.C. § 1738C).

2. J. D. Heyman, *The Marrying Man,* People, Mar. 29, 2004, *available at* http:// www.people.com/people/archive/article/0,,20149672,00.html; *see also* Tad Friend, *Going Places,* New Yorker, Oct. 4, 2004, at 42, *available at* http://www.newyorker .com/archive/2004/10/04/041004fa_fact_friend.

3. For an excellent chronology upon which much of this background is based, see Erin Allday, *Newsom was Central to Same-Sex Marriage Saga,* S.F. Chron., Nov. 6, 2008, at A1, *available at* http://www.sfgate.com/cgi-bin/article.cgi?f=/c/a/ 2008/11/06/MN1B13S3D3.DTL, and Rachel Gordon, *Newsom's Bold Move,* S.F. Chron. Feb. 15, 2004, at A1, *available at* http://www.sfgate.com/cgi-bin/article .cgi?f=/c/a/2004/02/15/TICKTOCK.TMP.

4. Letter from Gavin Newsom, Mayor of San Francisco, to Nancy Alfaro, San Francisco County Clerk (Feb. 20, 2004), *available at* http://news.lp.findlaw.com/ hdocs/docs/glrts/sfmayor21004ltr.html.

5. *See* Allday, *supra* note 3.

6. *See id.*

7. *See* Sue Rochman, *The Marrying Man,* Advocate, Apr. 8, 2008, http://www .advocate.com/issue_story_ektid52690.asp.

8. *See* Friend, *supra* note 2.

9. *Mayor Defends Same-Sex Marriages,* CNN.com, Feb. 22, 2004, http://www .cnn.com/2004/LAW/02/22/same.sex/index.html.

10. Friend, *supra* note 2.

11. Mike Weiss, *Newsom in Four Acts: What Shaped the Man Who Took on Homelessness, Gay Marriage, Bayview-Hunters Point, and the Hotel Strike in One Year,* S.F. Chron., Jan. 23, 2005, at CM7, *available at* http://www.sfgate.com/cgi-bin/article .cgi?f=/c/a/2005/01/23/CMGD9AHK721.DTL.

12. Weiss, *supra* note 11.

13. Harriet Chiang et al., *Mad Dash to S.F. City Hall to Say 'I Do,'* S.F. Chron., Feb. 14, 2004, at A1, *available at* http://www.sfgate.com/cgi-bin/article.cgi?f=/c/a/ 2004/02/14/MNG3R517C21.DTL; Gordon, *supra* note 3.

14. Chris Taylor, *I Do . . . No, You Don't!,* Time, Mar. 1, 2004 (quoting Randy Thomasson), http://www.time.com/time/magazine/article/0,9171,593499,00.html.

15. *Id.* (quoting Arnold Schwarzenegger).

16. *See Mayor Defends Same-Sex Marriages, supra* note 9.

17. A copy of the petition is available on the Web site of the California Judicial Branch, at http://www.courtinfo.ca.gov/presscenter/briefs/S122923P.PDF.

18. William Powers, *Cold Feet,* Nat'l J., Feb. 28, 2004 (quoting Newsom on CNN).

19. Weiss, *supra* note 11.

20. Allday, *supra* note 3 (quoting Dennis Herrera).

21. *Lockyer v. City of San Francisco,* 33 Cal. 4th 1055, 1119 (2004).

22. *Id.* at 1080.

23. *Id.* at 1117.

24. *Id.* at 1106.

25. *Id.* at 1120 n.42 (quoting Robert Bolt, *A Man for All Seasons* 66 (1962)).

26. *Id.* at 1120.

27. Heather Gerken, *Dissenting by Deciding,* 57 Stan. L. Rev. 1745, 1748–1749 (2005).

28. Perry Dane, *The Public, the Private, and the Sacred: Variations on a Theme of Nomos and Narrative,* 8 Cardozo Stud. L. & Literature 16 (1996).

29. *See California Supreme Court Nixes Thousands of Same-Sex Marriages,* New Standard, Aug. 13, 2004, http://newstandardnews.net/content/index.cfm/items/824 (quoting Newsom's statement).

30. *In re Marriage Cases,* 43 Cal. 4th 757, 809 (2008).

31. *Id.* at 821 (internal quotation marks omitted).

32. *Id.* at 823.

33. *Id.* at 853–854.

34. *Id.* at 857.

35. *Gay Marriage Upheld: Reactions to the Ruling,* L.A. Times, May 16, 2008, http://articles.latimes.com/2008/may/16/local/me-voice16.

36. *Id.*

37. *Id.*

38. *See* John Wildermuth, *California Majority Backs Gay Marriage,* S.F. Chron., May 28, 2008, at A1, *available at* http://www.sfgate.com/cgi-bin/article.cgi?f=/c/a/2008/05/28/MNOU10U8MB.DTL.

39. Of those polled, 53 percent also believed that a gay marriage performed legally in another state should be recognized as legal in their own state. *See* Press Release, ABC News / Washington Post Poll, Changing Views on Social Issues (Apr. 30, 2009), *available at* http://abcnews.go.com/images/PollingUnit/1089a6HotButtonIssues.pdf (summarizing results of ABC poll).

40. *See* Poll: Support for Same-Sex Marriage Grows, Posting of Brian Montopoli to CBS News Political Hotsheet, http://www.cbsnews.com/blogs/2009/04/27/politics/politicalhotsheet/entry4972643.shtml (Apr. 27, 2009, 6:30 p.m.).

41. Tony Castro, *Attorneys Theodore B. Olson and David Boies Join Forces in Prop 8 Lawsuit,* Daily News (L.A.), May 27, 2009, http://www.dailynews.com/news/ci_12461986.

INDEX

lawsuits filed by, 47–48, 81, 169, 170, 179–180; mashups in, 208–209; monopoly in, 201; peer-to-peer file sharing, 169, 185, 200; and piracy, 47, 81, 83–84, 194, 212–213; player piano in, 198–200; space shifting in, 81, 179–180

NAACP, 64, 65, 79–80
Native Americans: activism of, vii–viii, ix, 13; dispossessed of their land, 15, 55, 56
Natural disasters, 9; and doctrine of necessity, 153–154
Necessity: discretionary relief in, 163–164; doctrine of, 135–138, 152–156, 158, 191–193, 219; economic, 196; "expressive," 160–163, 217–219; rethinking, 190–197
Need: and adverse possession, 149–150; definitions of, 136–138, 154–155, 191; and redistribution, 156
Neij, Hans Fredrik, 88
Netanel, Neil, 48, 200
Neuwirth, Robert, 133
New Deal, 12, 28
New Jersey Coalition Against War in the Middle East v. J.M.B. Realty Corp., 163
Newsom, Gavin, 227–236, 238–239
Nkoli, Simon, 97
NLRB v. Jones & Laughlin Steel Corp., 28
Olson, Ted, 239
Outlaws: altlaws vs., 80–81, 82, 85; difficulty of definition, 76, 79; ideologically motivated (hackers), 84–86; of piracy, 84–85; and social meaning, 80
Ownership, fixed legal theories of, 86

Palfrey, John, 112, 116
Parchomovsky, Gideon, 10–11, 29, 189–190
Parker v. Stephens, 61
Patent, and compulsory licensing, 94, 95, 104, 106–108; and cyberspace, 36; inventors rewarded in, 90, 91; and

laws of nature, 41; misuse of, 220, 222; and monopoly pricing, 90–91, 95, 101, 105–106; and parallel importing, 94–95; for pharmaceutical drugs, 91–97, 193; and public health, 90–102; recent adjustments to, 13, 48, 176, 179, 201; subject-matter limitations of, 41; and TRIPS agreement, 92–97, 102–104
Patented inventions: built on prior inventions, 40, 41, 185; "experimental use" of, 90; initial costs of, 91; and self-actualization, 46
Pavlosky, Nelson, 118
Pharmaceutical drugs: and anthrax, 103, 107; in Brazil, 102–105; compulsory licensing of, 94, 102, 103–108, 196; costs of, 91; development life cycle of, 91; differential pricing of, 197; and Doha declaration, 107–108; generic substitutes for, 93, 99, 100, 102–103, 108, 193–194, 196; and HIV/AIDS, 92–105; off-label use of, 193, 195; parallel importing of, 94–95; and patents, 91–97, 193; and public entitlements, 106; and public health, 92–97, 196; research and development of, 103–104, 196; in South Africa, 93–98; and TAC, 97–102; and TRIPS agreement, 92–97, 102–104
Pierce, Tony, 5
Piracy: broadening definition of, 179–180, 211–212; and copyright law, 72, 212–213; corporate methods of control, 81; creativity vs. illegality in, 83–84; and criminal law, 72, 75–77, 177; and DeCSS, 71–77; in developing world, 83–84; difficulty of controlling, 46, 73; difficulty of defining, 83–84, 180; DRM systems vs., 71–76, 77; effect on sales, 194; and First Amendment, 72, 73, 75; and hackers, 84–86; of intellectual property, 31, 46–51, 82–89, 179; outlaws of, 84–85; outside rule of law, 83–84; space shifting, 81, 179–180; and trade-secret law, 72, 75, 77; as unauthorized copying, 46